DESTINY
IN THE DESERT
★ ★ ★ ★

This is the story of the making of a soldier's soldier—the man who made America swell with pride in our fighting men and women.

It is a story of H. Norman Schwarzkopf, who learned the meaning of duty through his own father's example . . . of hard schooling at West Point . . . of a still sterner school of combat in Vietnam . . . of enduring the fierce opposition to that war and applying its lessons . . . of amazing prophetic planning for defense of U.S. interests in the Middle East even before the Iraqi attack . . . and of the Gulf War behind the scenes, revealed by the man who made Desert Storm end in a blaze of glory.

SCHWARZKOPF
THE MAN,
THE MISSION,
THE TRIUMPH

★

RICHARD PYLE has reported on six wars for the Associated Press, beginning with Vietnam and including the Yom Kippur War, the Lebanon civil war, the Israeli invasion of Lebanon, the Iran-Iraq war in the Persian Gulf, and most recently Operation Desert Storm. He was in the Arabian desert days after Iraq invaded Kuwait, and was the only print reporter in the tent where General H. Norman Schwarzkopf summoned Iraqi generals to hear his surrender demands.

SCHWARZKOPF

THE MAN,
THE MISSION,
THE TRIUMPH

Richard Pyle

A SIGNET BOOK

SIGNET
Published by the Penguin Group
Penguin Books USA Inc., 375 Hudson Street,
New York, New York 10014, U.S.A.
Penguin Books Ltd, 27 Wrights Lane,
London W8 5TZ, England
Penguin Books Australia Ltd, Ringwood,
Victoria, Australia
Penguin Books Canada Ltd, 2801 John Street,
Markham, Ontario, Canada L3R 1B4
Penguin Books (N.Z.) Ltd, 182-190 Wairau Road,
Auckland 10, New Zealand

Penguin Books Ltd, Registered Offices:
Harmondsworth, Middlesex, England

First published by Signet, an imprint of New American Library, a
division of Penguin Books USA Inc.

First Printing, April, 1991

10   9   8   7   6   5   4   3   2   1

To
Terry Anderson,
Friend, Colleague, Hostage

Contents

Part Two
★ ★ ★ ★
SCHWARZKOPF IN HIS OWN WORDS

Preface

Less than a year ago, the name H. Norman Schwarzkopf was not known to many people around the world. Today, by virtue of his generalship in Operation Desert Storm, he has become an authentic American hero, an icon in desert camouflage.

Here was a military man who may have thought he had seen and done it all, yet in the waning years of his career he found himself drawn together with an event that would provide the final definition to his life as a soldier, a destiny in the desert.

As a reporter covering Desert Storm, I once had the occasion to ask General Schwarzkopf if he had ever thought of his experience in those terms. He pondered the question for a moment. "No," he finally said, "I never did." This book is an attempt to tell something about this remarkable public figure.

Acknowledgments begin and end with my wife, Brenda, who provided inspiration, encouragement, and coffee. She also devoted herself to tasks great and small, and deserves whatever the nation's highest award is for transcribing tapes under deadline pressure.

A similar medal for my friend and agent, Tim Hays, who was enthusiastic, supportive, and resourceful in helping the project along.

My editor at NAL/Dutton, Kevin Mulroy, his assistant, Mitch Horowitz, John Paine, who line edited the entire manuscript in forty-eight hours, all deserve special praise. The entire NAL/Dutton organization was splendid in its professionalism in bringing this endeavor to publication so quickly.

My sincerest thanks also for valuable assistance from a variety of people (in no particular order): Major Ed Evans, West Point '76; Mike D'Aquino, West Point; Ed Baumeister, Managing Editor, Shirley Bounchelle, Lisa Belknap, all of the *Trenton Times*; Larry Edwards, Valley Forge, MA; Shelby Scates, *Seattle Post-Intelligencer*; John Branon, Bob Haskell; Brig. Gen. (ret.) Ted Mataxis; John Carlend, Center for Military History; Jim Benagh; Gail Gallucci; numerous individuals past and present at U.S. Central Command, and others at the National Archives, who asked that they not be mentioned by name. And, again, to Brenda without whose support this could not have happened.

—RICHARD PYLE

New York
April, 1991

★ ★ ★ ★

I told my family: the first month of any military campaign, the guy in charge is a hero, and it's downhill after that.

It's gonna happen. It's coming my way.

—H. NORMAN SCHWARZKOPF
September 13, 1990

PART ONE

THE MAKING OF A GENERAL

Have You Ever Been in a Mine Field?

At nine o'clock sharp on the evening of February 27, a tall, burly man in U.S. Army desert camouflage fatigues watched for the nod from an Air Force colonel, then stepped quickly toward the podium in a fourth-floor ballroom at the Hyatt Regency hotel in Riyadh, the capital of Saudi Arabia. Briefly scanning the faces before him, he began: "Good evening, ladies and gentlemen. Thank you for being here. I promised some of you a few days ago that I would give you a complete rundown on what we were doing and, more important, why we were doing it—the strategy behind what we were doing."

To the rapt attention of some two hundred journalists and military officials in that ballroom, and millions of people watching on television in more than thirty countries, General H. Norman Schwarzkopf then delivered a hour's worth of startling detail on how the half-million-strong international military force arrayed under his command in Operation Desert Storm had surprised and overwhelmed an Iraqi army that ostensibly outnumbered his own by a two-to-one margin, an army that supposedly had been waiting in heavily fortified fighting positions behind successive barriers of sand walls, wide trenches of blazing oil, and mine fields so thick that no man or vehicle could cross.

Brandishing a chrome pointer in his thick hand, the general poked at charts showing how the Iraqi forces had been positioned by President Saddam Hussein's generals—infantry to the front, armor and mechanized forced behind them, the tough, politically reliable Republican Guards as a strategic reserve to be hurled at the enemy when the time came.

Using the charts, Schwarzkopf showed how allied air forces, having acquired complete air supremacy, had used it to batter the opposition in their underground bunkers and dug-in tanks around the clock, for five weeks. The air attacks had "taken out his eyes," so that the Iraqi commander could not know how Schwarzkopf's forces were being positioned for attack. The highly visible activities of a thirty-ship amphibious force in the Persian Gulf had induced the Iraqis to build elaborate beach defenses and turn their guns toward the sea, only to have massive land forces come directly at them, and around them, from the opposite direction across hundreds of miles of open desert. They advanced with a swiftness that simply bypassed many of the Iraqis, leaving them standing, dazed, beside their former bunkers, or wandering about in confusion until special units of allied soldiers came to take them prisoner and shepherd them to the rear.

Schwarzkopf tried to mention everyone involved in his coalition, or at least all the main players—the U.S. Army's 24th Infantry Division, which he himself had once commanded and now was the spear point of the allied drive into southern Iraq to the Euphrates River. Two Marine divisions had breached the Iraqi defenses in southern Kuwait in an "absolutely superb" textbook operation. Saudi Arabian troops had driven up the coast toward Kuwait City, the principal objective. Light, mobile French forces had penetrated northward on the far left to protect that flank from an Iraqi counterattack. America's famed 101st Airborne Division had seized Iraqi airfields to use as forward bases just south of the Euphrates. The British 1st Armored Division had punched north into Iraq, through the barriers, and then linked up with American armor and mechanized forces to wheel eastward toward Kuwait City, cutting off Iraqi escape. Finally the U.S. Army's Special Forces had mounted a variety of clandestine operations behind Iraqi lines to gather intelligence, destroy installations, and sow confusion.

Alternately scowling and smiling at some of the journalists' questions, Schwarzkopf listened patiently as one reporter asked whether the Iraqi barrier defenses might possibly have been overrated. Fixing the man with a laser-like stare, Schwarzkopf fired back: "Have you ever been in a mine field?" "No," admitted the cowed reporter.

"All there has to be is one mine, and that's intense. There were plenty of mines out there, plenty of barbed wire . . . not a fun place to be. I have got to tell you, probably one of the toughest things that anyone ever has to do is to go up there and walk into something like that and go through it." This was spoken by a man who once upon a time in Vietnam, had done that very thing—walked into a mine field to rescue a soldier of his battalion who had been wounded by a buried explosive.

He ticked off the Iraqi losses so far: 21 infantry divisions, five armored divisions, and three mechanized divisions destroyed or rendered "ineffective" out of 42 committed to the defense of occupied Kuwait. More than 3,000 of Iraq's 4,200 tanks destroyed. Fifty thousand Iraqi prisoners in allied hands and "mounting on a continuing basis." For the first time since the war had begun, he directly addressed the subject of Iraqi casualties, saying the onrushing allied forces had come

across "a very, very large number of dead" in the
bunkers and trench lines just above the border of Kuwait and Saudi Arabia. As for his own losses, Schwarzkopf said, they had been so low as to have been "almost
miraculous."

And he noted that the battle was not over. "I should
remind you that the war is continuing to go on. Even
as we speak, there is fighting going on out there. Even
as we speak, there are incredible acts of bravery going
on," he said, citing as his example the attempted rescue of a downed U.S. Air Force pilot by helicopters of
the 101st Airborne, one of which also had been shot
down, in southern Iraq. "It is not a Nintendo game,"
Schwarzkopf told his listeners. "It is a tough battlefield
where people are risking their lives at all times. There
are great heroes out there."

When another reporter asked the general what he
thought of Saddam Hussein as a military strategist,
Schwarzkopf flashed a large grin, conveying his delight
at this opportunity to express his opinion on the Iraqi
leader, knowing full well that Saddam himself might
well be among the millions around the world who were
watching this event by way of live satellite-fed television. Leaning on the wooden podium like the West
Point professor he once had been, he gestured with one
hand and delivered a scathing verdict: "He is not a
strategist, nor is he schooled in the operational arts,
nor is he a tactician, nor is he a general, nor is he a
soldier. Other than that, he's a great military man."

Schwarzkopf's mood turned instantly grim again as
he spoke of Saddam's soldiers, who during their six
months of rule over Kuwait were alleged to have committed outrages including murder, arbitrary executions, torture, and rape, and to have kidnapped thousands of young Kuwaitis in the previous few days. The
perpetrators of these "unspeakable atrocities" were
"not part of the same human race that the rest of us
are," said Schwarzkopf. When pressed by a reporter for

more details of what had gone on in Kuwait, he snapped, "No sir, I wouldn't want to talk about it."

At the end, Schwarzkopf spoke again from his general's heart, saying that he was "very thankful for the fact that the President of the United States has allowed the United States military and the coalition military to fight this war exactly as it should have been fought, and the President in every case has taken our guidance and our recommendations to heart, and has acted superbly as the Commander-in-Chief of the United States."

One newspaper, borrowing the phrase that Saddam himself had used weeks earlier to refer to the battle that was then impending, called Schwarzkopf's report "the Mother of All Briefings." And indeed, his performance on that cool Riyadh evening set a new standard for events of the kind. Reporters who had covered a half dozen other wars conceded they had never heard anything quite like it: an information blitzkrieg, as dazzling in its own way as Desert Storm itself—one of the most successful, if surprisingly one-sided, operations in modern military history.

In Vietnam, the reporters remembered, General William Westmoreland had never given such a detailed, lucid account of any military operation, confining himself instead to occasional stiff, self-serving appearances before the press in which he sought to portray an unrelentingly bad situation in optimistic pastels. None could recall Westy's successor, General Creighton Abrams—a gritty tanker who happened to be a particular hero of Schwarzkopf's—ever giving a group briefing at all, let alone an hour's worth of hypnotic show-and-tell while the battle was still in progress.

Back home in America, the briefing had been seen on television during the noontime lunch hour on the East Coast and at nine o'clock in the morning on the West. All across the country, people cheered and applauded, or just watched in fascination. And as the television tape was played over and over again on the

Cable News Network, and broadcast in excerpts on all the other networks, the country was suddenly abuzz.

Even before he addressed the media and a global audience on that February evening in Riyadh, only the most inveterate of hermits did not know who H. Norman Schwarzkopf was.

Just six months earlier, an obscure military officer running an equally obscure headquarters on the west coast of Florida, he would have seemed an unlikely candidate for instant world fame. Yet here he was at center stage—a bulky, lumbering figure with an almost cherubic face and thinning hair, six feet four and pushing two hundred forty pounds, in size eleven-and-a-half combat boots that he had designed himself. He was left-handed and wore a watch on each wrist to keep track of the eight-hour time difference between Washington and Riyadh.

On his field tunic, Schwarzkopf wore the four stars of his rank, the Combat Infantryman's Badge, the wings of Master Parachutist, and his name—the barest essentials that would tell another soldier who he was. Not displayed were the three Silver Stars for valor, the two Purple Hearts for wounds, or the dozen-plus other commendations that he had earned in thirty-five years as a professional soldier.

He was friendly and verbose, tending to ramble when he talked, always saying "very, very" and "many, many" when one of either would suffice. He laced his speech with typical American colloquialisms, but was careful in his use of expletives, although he certainly knew them all. He was notoriously hot-tempered but usually quick to forgive. He did not like being called "Stormin' Norman," believing that it suggested, as he once said, "somebody who's mad all the time and raising hell, and that's not me."

He was described in an official biography as having an IQ of one hundred seventy. Close associates said he had a photographic memory, never forgot what anyone told him, and would immediately question the individual who offered a revised version of what had been said previously. They also said that in planning a military operation he welcomed ideas from subordinates. He spoke contemptuously of his Iraqi adversaries but cautioned aides not to underestimate them.

He could become visibly emotional about the American flag and other patriotic symbols of the country he had sworn to defend, and die for if necessary. He was a faithful family man, lover of animals and the outdoors. He made it clear that nothing, other than his family, was as important to him personally as the troops under his command. And for that reason he loved, and carefully nurtured, the image of himself that had begun with the nickname given to him by his soldiers in Vietnam, two decades earlier: "The Bear."

2

A Respectful Awe

Interestingly enough, the name H. Norman Schwarzkopf had been a household word before. In 1932, the infant son of the aviation hero Charles A. Lindbergh was stolen from a second-floor bedroom at the family's newly built estate near the small town of Hopewell in central New Jersey. Located about halfway between Philadelphia and New York, the area was remote enough to give the Lindberghs the privacy that they increasingly had craved after years in the public eye.

When the kidnapping of their firstborn, twenty-month-old Charles A. Lindbergh, Jr., occurred on March 1, 1932, it touched off a national wave of outrage and public curiosity. Spurred by the biggest crime story since the St. Valentine's Day massacre in Chicago three years earlier, hordes of reporters, thrill seekers, amateur criminologists, and self-styled clairvoyants flocked to the area. Many of them joined the police and volunteer searchers tramping across barren fields and hollows, seeking clues to the child's disappearance.

Holding the line against the unwanted invaders was Colonel H. Norman Schwarzkopf, a 1917 West Point graduate and former World War I cavalry officer. In 1921, at the age of twenty-five, he had been hired away from his job at a Newark department store to organize and head New Jersey's new state police force. A stocky, dapper figure with a close-cropped moustache, deep-set, penetrating eyes, and an almost Prussian bearing, this son of German immigrants had built the force, beginning with eighty-one troopers chosen from sixteen hundred applicants, along paramilitary lines. As superintendent, he held the rank equivalent to a regimental commander, earning nine thousand dollars a year.

Appointing himself, with the governor's approval, as chief investigator in the case—kidnapping was not yet a federal crime, but would become one under the subsequent act of Congress known as the Lindbergh Law—Colonel Schwarzkopf presided over a sensational four-year inquiry that became increasingly politicized and immersed in controversy, with charges of mishandling, police corruption, falsified evidence, and eventually claims that the German-born carpenter arrested for the crime was railroaded to the electric chair.

Although Schwarzkopf's military credentials were considered impeccable, skeptics questioned whether his former job as chief of deliveries for a hometown department store had qualified him to investigate the nation's latest "crime of the century." In taking charge of the inquiry, Schwarzkopf set up his command post in the Lindberghs' garage, and from the start he was highly protective of the world-renowned flier and his wife, Anne Morrow Lindbergh, who sought desperately, in their grief, to protect themselves from the prying public. To this end, Colonel Schwarzkopf established a firm policy in which only he spoke for the officials on the case—and rarely at that. A contemporary newspaper account from the Brooklyn *Daily Eagle* complained: "The secrecy which shrouded plans at military headquarters in France as to intended movements of the A.E.F. [Allied Expeditionary Forces] was no greater than the care with which Schwarzkopf hid from the public what was or was not being accomplished by his investigators."

The writer, who evidently had asked for a personal interview with the colonel and been turned down, explained to his editors that Schwarzkopf had given "personal interviews" to the press "on but two occasions," and "both of these were mass interviews. At neither would he answer any questions, confining his remarks solely to the task of informing newspaper men what type of questions would not be answered."

After the Lindberghs paid a fifty-thousand-dollar ransom through a self-appointed intermediary, an elderly New York City doctor, to mysterious recipients in a Bronx cemetery, Colonel Schwarzkopf was hard put to explain why the child was not returned safely to his parents. Then, on May 12, the boy's badly deteriorated body was discovered in a shallow grave in a wooded swamp near Hopewell. Amid screaming headlines the focus shifted to a search for the kidnappers.

For the next two years Colonel Schwarzkopf's investigators, with a welter of unsolicited advice from politicians, newspaper editorial writers, other police agencies, and the New Jersey governor's office, chased one false lead after another. They collected and catalogued every letter, from well-meaning citizens and cranks alike, and coped with a series of peripheral mysteries that usually had nothing to do with the case, but provided a field day for the insatiable press.

There was, for example, the untimely death of a Lindbergh servant from peritonitis, and later the apparent suicide of Mrs. Lindbergh's mother's maid shortly before she was to be questioned by police. Lindbergh himself emerged from seclusion several times to make private contact with persons claiming to have knowledge of the case; all proved to be charlatans or crackpots.

Through it all, Colonel Schwarzkopf was the star player in the affair, a familiar figure in newspaper photographs, whether in his military-style state police uniform with cavalry boots and Sam Browne belt, or civilian suit with a bow tie and straw boater.

On August 22, 1934, a month to the day after the notorious Midwest bank robber John Dillinger was gunned down by FBI agents in Chicago, Colonel Schwarzkopf's search for the Lindbergh killer was temporarily put on hold as he celebrated the birth of his third child, a son, in Trenton. The boy was named H. Norman Schwarzkopf, Junior. But the father, who was said to have detested his first name, Herbert, stipulated the the *H* in his son's name would stand alone.

Less than a month later, Colonel Schwarzkopf had another reason to rejoice. On September 19, he was able to announce the arrest of a prime suspect in the Lindbergh case. He could not, however, claim that his relentless investigation had finally cracked the case. The credit went to a Bronx filling-station attendant, who had received a bill in payment for gasoline and alertly noticed that it bore a serial number from the Lindbergh ransom. Following up that lead, police in the New York borough investigated Bruno Richard Hauptmann, a carpenter, and reported finding more of the Lindbergh ransom money hidden in his garage.

Hauptmann, a recent immigrant from Germany whose English was poor, claimed that he had gotten the marked bills from a friend repaying a personal loan. He could offer no alibi for the time of the kidnapping except for the insistence of his wife, Anna, that he was at home.

Hauptmann's refusal to admit to the crime was seen as highly uncooperative, and as authorities built a case against him on the strength of circumstantial evidence—some of it questioned at the time as highly dubious but accepted nevertheless—it became clear that he had little chance of escaping the law.

The prime exhibit in the prosecution's case included a hand-built wooden ladder that the kidnapper had used to climb into the Lindbergh baby's bedroom.

Defense attorneys argued that no self-respecting carpenter would make such a crude ladder, but a government forensic expert testified that pieces of the ladder showed saw blade striations that linked it directly to Hauptmann. In 1936 he was convicted in a six-week trial in Flemington, New Jersey, and went to the electric chair.

At the time, there were those who deplored the circus-like atmosphere of the trial, and some who questioned whether the investigation had been fair or even competent. It was noted, for example, that Schwarzkopf had allowed Lindbergh to have the baby's body cremated almost immediately after it was found, leaving forever unclear the exact cause of death that an autopsy could have established. New Jersey's governor, Harold G. Hoffman, had enough misgivings to tell Colonel Schwarzkopf in a private letter that "had ordinary sound police methods been used following the commission of the crime, many doubts entertained today might have been eliminated." The feud led Hoffman to refuse to reappoint Schwarzkopf as state police superintendent.

More recent years have seen a spate of books and articles about the Lindbergh case, many of them questioning sharply the conduct of the investigation and suggesting that Colonel Schwarzkopf was, at the very least, overzealous in finding a solution to satisfy the Lindberghs and, at the worst, played an instrumental role in the scandalous frame-up of an innocent man. Although the Lindberghs put the tragedy almost totally behind them—Anne Lindbergh, in particular, was said to have never mentioned the case for the rest of her life—they were reported to have believed completely in Hauptmann's guilt and did not question Colonel Schwarzkopf's conduct of the case.

In 1981, material from New Jersey police and FBI files, released under the Freedom of Information Act, revealed a series of events that cast serious doubt on the investigation. One item indicated that the state police had tried to bribe a witness into saying he had seen Hauptmann near the kidnap site. Others revealed that police had suppressed facts or experts' statements concerning the handwriting on ransom notes, fingerprints on the ladder, and other discomforting bits of information.

After Governor Hoffman refused to reappoint him, Colonel Schwarzkopf became president of a New Jersey bus company, and later the narrator on the popular weekly radio show, "Gangbusters," which dramatized real-life stories, mostly in the Dillinger mold. The program opened with the sound of police sirens and machine-gun fire and ended with Schwarzkopf giving a "nationwide clue" that occasionally led to the apprehension of a felon wanted by the FBI.

Having been too young to recall any of the machinations of the Lindbergh case, H. Norman Schwarzkopf, Jr., has said his first recollection of his father is from those days when as a small boy, he was allowed to stay up on Friday nights to listen as his father and the radio cops on "Gangbusters" brought the crooks to justice.

"The other thing I distinctly remember about my father was how all the people who worked for him admired and respected him," the younger Schwarzkopf told one interviewer. "He was almost like—I don't want to say like a god because that's an inappropriate choice of words—but when my father was around, people were almost in awe of him. It was a respectful awe, not a fearful awe. I guess all fathers to their sons have an aura of being a superman, but my father was even more than that."

When the United States entered World War II, the elder Schwarzkopf was soon back in uniform—this time as an Army colonel. In early 1942, after giving his West Point sword to his eight-year-old son and telling him, "Now you're the man of the house," Schwarzkopf was dispatched to Iran, where he was assigned to build a security force for the country that was then serving as the base for a major United States commitment to help the Soviet Union in its struggle against Nazi Germany.

Some 30,000 American military personnel made up the Persian Gulf Command, mainly logistics specialists and engineers, whose main job was to expedite the movement of Lend-Lease military supplies and equipment to the Soviets through this far-flung but relatively secure back door. The engineers laid out roads to carry the supplies northward, and built harbors, including the northern Iran port of Khorranshar, in the Shatt-al-Arab waterway that Iran shared with Iraq, and Bandar Abbas in the Strait of Hormuz, the strategic passage linking the Persian Gulf with the Arabian Sea and the Indian Ocean.

The United States, which for decades had seen its attempts to gain influence in the increasingly important Gulf oil states thwarted by the colonial British, was also running civilian advisory missions in wartime Iran in finance, public health, farming, irrigation, and other fields. But none would prove more important than the project that belonged to Colonel—and later Brigadier General—Schwarzkopf: the training of a national police force.

Shortly after the end of the war in 1945, Soviet Premier Josef Stalin refused to abide by a wartime treaty that required the withdrawal of foreign troops once hostilities had ended, seeking instead to stir up civil unrest in the Iranian province of Azerbaijan adjoining the Soviet Union. Stalin's immediate hope was to pressure the Iranians into granting him an oil concession similar to those awarded the British and Americans; Western diplomats saw the long-range objective as establishing a Moscow foothold in the Persian Gulf, with its oil and warm-water ports. As far back as 1940, they noted, Foreign Minister Vyacheslav Molotov told the Germans, then Soviet allies, that Soviet territorial ambitions "lie south . . . in the direction of the Persian Gulf."

The constabulary of 21,000, organized and trained

by Schwarzkopf, was credited with an instrumental role in putting down the Azerbaijan rebellion, after which some adroit diplomacy by the United States, Britain, and Iran defused the confrontation with the Soviets, ending what has been called by some the first significant crisis of the Cold War.

That same year, now going on twelve, Norman Jr. joined his father in Iran. They hunted and rode horseback together in the desert. The younger Schwarzkopf also learned the fine points of shooting from his father, who had been a sharpshooter at West Point, and while commander of the New Jersey state police was also a member of its pistol team, once holding the department record of 99.1 in right-hand shooting.

Young Schwarzkopf picked up some of the Farsi language, including a few of the more common swear words. He found that the Iranians, like the people back home, admired and respected his father. Years later, as a victorious general in his own right, the son would tell an interviewer that his father's memory had been an inspiration. "I probably thought about him more since I've been over here than I have in many, many years," he said. "I just mean that many times I've thought that if he was looking at me now, I know he would be proud."

In the years that followed, young Norman went to school in Europe as his father remained in the Army, serving in Germany and Italy. In 1948, he was deputy provost marshal in Berlin, under General Lucius D. Clay, the U.S. military governor, and led an anti-smuggling campaign. Later he spent two years as chief of the U.S. military assistance group in Italy, before retiring as a major general.

By the early 1950s, however, he was back in Iran, this time as a security adviser to a right-wing Iranian political activist named Fazollah Zahedi.

In 1951, Iran's ultranationalist leader, Mohammed Mossadegh, seized Iran's British-operated petroleum industry, prompting British and other Western oil interests to retaliate with a boycott that kept Mossadegh from finding buyers for his newly acquired resource. Within two years Western governments—namely the United States and Britain—saw ominous signs that the fiercely independent Iranian firebrand was moving closer to the Russians.

Having suppressed one Soviet-backed communist threat in Iran, they were unwilling to let Moscow gain any power there by default. After a cutoff of all U.S. aid to Iran failed to intimidate him, Mossadegh was overthrown in a coup d'etat engineered primarily, according to most accounts, by the U.S. Central Intelligence Agency, with a certain amount of British help. General Schwarzkopf was widely regarded as having played a crucial role in the affair, and his patron, Zahedi, served briefly in power until the Shah Mohammed Reza Pahlevi took over, to reign for the next two decades.

Returning to the United States in late 1951, the elder Schwarzkopf became coordinator of New Jersey's public safety and law enforcement division. He won plaudits for an investigation of corruption on the New Jersey docks, and in 1964 he was put in charge of another probe into the state's Division of Employment Security, which by coincidence had been headed since 1938 by Hoffman, the former governor.

Schwarzkopf never got the goods on Hoffman, but the ex-governor told friends shortly before he died of a heart attack in 1954 that after his nemesis's inquiry was "getting pretty close." In a letter opened after his death, Hoffman confessed to having embezzled thousands of dollars from a South Amboy bank to finance his political career.

Thus vindicated in his feud with Hoffman, the elder Schwarzkopf died in 1958 at age sixty-three. In 1971, the state honored his long service in New Jersey law enforcement by naming a new training center after him at Sea Girt, the location where he had turned out his first batch of eighty-one officers and troopers fifty years earlier.

Nor was H. Norman Schwarzkopf, Sr., forgotten in Iran. When table talk at a recent social gathering in Riyadh turned to the subject of the present-day General Schwarzkopf, the Iranian-born wife of a prominent Saudi businessman heard for the first time how the general's father had built the Iranian national police, and played a key role in bringing the shah to power. "Well," she said, "that explains why there is—or used to be—a Schwarzkopf Square in Tehran."

3

He Always Had to Be the Good Guy

In March 1929, the *Newark Sunday Call* carried a feature story about a hometown hero, Colonel H. Norman Schwarzkopf, the "trim, handsome, blond young man" who for the previous eight years had been making a name for himself in national law enforcement circles as the superintendent of the New Jersey state police. It was an effusive, admiring article, typical of the newspaper style of the day, describing its subject as "a West Point man—and all that that implies," and a "Newarker through and through."

In the final paragraph, the writer added that "he is unmarried, though one wonders how he ever escaped leap year." In closing, the reporter observed that "Apparently, he is 'safe' until 1932 rolls around."

Schwarzkopf, perhaps with the same penchant for secrecy that later characterized his conduct of the Lindbergh kidnap case, had not told the reporter everything. On October 3 of that same year, an item in the

Trenton Times, which by now also claimed Colonel Schwarzkopf as a hometown celebrity, announced his engagement to Ruth Alice Bowman of New York City, a native of Trenton, where she had been an assistant supervisor of nurses at Mercer Hospital. "The wedding will be an event of November," it said.

The newlyweds set up housekeeping in the Trenton area, where Schwarzkopf maintained his office at state police headquarters. Two daughters, Ruth Ann and Sally Joan, were born in the first years of the marriage. On August 22, 1934, the *Trenton Times* carried this item on page ten.

"Colonel and Mrs. H. Norman Schwarzkopf, of Pennington, announce the birth of a son, H. Norman Schwarzkopf, Jr., at Mercer Hospital today. Mother and child are reported doing well under the care of Dr. Henry M. Rowan. This is the third child, the other two being girls. Colonel Schwarzkopf is superintendent of the New Jersey state police."

Not long after, the Schwarzkopf family moved from Pennington, north of Trenton, into a large two-story brick home with green shutters on Main Street in Lawrenceville, a Trenton suburb on the highway to Princeton. It was in this house, now registered on the state list of historic places, that young Norman spent the first twelve years of his life, until 1946, when the colonel—by then a brigadier general in the Army—sent for the family to join him in postwar Iran.

Former boyhood friends describe a typical growing up. "If we weren't playing cops and robbers, we were playing cowboys and Indians," one of them recalled in an interview in the *Trentonian* newspaper. "And Norman—well, he always had to be the good guy." Another boyhood acquaintance, Paul Mott, told the newspaper he remembered Norman as "a brat" who was very protective of his sisters and "always seemed to get in the way" when he tried to talk to pretty, blond Ruth Ann.

Other vignettes add to the portrait of young Norman

in the 1930s and early 1940s, years in which Europe was being threatened, then wracked, by war. In addition to being a fine athlete, he was an amateur magician—a popular hobby among youth of that time. Imagine the boy, already big for his age and smarter than most of his playmates, poring over the mail-order catalogues of the time that specialized in magic tricks and enticed youthful customers to "amaze your friends" with a disappearing coin, or "be the first on your block" to own a secret periscope that could see around corners.

He rode the bus to public schools in Princeton, five miles north of Lawrenceville. The Schwarzkopfs, who were Presbyterian, infused their offspring with values of fair play and respect for the individual. Norman Jr. has told a story of riding the bus one day and, out of courtesy, giving his seat to an old black woman, only to have the other whites on the bus make fun of him.

He says that on arriving at home, he asked his mother whether he had done something improper, and he quotes her response: "Remember this. You were born white, you were born Protestant, you were born an American. Therefore you're going to be spared prejudices that other people will not be spared. But you should not forget one thing. You had absolutely nothing to do with the fact that you were born that way. It was an accident of birth that spared you this prejudice."

In telling that tale, Schwarzkopf added, "I just grew up liking people. I tend to judge them on what kind of human beings they are, and I like to be judged the same way. I like the people to look at the net worth of Norman Schwarzkopf, and I hope that they judge me on what kind of heart I have in me."

Norman's two sisters were already students at Smith and Wellesley colleges when he returned from Europe in the fall of 1951 to enroll at Valley Forge, a military academy near Philadelphia that was founded in 1928. In the application, sent in the winter of 1950, the senior Schwarzkopf had told the school: "Norman is most anxious to become a cadet at the United States Military Academy." Pointing out that he himself was a 1917 graduate of West Point, the father added, "Naturally, I heartily concur in his ambitions."

Having first learned to play football in high school in Germany, young Norman now applied his talents as a tackle on the Valley Forge team and shot-putted on the track team. At age seventeen, he was six feet two inches tall and weighed two hundred three pounds. He also was the star of the debate team, editor of the school yearbook, *Crossed Sabres*, and maintained top grades, graduating in 1952 as the valedictorian of his class of about one hundred fifty.

The baccalaureate speaker that year was retired General Anthony McAuliffe, famed for his role as the commander who had replied, "Nuts," when the Germans demanded that he surrender his trapped paratroopers at Bastogne in the December 1944 Battle of the Bulge.

It was then, too, that classmates annoyed the now strapping youth by supplying a name for the mysterious stand-alone *H* in the yearbook. It was Hugo.

Only three percent of Valley Forge graduates go on to a military career, and Schwarzkopf was one of the few in his class who became a professional soldier. His classmates included Paul Roebling, a descendant of the Civil War officer who had later built the Brooklyn Bridge, William Tiefel, a prominent hotel executive, and the late Allan P. Jaffé, who would rediscover, promote, and play with the Preservation Hall Jazz Band in New Orleans. Three years behind him, in the class of 1955, was John Yeosock, who in 1990 would be the three-star general in direct command of ArCent, the Army forces under Schwarzkopf's overall command in Operations Desert Shield and Desert Storm.

Years later, after he became famous, Schwarzkopf wrote a letter to the school in which he said, "West

Point prepared me for the Army. Valley Forge prepared me for life."

In the fall of 1952, Norman Jr. realized his long cherished ambition to become a cadet at the U.S. Military Academy, following in his father's footsteps. Nor did the legacy end there. He inherited his father's old nickname, Schwarzie. In his plebe, or freshman, year, the traditional hazing by upperclassmen included frequent demands that he imitate the sounds of screeching brakes, police sirens, and chattering machine-gun fire that had opened his father's "Gangbusters" radio show.

At the Point, Schwarzkopf, now a hulking six feet three, played football, soccer, wrestled, and was active in the weightlifting and German clubs. Always a music lover, he led the Cadet Chapel Choir, singing tenor. He graduated in the top ten percent, number 42 in a class of 485.

His heroes were, of course, military leaders. At West Point he became a great admirer of Alexander the Great, who succeeded in conquering most of the known world in the third century B.C. Although his deeds are recorded only in scraps of fact and a lot of mythology, the Macedonian warrior-king was noted as a master tactician who used his forces with great skill and lightning speed. But he possessed one quality that set him apart as a general, in Schwarzkopf's view: "Everything his troops did, he could do and better."

Schwarzkopf also was attracted to two of the Union's greatest leaders in the Civil War, generals Ulysses Grant and William T. Sherman, both as "muddy boot soldiers" who maintained the common touch with their soldiers despite the stars on their shoulders. He said that Sherman, who was known to his hardened Union veterans as Uncle Billy, "truly understood the horror of war but when required to execute a war, did so and hated every minute of it."

Looking ahead, yet another hero, in later life, would be a man under whom Schwarzkopf personally served.

General Creighton Abrams, who took over the command of United States forces in Vietnam in mid-1968, was another iron-tough individual who looked upon war as an abomination but went all out to fight it, to destroy his enemy, on the theory that the sooner and more effectively it was done, the more lives among his own troops would be saved in the long run.

Abrams, who with his craggy features and habitual cigar, seemed almost the reincarnation of Grant, had been known as General George Patton's favorite tank commander in World War II, leading the battalion that broke the siege of Bastogne during the Battle of the Bulge. His no-nonsense manner was in sharp contrast to the flashy William Westmoreland, whom he replaced in Vietnam and whom Schwarzkopf bluntly refers to as "a horse's ass."

But Abrams, he told an interviewer from *Life* magazine recently, "epitomized to me what the professional military should be all about. He was totally candid. He had a great expression that I think about a lot. He said, 'Did you ever think what a great army it would be if no one worried about who got the credit?' That's the way I like to do things. Get the job done and then sort out the credit later."

Colleagues at West Point recall that in his senior year, Schwarzkopf, who planned to choose the infantry as his branch of service, recruited many of his classmates to do the same, shunning the more glamorous artillery, which customarily attracted the top students. His degree was a bachelor of science, but like many West Pointers, no major. The future would be military, but within that framework, an open book and up the ladder.

Schwarzkopf has said he always considered the command of a division—a two-star general's assignment—to be his ultimate objective, and that anything beyond that was a bonus. But his academy roommate, General Leroy Suddath, told the *Los Angeles Times* in an interview in 1991: "Norm aimed for the top and expected to reach it. When he got his first star, he was already looking forward to his next promotion. He's always been looking for positions of greater responsibility."

The 1956 edition of *Howitzer*, the West Point yearbook, remixing his name as "Norman H. Schwarzkopf," depicted a young man with a pleasant yet serious expression, but offered little in the accompanying paragraph to foretell the future: "Schwarzie's far-flung travels from New Jersey to Iran have made him a connoisseur of life. His afternoons at West Point were filled with soccer, tennis, and wrestling, an excellent competitor in each. His genial personality has won him many friends. His spirit is his greatest asset and will assure him success."

At that it was an considerable improvement on the entry that his father had suffered in the 1917–18 edition of the *Howitzer*, which had described the elder Schwarzkopf as being shaped "like a beer keg . . . No one would suspect from his anatomy that our genial German gink is built for speed, and he isn't—but oh, my, what a wallop when he lands!"

While the "genial German gink" had landed immediately after West Point graduation in France, where he served as a lieutenant and then captain of artillery in the last year of World War I, the post-graduation years for Norman Jr. were typical for a young Army officer with no war to fight but with one ever on the horizon.

In that year the Cold War was moving toward its period of deepest freeze. The Army was tinkering with its organizational structure, substituting a "pentomic" system of battle groups for the traditional divisions. But outwardly it still resembled what it had been in World War II and Korea, and its top leaders, as well as many of its senior line officers, were veterans of those battlefields. Schwarzkopf had entered West Point in the middle of the Korean War, and once in the ranks he encountered some of the disillusionment that lingered from that ambiguously resolved conflict.

From October 1956 until the following March,

Schwarzkopf attended the Infantry School at Fort Benning, Georgia—the first and most important postgraduate course in his chosen field of military endeavor. There he gained his paratroop badge and learned firsthand the soldierly skills that had been taught as theory on the plain overlooking the Hudson, but now would make him fully qualified to wear the sky-blue scarf and piping of the infantry.

Schwarzkopf found his first regular assignment as a platoon leader and later executive officer of Echo Company, 2nd Airborne Battle Group, 187th Infantry, at Fort Campbell, Kentucky. The 187th Regiment, part of the 101st Airborne Division, was noted for Korean War service in which it acquired one of the Army's quainter nicknames—the Rakkasans. The Japanese word for paratrooper, it literally meant "falling down umbrellas."

In July 1959, by now a first lieutenant for over a year, Schwarzkopf was assigned overseas for the first time. The first two years in Europe was a mixture of beetle-crusher and staff duty—platoon leader, liaison officer, reconnaissance platoon leader, liaison officer again. In July 1960, as tension grew over a possible confrontation between the West and the U.S.S.R. over Germany, Schwarzkopf won a plum assignment as aide-de-camp to the Army's commanding general in Berlin. It was a lesser role, but somewhat reminiscent of the post that his father had held a few years earlier, as deputy provost marshal in that same divided city.

Promoted to captain in July 1961, Schwarzkopf reported in September for another eight-month training period at the Advanced Infantry School at Fort Benning. His Berlin assignment had ended the very week that the Wall was going up, remaining for three decades the most enduring symbol of the Cold War.

Like most career military officers, who earn civilian degrees in a vast range of fields that often, on the surface, appear to have little relevance to their chosen pursuits, Schwarzkopf found time to expand his knowledge in a field for which he had shown considerable

aptitude while at West Point. On graduation from the
Fort Benning school, now wearing the chest badge of
Master Parachutist—and with back pains to prove it—
Captain Schwarzkopf enrolled in a master's degree
course in engineering at the University of Southern
California.

For the next two years, from June 1962 to June 1964,
while the young officer immersed himself in the study
of missile mechanics, the world was changing quickly,
and dangerously. Even before the Berlin crisis, Cuba
had gone communist under the charismatic Fidel Cas-
tro. President Kennedy, humiliated by the Bay of Pigs
fiasco, had recouped in October 1962 by staring down
Soviet Premier Nikita Krushchev in the missile crisis.
The Berlin Wall was reinforced with mine fields and
guard towers, and extended all along the border between the two Germanys.

Vietnam, a place that few Americans could readily
locate on a map, had become somehow vital to U.S.
interests, enough so that military advisers had been
sent there to help the local government fight off a
communist insurrection. If this was not done, the
theory went, all of Southeast Asia would fall under
Moscow's or Peking's domination like a row of domi-
noes. On November 1, 1963, the government in Saigon
was overthrown by a cabal of disgruntled generals and
its president, Ngo Dinh Diem, murdered, along with
his adviser and brother, Ngo Dinh Nhu. The brother's
widow accused Kennedy of scheming with the generals. Three weeks later, Kennedy, too, was murdered, by
a strange man who the authorities claimed was a loner
yet was shown to have murky Soviet and Cuban con-
nections. The widow Nhu called it "chickens coming
home to roost."

During this same period the United States began to
get a grip on its rocketry problems, and the NASA
space program moved into full gear with a series of
successful Mercury astronaut orbits and some deep-
space probes, restoring confidence in American tech-

nology and making it respectable to have a master's degree in missile engineering.

By June 1964, when Norman Schwarzkopf emerged from the Los Angeles campus with his own degree, Lyndon Johnson had been president seven months, proclaiming his intent to create a Great Society of racial and social equality in the United States. Johnson also pledged to continue sending aid to troubled areas abroad, where communist subversion and insurgency threatened the existence of struggling democracies. But, he added, "we are not about to send American boys nine or ten thousand miles from home to do what Asian boys ought to be doing for themselves."

Armed with his new diploma and a storehouse of technical knowledge, Schwarzkopf returned to West Point to serve as an instructor in the Department of Mechanics. It would be another year before the bugle summoned H. Norman Schwarzkopf, Jr., to the real task for which he had been prepared.

4

You're Talking Human Lives

In the spring of 1965, as the academic year at West Point was drawing to a close, Captain Schwarzkopf received his orders for Vietnam. As a young officer with career ambitions, he had of course volunteered, and the military academy had approved the request, on condition that he return afterward to finish his scheduled three-year teaching assignment.

He took a Military Airlift Command flight to Saigon to become one of some 80,000 Americans who by that time had already flowed into the Southeast Asian country.

His assignment was as an adviser to the South Vietnamese Army's Airborne Division. This was one of the three elite units of the country's military, the others being the Ranger Division and the Marine Division. All three were largely manned by soldiers of northern birth who had come south with their families to escape communism after the Geneva Accords that ended the war with France in 1954.

The exodus of about one million was composed largely of Roman Catholics rather than Buddhists. This, along with a strong anticommunist sentiment, was thought to make the transplanted northerners more dedicated to the Saigon government's cause and more highly motivated in fighting against the Vietcong than the native southerners—from whose midst, after all, the Vietcong insurgency had sprung.

The political reliability of the Airborne troops had caused them to become Saigon's palace guard. One of the unit's three brigades, or at least a battalion, was always stationed close by the presidential palace, bivouacked in the parks and under the tamarinds and plane trees that shaded the decaying old French colonial city from the shimmering tropic heat.

June 1965 was a dark time in Vietnam's turbulent history. The build-up of American forces was in its early stages. A few months earlier, the first contingent of U.S. Marines had disembarked near Danang, in the northern part of South Vietnam, to be met not by hostile fire but by lithe Vietnamese girls in traditional *ao dais*, offering garlands of flowers.

Since then, however, the situation had turned grim. Communist forces had launched a series of coordinated attacks across the country, not unlike the Tet Offensive that would occur two-and-a-half-years later. In Saigon, two Vietcong terror bombs blew up a floating restaurant, killing and wounding some of the Americans who frequented the place. An increasingly beleaguered government appealed for help, and President Johnson responded by sending the Army's famed 1st Infantry Division, the "Big Red One," and a host of other units to help stem the tide. The American public was just beginning to take a closer look at what the war in Vietnam was about.

The situation was especially bleak in the Central Highlands, where the North Vietnamese—known then as PAVN, for People's Army of Vietnam—had for the first time entered the conflict in sizable numbers. In II Corps, as the region was known on military maps, the PAVN and indigenous Vietcong launched a series of coordinated attacks. Staging the assault from across the border in Cambodia, the communist forces were on the verge of cutting II Corps in half, isolating the highlands from the coast. Retired Brigadier General Ted Mataxis, at that time the senior American military adviser in II Corps, recalls that ambushes and attacks along the roads had isolated Pleiku, the biggest city and capital of the highlands, and "every province capital and every district capital was cut off from every other one."

Into this maelstrom came H. Norman Schwarzkopf, fresh from his year of teaching at West Point, two months shy of his thirty-first birthday and about to be promoted to major at the start of his first combat tour.

After a period of orientation at MACV—U.S. Military Assistance Command Headquarters—in Saigon, Schwarzkopf was sent up-country to Pleiku. He found II Corps to be rugged mountain country populated mainly by Montagnards, the mountain tribes ethnically different from the Vietnamese, who spoke different tongues and regarded the lowlanders with the same mixture of fear and contempt that the Vietnamese displayed toward them.

The 'Yards, as Americans called them, had been recruited as mercenaries to garrison the chain of U.S. Special Forces camps placed along the Cambodian border to watch for infiltration by the North Vietnamese. The Green Berets considered their CIDG, or Civilian Irregular Defense Group, troops to be better fighters and more trustworthy than the South Vietnamese, whose reputation as soldiers was subject to much scorn, some of it undeserved.

Within a month of arriving, Schwarzkopf pinned on his major's gold leaves. But even before that occurred, he had his first taste of the war. It was not what he had expected, and it brought his name immediately to the attention of superiors.

"We were getting ready to go into a military operation during the Ia Drang Valley campaign, and had been given this wonderful operations order written in total for Leavenworth style by the senior Vietnamese headquarters," Schwarzkopf recalled in a 1990 interview. "Then I discovered that, contrary to the order, we had no fire support or any advance air strikes.

"So I went back and advised by Vietnamese counterpart not to go. Three or four hours later, I was hauled in before an array of colonials. 'Captain,' one of them said, 'how dare you say not go? Who are you to decide what adequate air support is?'

" 'Sir, with all due respect,' I answered, 'when I'm the senior man on the ground and it's my ass hanging out, adequate air support is about a hundred sorties of B-52's, all in direct support of me. I may be willing to accept something less, but that's just barely adequate when it's my butt on the line.'

"Of course, they got furious. But that's my approach to military operations. You're talking human lives, and my responsibility is to accomplish the objective with a minimum loss of the troops under my command. That's my job—not just accomplishing the mission."

Bold stand that it was, Schwarzkopf survived the colonels' ire. But he would find repeatedly that Vietnam was not a war in which a field officer could depend on support from the rear of any kind.

Among the principal targets of the North Vietnamese offensive were the Special Forces camps guarding natural infiltration routes from Cambodia. In June, a regular North Vietnamese unit, the 32nd PAVN Regiment, attacked one of these at Duc Co, which guarded Highway 14, an old French-built, two-lane blacktop thirty miles southwest of Pleiku and seven miles from the border.

For two months the four hundred camp defenders and their twelve-member Green Beret A-team were surrounded, surviving on food and ammunition that was air-dropped daily into the compound. Every supply plane that approached the camp encountered a barrage of ground fire from the communist forces ringing the camp, and several were shot down. Air strikes and artillery pounded the enemy, estimated to number about three thousand, inflicting unknown casualties. About sixty of Duc Co's defenders were killed, including two Americans.

On August 3, the communist forces attacked in strength, hoping to overrun the camp and end the siege at last. The situation became critical, and a thousand Airborne troops loaded on helicopters at Pleiku to relieve the camp. Major Schwarzkopf was senior man among the handful of advisers who went along. The paratroopers made it into the camp and organized themselves for a counterattack to drive the enemy from the terrain around the camp, but were driven back, taking numerous casualties.

The fighting intensified over the next few days as the communist forces refused to pull back despite constant pounding by artillery and air strikes. By August 5, Schwarzkopf's unit had been split apart and three elements, fighting separately, were in great danger. The major braved heavy enemy fire to recover and treat a handful of wounded Vietnamese paratroopers, then led them to safety. After that he returned to find the other groups and pulled them back as well.

Four days later, another Vietnamese relief force, including everything from Marines to local "ruff puff" irregulars, headed down Highway 14 toward the Duc Co. They ran into a major ambush. Mataxis, who watched the action from a helicopter, said the North Vietnamese "came out of the woods in platoons." Allied aircraft were called in to hammer the enemy with bombs and napalm. "We had so many planes that they were stacked up, waiting for permission to attack," he says. But the relief force, reeling from the ambush with heavy losses, pulled back and never reached Duc Co.

Around August 17, the recently arrived U.S. 173rd Airborne Brigade was flown to Pleiku and sent to relieve the camp. This time the move succeeded. The North Vietnamese broke off the siege of Duc Co and vanished across the border into Cambodia.

Schwarzkopf recalls that he helped to stack the bodies of the dead paratroopers during the fight for the camp, and a much published photograph shows a tall young American, unmistakably Schwarzkopf in fatigue cap and shoulder-slung assault rifle, helping to carry a wounded Vietnamese soldier. (According to Schwarzkopf, the photographer was Peter Arnett, then an Associated Press reporter covering the Vietnam War.)

The battle of Duc Co was declared a major victory for the South Vietnamese, and to put the official stamp on it, General William Westmoreland flew from Saigon to commemorate the event. Schwarzkopf recalls that "the sky full of helicopters" as Westmoreland arrived with an entourage of dignitaries and news correspondents.

Schwarzkopf said the television crews had started setting up their cameras when Westmoreland asked, " 'Who's the senior American adviser here?' and I stepped forward, saluted, and said, 'Sir, I am the senior American in the camp, Major Norman Schwarzkopf.'

"And Westy turns around to the press and says, 'Wait a minute, you fellows, I want to speak privately with the major here.' Then he takes me off to one side and says in a low voice, 'Major, how's the food?' And I said, 'Well, General, we've been under siege here and getting only air drops.' Westmoreland says, 'I see,' and then he says, 'Well, Major, are you getting your mail?' "

A few months later, Schwarzkopf was awarded the Silver Star, the third highest American military decoration for valor, for his heroism in rescuing and reorganizing the divided paratroopers at Duc Co. It was the first of three Silver Stars that he would earn in the Indochina conflict.

The second came six months later, on Valentine's

Day 1966. This time, according to the citation, Schwarzkopf was leading a paratrooper assault on a strongly defended Vietcong position. "Exposing himself to intense hostile fire, he was wounded four times yet refused to take cover or medical evacuation until consolidation of the objective and the evacuation of wounded subordinates was completed."

After ten months, MACV pulled Schwarzkopf out of the field and assigned him to a rear-area slot as senior staff adviser for civil affairs to the Airborne Division. Then he was returned to the United States and back to West Point. As agreed, he resumed his teaching post in the Department of Mechanics, this time as an associate professor. From there he went to the Army's Command and General Staff College at Fort Leavenworth, Kansas, for another year, completing the course in June 1969.

It was during this time, too, that Schwarzkopf met his fiancée, Brenda Holsinger, who at the time was a Trans World Airlines flight attendant. They were introduced at a West Point football game in 1967 and married the next year, before he got new orders—back to Vietnam.

In June 1969, now a lieutenant colonel, Schwarzkopf arrived in Vietnam just as President Richard Nixon's Vietnamization program, to turn the main responsibility for the war over to the locals, was moving into high gear. Schwarzkopf was assigned as executive officer to the chief of staff at MACV Headquarters, located at Tan Son Nhut air base on the outskirts of Saigon.

The U.S. military was showing inordinate signs of wear and tear. Ever since the Tet Offensive a year and a half earlier, public confidence and support for the military had been eroding back home, and it was having its effect on the troops in the front lines.

Militarily, the enemy was being beaten; but then the enemy in Vietnam was always being beaten, they just never seemed to lose. American forces numbered about 500,000. Disciplinary incidents in the ranks were increasing, and drugs were beginning to eat away at the

Army like a cancer. The murder of more than one hundred Vietnamese civilians at My Lai had happened more than a year earlier, but was still a dirty little secret, to be revealed in a few months' more time. Six Green Beret officers would be charged with murdering a double agent but absolved before trial, on orders from the Pentagon. The name of the game for career officers was "getting your ticket punched."

Norman Schwarzkopf has said of what he found in Vietnam the second time: "It was a cesspool."

By December he had gained what he wanted, a field command. He was transferred to the Americal Division at Chu Lai, on the central northern coast just below Danang. He took over as commander of the 1st battalion, 6th Infantry, 198th Infantry Brigade.

The Americal—officially the 23rd Infantry Division—had been organized in Vietnam in 1968 by combining three formerly independent infantry brigades, the 196th, 198th, and 11th. From the beginning the new organization had had problems. As a provisional unit, it lacked the historical tradition or esprit de corps that helped sustain other divisions in Vietnam, such as the 1st Infantry, the 1st Air Cavalry, or the 101st Airborne. Even the name Americal was borrowed, from a similar unit organized at New Caledonia in World War II. The new division, like its predecessor, wore a patch design of the Southern Cross. It was to become, in many ways, a star-crossed division, with a reputation as a catchall for troops that commanders elsewhere wanted to be rid of. This applied in particular to the 198th Infantry, which became known as the "dollar ninety eight."

In its defense, probably no American unit in Vietnam had a tougher place in which to fight than the Americal Division. The coastal plains along the South China Sea were heavily populated, and few areas of the country, except possibly the Mekong Delta, fostered more sympathy and support for the Vietcong insurgency. Troops of the Americal Division approached

almost every village with the assumption that no matter how "pacified" it might be in the Saigon command's rating system, they would encounter hostility.
That this was unfriendly territory was reflected in
statistics—in 1970, figures showed that more than
three fourths of the Americal Division's battlefield
casualties were from booby traps and mines. The psy-
chological effect of that was even more corrosive on
division morale.

In the Americal, Schwarzkopf ran into Mataxis
again; their paths would continue to cross over the
years. The older man was now a brigadier general, sent
back to Vietnam by Westmoreland to be the assistant
division commander in the Americal Division. He remembered Schwarzkopf from the Duc Co days and
came to regard him as one of the division's best battalion commanders, one whose field reports could always
be trusted. "He was a hell of a good man, rock solid,
right on the bubble all the time," Mataxis says today.

During this time two incidents occurred that would
haunt Schwarzkopf in later years. On February 17,
1970, two members of Charlie Company of the 1st
Battalion, 6th Infantry, was killed by a "short round"
from an American artillery gun. The shell was fired as
intended but hit a treetop, hurling red-hot shrapnel
into the troops' position.

The parents of one soldier, Sergeant Michael Mullen,
later accused Schwarzkopf of being responsible for the
death of their son. Schwarzkopf denied it then and still
does. He says calling the artillery fire was the kind of
tragic mistake that sometimes occurs in combat, for
which blame cannot always readily be placed. The
story, recounted in detail in a 1976 book, *Friendly Fire*,
by C.D.B. Bryan, has been seen by some as a metaphor
for the nation's agony over the Vietnam experience. In
the book, Schwarzkopf is quoted as telling the author
that Mullen's death was "a terrible, terrible tragedy . . .

but I don't think it was an error of deliberate negligence."

("Friendly fire" would trouble Schwarzkopf again during Operation Desert Shield, when a number of Americans would be killed by misdirected fire from U.S. aircraft attacking Iraqi targets on the battlefield.)

Three months after the artillery incident, Schwarzkopf was commanding another operation, this time in the Batangan peninsula south of Chu Lai. Within the Americal's area of operations, no area was more dangerous than the Batangan. It was where the My Lai incident had occurred more than two years earlier, and still had a number of hard-core VC units operating in its villages.

On May 28, 1970, Schwarzkopf was orbiting in his UH-1 Huey command and control helicopter as troops on the ground conducted a sweep. The radio suddenly crackled with the word that some members of Bravo Company had blundered into a mine field. Two officers had been wounded and other soldiers were trapped, unable to move for fear of triggering more mines. Although a medevac helicopter was on the way, Schwarzkopf ordered his pilots to land and pick up the wounded. Then he began to thread his way on foot into the mine field, telling his frightened troops to walk out the way they had come, keeping a distance from each other but stepping only in each other's tracks.

As they moved gingerly toward safety, a GI stepped on a mine. It hurled him in the air, breaking a leg. Shrapnel sprayed Schwarzkopf and his artillery officer, Captain Bob Trabbert, who had arrived with him on the helicopter. The soldier was panicked, screaming. Schwarzkopf, fearing he would touch off yet another mine, moved slowly toward the wounded man, his knees buckling. As he reached the wounded man, he called back to Trabbert to find something to splint the leg. Trabbert handed his knife to another soldier to cut a branch from a nearby tree. In moving toward the tree, the man stepped on another mine. The explosion killed him and two others standing nearby. Trabbert lost a leg and an arm but survived.

Schwarzkopf has said numerous times since that he saw himself as having had no choice but to risk his own life to get the troops out of the mine field. The action earned him his third Silver Star and a second Purple Heart. But those medals were small consolation for the pain of what had occurred, and when he finally left Vietnam two months later, it was with a bitter taste—made even worse by his discovery that back home, the country had turned against the military.

He found that returning servicemen were villified as murderers and "baby burners." He resented it because he hadn't done any such thing. He even got into an argument with one of his sisters, who had been a peace marcher, although he later apologized to her.

The whole experience made Schwarzkopf wary about future wars. In 1971, a year after his return, he told *Friendly Fire* author Bryan:

"Now, this is going to make me think long and hard before I go to war again. This is me, Norm Schwarzkopf, personally. I don't think there will ever be another major confrontation where the armies line up on both sides. If that happens, it's inevitably going to be nuclear weapons and the whole thing. So I think all wars of the future are going to be—and again, God forbid, I hope we don't have any. War is a profanity. It really is. It's terrifying. Nobody is more anti-war than an intelligent person who's been to war. Probably the most anti-war people I know are Army officers—but if we do have a war, I think it's going to be similar in nature to Vietnam and Korea. Limited in scope. And when they get ready to send me again, I'm going to have to stop and ask myself: 'Is it worth it?' That's a very dangerous place for the nation to be when your own army is going to stop and question."

Schwarzkopf's prophecies about future wars didn't exactly prove out—there would be, along with Grenada and Panama, another major confrontation, called Desert Storm. There would be no nuclear weapons, no reprise of Vietnam. And when the time came, nobody had to ask Norman Schwarzkopf whether he would be available. But the Vietnam memories did not fade. In a recent *Life* interview, he recalled his experience there again: "Ordinarily, commanding an infantry battalion is the highlight of a military career. Let me tell you, mine wasn't. It was because of all the stuff going on back in the States. No one wants to go to war, but if you go, you like to think that your country is behind you."

5

I Don't Need This Gaff

The return from Vietnam was fraught with unhappy encounters. People even spat on soldiers in uniform. Although Schwarzkopf says, defiantly, that nobody ever dared do that to him, he was insulted several times while speaking to civic groups and other audiences, even to the point of asking him whether he had "napalmed babies." He considered leaving the service and looking for a job in the civilian sector. "I don't need this gaff," he recalls telling others. But eventually he was able to come to terms with the Vietnam aftermath, recognizing that "if I didn't, it would destroy me." He also decided to stay with the Army in the hopes that the problems left over from the Vietnam experience could be fixed, and that he could play a part in fixing them.

But there would be further reminders in years to come. Schwarzkopf recalls "one of the blackest days of my life," the day in 1975 when he learned, while stationed in Alaska, that the Saigon government had finally fallen to the communists.

"I had got very close to many of the Vietnamese, and I recognized that what they were fighting for was good," he said. "I asked myself about the thousands of lives lost, the many years of U.S. involvement and the cost to the taxpayers, not to mention the families of the people who were killed, and what was it for? At that time it appeared that it was for nothing. I'm not sure it wasn't a piece of the Berlin Wall coming down and being played out elsewhere."

Soon after returning, he underwent surgery at Walter Reed Army Hospital in Washington to repair long-standing back problems, aggravated by what he calls "too many parachute jumps."

The next few years brought a variety of assignments for the Schwarzkopfs, as their family grew. Daughter Cynthia was born in 1970, daughter Jessica two years later. A son, Christian, came along in 1977. During the years from mid-1970 to 1983, the family lived mainly in the Washington area. But there were numerous moves—to Fort Richardson, Alaska, where Colonel Schwarzkopf was deputy commander of an infantry brigade; to Fort Lewis, Washington, where he commanded a brigade of the 9th Infantry Division; and to Hawaii, where he was deputy director of plans for the U.S. Pacific Command. While there, Brenda Schwarzkopf proudly assisted with the formal pinning on of his first star.

In all this time, he never quit soul searching on the matter of Vietnam and the doubts it had raised in his mind. He had told the author of *Friendly Fire* that at some point he might have to stop and ask himself whether an order he had been given was worth it.

In 1986, while at Fort Lewis, he told the *Seattle Post-Intelligencer* in an interview that he had come to terms with this during the Grenada invasion three years earlier.

"I thought a lot about the role of the military and the role of the Army and my place in it after the Vietnam War, as I think any professional who had any sensitivity at all had to do," Schwarzkopf told the reporter. "I was able to reconcile my role in the military and also the role of the military in regard to the country. The bottom line of all that is that the country can never dare risk having a military that, when asked to carry out legitimate orders, is given the option of refusing those orders. I think that places the country in a very dangerous position. If they think they would ever turn an order down, the morally correct thing to do is choose another profession."

He said he had given thought to leaving the military more than once, including whether to retire after twenty years. "But I don't think I did for long," he said. "People ask me, when did I decide to make the Army a career. I never decided to make it a career. I always decided not to get out yet is what it boils down to."

He said then that when he did leave the military, he wanted to be choosy about a second career. "I will be candid with you and tell you what I *don't* want to do," he said, "and that is to work for the so-called military–industrial complex. I don't want people to use me or my contacts and friendships. I would hope that when they hire me, they would be hiring Norman Schwarzkopf, not General Schwarzkopf.

"It's okay to hire General Schwarzkopf if they think he has management ability, but not because he knows Joe Blow who happens to be in the procurement business, and therefore they think they can get special contracts."

There followed another two-year assignment in Europe, as assistant division commander of the 8th Infantry Division (Mechanized), then a return to Washington for yet another obligatory Pentagon desk assignments, this time as director of personnel management for the Army. Schwarzkopf was now a major general.

In June 1983, Norman Schwarzkopf was back in fatigues. He was named commanding general of the 24th Infantry Division (Mechanized) and its home post at Fort Stewart. At the time it was the culmination of his dreams. As a young officer at West Point, he had thought the command of a division was the best that anyone could hope for in an Army career.

One Sunday in October 1983, Brenda has recalled, the general came home and said: "I have to go. I can't tell you where." He was gone, and two days later she learned, along with the rest of the country, that U.S. forces had invaded Grenada.

Few people knew immediately where Grenada was located. Although the government's pro-Soviet leanings and close ties with communist Cuba were an irritant to United States policy in the Western hemisphere, it hardly seemed the sort of place that Washington would regard as having sufficient strategic value to merit a full-scale military invasion.

Discovered in 1498 by Christopher Columbus on his second trip to the New World, it was a tiny island, one of the Windwards, about ninety miles off the coast of Venezuela. It has a population of about eighty thousand people, mostly French-speaking and of African descent, and an economy heavily dependent on nutmeg and other spices.

The Grenada crisis had risen like a Caribbean hurricane. A military-led coup d'etat, with the backing of the Cuban government that had military advisers on the island, had deposed Prime Minister Maurice Bishop. The conspirators led by the Grenada military commander, Hudson Austin, and the radical leftist deputy premier, Bernard Coard, had put Bishop under house arrest. He was set free by his supporters, then recaptured. As the crisis deepened, Bishop and several of his close associates were murdered, and surviving members of his party and government appealed for help from the United States.

A sizable operation, employing all four services under the command of a Navy admiral and code-named Urgent Fury, was organized to retake the island. The plan had all the basic elements of an raid—capture the island's two airfields, the radio and television station, free the prisoners held by the rebels, and restore order.

It also called for the rescue of about a thousand Americans, many of them students at a medical school on the island.

The expectation was that it could be accomplished in twenty-four hours. As part of the planning, news media were to be kept away until the situation on the island was stabilized and secure. On October 25, a U.S.-led force with token representatives from several other countries in the region, attacked. To critics who shrieked that it was an act of imperialist American aggression, President Ronald Reagan replied that the mission was necessary to rescue the medical students.

When Schwarzkopf got the word to saddle up, he thought at first he was headed to Lebanon, where a U.S. Marine barracks had been blown up by a truck bomb the day before. His Grenada assignment, according to published accounts, was to serve as the Army's chief adviser to the commander, Vice Admiral Joseph Metcalf III, on what was primarily a naval operation even though it involved all the services.

The Grenada operation did not go like clockwork. Some of the confusion was ascribed to the joint forces arrangement, the same problem that had plagued the Desert One rescue operation in the Iranian desert almost three years earlier. Not all communications gear was compatible, meaning that members of the different services had trouble communicating with each other. (The tale of the Army officer who had to make a credit-card call to the United States in order to call in naval gunfire is apparently apocryphal, although permanently ensconced in American military lore.)

As Schwarzkopf has recalled, the 800 Cubans on the island did not surrender meekly as some had expected, but fought back against the advancing Americans. Anti-aircraft crews, Cuban-trained, also stayed at their posts and shot it out with the attacking American helicopters. And one American air strike hit a hospital by mistake because of faulty map coordinates.

Matters could have been worse, had it not been for

an element of luck. One of the first objectives of the attack was an airstrip that was so close to the shore that officer, feared winds could drive parachuting U.S. Army Rangers into the water. The choice was to drop from only five hundred feet, which would put them on the ground, but at the risk of severe injuries. Moreover, the Americans were unaware that antiaircraft guns were emplaced on high ground near the strip. That could have been devastating that not the guns been mounted in such a way that they could not depress their barrels below seven hundred feet. Thus then were unable to hit the planes as they dropped the parachutists.

Schwarzkopf recalls that while aboard the helicopter-assault-carrier USS *Guam* on the way to Grenada, he had misgivings as to whether the United States should be committing its military forces to that particular cause. "I asked myself why on earth the U.S. was getting involved in Grenada. Then I said, 'Schwarzkopf, just let it sort itself out. You're an instrument of policy. You don't make policy.'"

But not until the second day on the island did he become convinced that the mission was justified. Flying into the capital of St. George, he saw some words scrawled on a wall. "I have seen that sign on walls all over the world—in Berlin, Vietnam, Tokyo, and even on the walls of the Pentagon. It always says something like 'Long live Marxism' or 'Down with the U.S.,' but as the helicopter got closer and I could read it, I saw that it said, 'God Bless America.'"

Later on, the images of the American medical students arriving back in the United States and dropping to their knees to kiss the ground helped him to become "one hundred percent sure we did the right thing in Grenada.

"First of all, it was healthy for the military to have been involved in an operation that the American public has resoundingly endorsed," he said, looking back on the Grenada episode. "Also, it was very good to be

involved in an operation that was recognized by everyone as a very successful one, given the recent history
of the armed forces in Korea, which some people considered a tie, and Vietnam, which others felt was a
defeat."

Although judged a qualified military success, Grenada would have its own kind of fallout. The decision
by Metcalf to bar the press for the first part of the
operation had outraged the news media in the United
States. Many reporters had managed to make it to the
island on their own; some were rounded up and detained by military officials after they stepped ashore.
Many military people felt the press was getting what it
deserved after Vietnam. To the media, of course, it was
blatant censorship, running counter to the letter and
the spirit of the First Amendment and the American
public's "right to know."

Eventually the dispute shifted to dialogue, as journalists and generals sat down in Washington to search for
ways to accommodate each other's needs and priorities
in time of war. The result was the "media pool" system. Eight years later, it would be put to its biggest
test in the Saudi desert.

After Grenada, and the completion of his stint as
commander of the 24th Infantry, Schwarzkopf was
transferred back to Washington for his third tour of
Pentagon duty since Vietnam. He served eleven
months, beginning in July 1985 as Assistant Deputy
Chief of Staff for Operations and Plans. Awarded his
third star on July 1, 1986, he returned to Fort Lewis for
a year as Commanding General of I Corps. Then it was
back to Washington yet again as Deputy Chief of Staff
for Operations and Plans. In a second role, he served as
the Army's senior member on the Military Staff Committee at the United Nations, a post that helped
Schwarzkopf hone the diplomatic skills he would require in his next, and most important, assignment.

$\star$ $\star$ | 6 | $\star$ $\star$

His Own Stamp of Approval

The headquarters of United States Central Command was housed in several buildings erected for the purpose at MacDill Air Force Base, across the bay from Tampa. CentCom, as it was called, evolved in 1983 out of the former Rapid Deployment Joint Task Force that was created during the Carter administration, and had come to grief in the aborted effort to rescue hostages from the American embassy in Tehran in 1980.

General P. X. Kelley was the first commander in 1980–81, going on to become commandant of the Marine Corps. His successor, Army General Robert C. Kingston, remained in charge as the transition was made in January 1983 from the RDF to Central Command, and continued as commander-in-chief until late 1985, when he was replaced by George B. Crist.

Crist was a flinty four-star Marine general who had made it to the top—somewhat miraculously, for a Marine—without ever having commanded a battalion in combat. However, he had been a combat field adviser to the South Vietnamese Marines, and went on to earn a reputation as an organizational genius. He also was a terrifying boss who, in the words of one subordinate officer, "ate colonels for breakfast." Stories were legion at MacDill of how Crist would fire on the spot any briefing officer who did not have an immediate answer to a question. The officers, while looking for new assignments, tended to gather at an area of the base known as the "molehole," where, according to one former CentCom officer, "they played a lot of golf." He said that after a while it became something of a badge of honor to have been fired by the fire-breathing Marine.

When Crist came up for retirement in November 1988, some of the Pentagon betting on his successor focused on Navy Admiral Henry C. Mustin. The fact that a Marine general and not a naval officer had run the headquarters through the recent Gulf "tanker war"—essentially a naval operation, after all—had already rankled some feelings. In keeping with the joint character of the headquarters, they felt it should now be the Navy's turn. But when the time came, the Pentagon reached into its own corridors to pick out an Army officer, H. Norman Schwarzkopf, Jr. He was a top-grade strategic thinker, who as Deputy Chief of Staff for Operations and Plans, and senior Army member on a United Nations-related committee, had sat in on arms-reduction talks with the Soviets. He was also a combat veteran with knowledge of the Gulf region, and eligible for promotion to full general.

At CentCom, the changeover from Crist to Schwarzkopf was like a breeze sweeping in off Tampa Bay. While everyone acknowledged that the crusty Marine was brilliant, most junior officers were terrified of incurring his wrath. The first thing new arrivals heard was about Crist giving the instant boot to any "oh-six" who fumbled a question.

Some officers in the Public Affairs Office, who had

been involved in handling the media pools in the Gulf, said Crist had never once visited their office. "On the day he retired, he just walked out without saying thank you or good-bye or anything," one said. Ironically, Crist had gone to great lengths during the "tanker war" to assure that the media pools had access to events. He told one interviewer that the Grenada invasion, where he had been a Pentagon observer, had taught him that "the press can do a hell of a lot better job than the military" in telling the story. It was a different George Crist, too, who turned up with blue blazer and affable manner as CBS military analyst during Operation Desert Storm.

According to former associates, one of Schwarzkopf's first moves after arriving at Tampa, wearing his brand-new four stars, was to assure the Central Command staff that although he had no patience with slackers, he would "not be a firing CINC" in the tradition of George Crist. "He went through all the offices and introduced himself to everybody. He wanted a new image for the place, and he was really a hail-fellow-well-met. It didn't take him long to get around and get to know the people he was working for."

Schwarzkopf also introduced new family-day gatherings at CentCom, an aspect of military life in which his all-business predecessor had shown little interest. "He had a big picnic tent put up outside, and he brought in tanks and other equipment, and put it on display for the families to see," recalls one who was there at the time. "I guess it reflected the fact that here was a very senior officer with a young family."

Despite the vast differences in personality, some associates saw some similarities in the two generals. One officer who had seen them both in action says, "Schwarzkopf was like Crist in that you had to prove yourself to him. And they both have phenomenal memories. If you told either of them something once and then gave them a different version later, you'd better be able to explain why." Both also were quick to

anger, but whereas Crist had zero patience with someone who had not done his homework, "Schwarzkopf
would explode, and they'd turn it around. He got their
attention, but the next day it was forgotten. No
grudges."

One of Central Command's functions was to hold
command briefings for American ambassadors, diplomats, and other senior officials who were being assigned to duties in a given region, and Schwarzkopf
took steps to have these expanded and enlivened. "He
wanted the briefings to be more interesting, more up-
beat, and enthusiastic briefings that these people could
really understand," said a former aide. "He wanted to
have his own stamp of approval on the command briefings."

First of all, he wanted to find out where matters
stood, the first priority being a review of Central Command itself in the immediate aftermath of the Iraq–
Iran war, which had ended three months earlier. Although none of it was exactly news to him, Schwarzkopf found himself in charge of a headquarters with
overall responsibility for U.S. military activities in a
vast region of nineteen countries, stretching from
Egypt, Sudan, and Kenya in northeastern Africa, some
three thousand miles across the heart of the Arab world
to the Asian subcontinent, and more than three thousand miles from north to south. It was an area larger
than the continental United States, and a region of
extremes, with deserts below sea level and mountains
over 24,000 feet, meaning temperatures ranged from
well below freezing to over 180°F.

Its concerns included the oil-rich and politically explosive Persian Gulf, where Iraq and Iran had just
fought one of the century's longest and bloodiest wars;
Afghanistan, whose communist government was still
battling an insurgency after the Soviet withdrawal, and
such politically turbulent countries as Ethiopia, Jordan,
and Pakistan.

The region contains about seventy percent of the

world's oil reserves and three of its most strategic choke points—the Suez Canal, the Bab el Mandeb at the lower end of the Red Sea, and the Strait of Hormuz. It did not include Israel, Lebanon, or Syria—the countries making up the other major trouble spot in the Middle East.

Central Command's overall mission was to guarantee that the United States and its allies continued to have access to Persian Gulf oil, maintained an "effective and visible" U.S. military presence, helped friendly states build and maintain their defense and security, and deterred threats to the region's stability by the Soviet Union or other states.

A basic element of the Soviet deterrence policy was the so-called Zagros Doctrine. This Cold War concept, dating back forty years, held that the Soviets, in their never ending ambition to gain access to the Gulf with its oil reserves and warm-water ports, would strike southward through Iran, and the United States would deploy forces there to block the advance in the rugged Zagros Mountains of western Iran.

More than 200,000 troops of all four services were designated as on call to CentCom in a time of crisis. Whether they could have fulfilled the requirements of the Zagros Doctrine was unclear, as was the means by which they could be transported.

One of the glaring weaknesses of the United States military at that time was the shortage of transportation. The U.S. Merchant Marine, so vital in World War II, had virtually disappeared by the early 1980s. A massive program was initiated then to provide fast cargo vessels, mainly by buying and converting existing ships, to pre-position them with supplies in a given region, and to carry entire Army or Marine divisions with their equipment. These ships, along with the Air Force's cargo and personnel-lift capability, eventually would be put to the litmus test in Operation Desert Shield.

As a unified, or joint, headquarters, Central Command was subjected to a great deal of scorn from critics within and without the military. With no visible hardware, no tanks conducting exercises nearby, it looked like a do-nothing bureaucracy, where the main activity was maneuvering papers from in-box to out-box. The corridors were thronged by officers and enlisted people in Army green, Marine olive, and the blues of the Air Force and Navy. Just what they all did was a puzzle to outsiders and a subject of much ridicule among military traditionalists.

Such headquarters was like a miniature Pentagon, and detractors felt that it was more likely to generate confusion than foster cohesion among their combat elements. Instead of resolving problems of inter-service rivalry, they tended to get caught up in the same old Pentagon politics and intrigues. The biggest problem with the military's jointness concept, these critics said, was that it required every service to have a role in a given operation whether it was really needed or not.

The worst example cited by these critics was the 1980 Iran hostage-rescue operation, in which the Army commando force was given an insufficient number of poorly maintained Navy helicopters and Marine Corps pilots who had not flown these particular aircraft before, and could not even train on the carrier's deck for fear of giving away the game to Soviet spy ships.

Among the severest critics of the joint system was former Secretary of the Navy John F. Lehman, Jr., who in a 1988 book, *Command of the Seas*, ridiculed Central Command as "one thousand uniformed bureaucrats (850 Army and Air Force, 150 Navy/Marine) to run the Gulf operations, and for pork-barrel reasons, located at Tampa, Florida." Lehman said that Admiral James "Ace" Lyons, a former commander of the U.S. Pacific Fleet, had been forced to retire from the Navy in 1987 after arguing that "running a dangerous naval operation in the Gulf from a bureaucracy in Florida was unworkable and would lead to disaster."

Supporters of joint commands, on the other hand,

argued that the United States was unlikely to fight any kind of war in which any of the services—Army, Navy, Air Force, or Marines—would not be needed. A unified headquarters was the best way of assuring that the best available forces could be brought to bear under one commander to carry out the mission. Nowhere, contended Central Command's defenders, did this seem more appropriate than in the Persian Gulf region, the farthest-flung of all areas where the United States had major strategic interests but no significant military establishment already in place.

In Europe, there were the forces of NATO, dominated by the United States; in Asia, U.S. air and naval forces operated full-time from bases in the Philippines and Japan, and a U.S. infantry division helped to anchor South Korea's defense against another invasion from the north.

CentCom, however, was halfway around the world from its assigned area of responsibility, making logistics its first and foremost problem in any crisis. There were no permanent American bases in any of the nineteen CentCom countries, and the creation of a forward headquarters with logistics bases in the region was the most avidly sought-after objective of its commanders.

It was not as if the United States had no military presence at all in the region. Although few Americans were aware of it, at least before 1987, the Navy had maintained a permanent small fleet of four to six warships in the Persian Gulf since 1949. Known as the Middle East Force, it had the assigned mission of showing the American flag and demonstrating to the Arab governments in the region that the United States was a friendly power, ready to assist them in any peaceful endeavor if asked, help out in emergencies, and especially to help guarantee that the international sea-lanes of the region were kept open.

More to the point, it was a reminder to all—including the British, who in the beginning had not wel-

comed the Americans into their former colonial
stronghold—and especially the Soviet Union, that the
Gulf and its oil were of great strategic importance to
the United States.

The determination to assert its interests in the oil-
rich Gulf region had been redefined after the collapse
of the shah of Iran's government in 1979, followed soon
afterward by the Soviet invasion of Afghanistan. These
events precipitated the Carter Doctrine, which declared that any attempt by an outside power to take
over the Persian Gulf region "will be regarded as an
assault on the vital interests of the United States, and
such an assault will be repelled by any means necessary, including military force."

In a major crisis in this area, U.S. military planners
clearly saw that all the services would be involved.
Army troops would need Air Force airlift and Navy
cargo ships to move their heavy equipment for desert
warfare. The Marines would of course be transported
by Navy ships. The Air Force would rush its fighter
bombers to the area, but the Navy's carrier-based jets
would already be on the job.

Earlier on, American military engineers had built a
number of air bases in the Saudi desert, and in 1988
they completed another on the southern end of Bahrain
island. Ostensibly this base was to be used by the
Bahrain Air Force, but with a runway reported to be
eight miles long, it was far too big for that purpose.
Just what it was really for was, for a long time, anybody's guess.

General Crist had said many times that a permanent
U.S. headquarters in the area was desirable, and he
carried that message to the Arab leaders on his frequent visits to the region. When a press report circu-
lated in late 1988 that the United States had finally
obtained permission from an unnamed country to set
up such a forward headquarters, Crist emphatically
denied it. Shortly thereafter, when he replaced Crist as
the CINC, so did Schwarzkopf.

On his first trip to the Gulf region after taking over, Schwarzkopf attended the change-of-command ceremony in which Rear Admiral William M. Fogarty replaced Rear Admiral Anthony Less as commander of the Middle East Force. On the bridge of the Navy's Gulf flagship, USS *La Salle*, moored at Bahrain, Schwarzkopf told reporters that the United States' actions during the Iraq–Iran war, namely the commitment of an expanded naval force to protect commercial shipping against Iranian attacks, had given Washington "a great deal of credibility" among the Arabs.

But he said the report that this had earned the United States approval to set up a forward military headquarters was untrue and had come as "just as much a shock to me as it did to a lot of other people that read it." He went on, "What the article said was that Central Command was getting ready to move out of Tampa and move over here to the Middle East. You know that's always been an objective of CentCom. We would like to have a headquarters over here someplace. We'd like to establish our U.S. presence here, and a headquarters here is a commitment.

"Also, it's an awfully long way to travel, you know, back and forth, every time you come over here. It would be a lot easier to coordinate some of the things we have to do. On the other hand, I would tell you that the last estimate we had was it was going to cost a lot of money if we ever decide to build a headquarters over here. And to be candid with you, in the current environment in Washington with regard to money for the military, particularly for construction, I doubt seriously if we're going to see any sort of a headquarters presence over here during my duration as the CINC and maybe several that follow me."

In the early days of Operation Desert Shield, Crist, speaking from his Florida retirement home, told a reporter that the press report two years earlier had been essentially correct. The Central Command headquarters was to have been located at the huge secret airbase at the southern end of Bahrain island, but the deal was never consummated, evidently for either political or budgetary reasons or a combination of both. When asked why he had denied the story two years earlier, Crist laughed. "I lied," he said.

The plan for a forward Central Command headquarters was anything but dead, however. In March 1991, Schwarzkopf himself confirmed that talks were again under way toward setting up a CentCom Forward in the Gulf region. While he did not confirm directly that Bahrain was still the proposed site, that was acknowledged by Bahraini officials.

After the shah fell and a fundamentalist government took over in Tehran in 1979, the U.S. presence took on even more importance. The Saudis and the sheiks who controlled the other Trucial states along the west coast of what they called the Arabian rather than the Persian Gulf took seriously the Ayatollah Khomeini's pledge to export Iranian-style fundamentalism throughout the Muslim world.

The Gulf rulers, in every case Sunni Muslims, feared the Iranian appeal would spread among their Shi'ite populations, which in some cases were the majority. So although these leaders publicly objected to the military presence of any Western superpower in the Gulf, they privately welcomed a bulwark against Iranian subversion or aggression. Their misgivings about the United States had to do with whether Washington would have the means or the resolve, when the crunch came, to maintain its commitment so far from home.

In September 1980, Iraq President Saddam Hussein baited Iran into a war over control of the Shatt-al-Arab waterway, the outlet to the Gulf that formed part of the border between the two historic enemies. This added a new element of crisis. Kuwait, next door to Iraq and dangerously close to the area of fighting, was particularly vulnerable to being caught up in the conflict. But all the Gulf states, valuing their relationship with Iraq, an Arab country, and fearful of Iran as regional power, were worried that they might become unwitting victims of the quarrel. While declaring public neutrality, the Saudis and Kuwaitis privately sided with the Iraqis by providing financial support and materiel to Baghdad.

In what would become known as the "tanker war," the Iraqis in 1984 began using aircraft to launch bombs and missiles against Iran's oil shipping, terminals, and coastal refineries in an effort to disrupt the oil lifeline that was paying for Iran's war effort. The Iranians, unable to retaliate against Iraq's nonexistent oil fleet, instead used gunboats and armed speedboats to attack commercial shipping in the Gulf, hoping that other governments would then pressure Baghdad to end the war.

Although the Iranian attacks were random, they concentrated on vessels of Kuwait and Saudi Arabia, the two countries that were providing the most financial support for Iraq. In all, some four hundred ships were damaged and several sunk in the four years from 1984 until the war's end in 1988.

The United States, meanwhile, had a ringside seat for the Iraq–Iran war in its early years. American advisers were training Saudi crews in the use of AWACS, the flying radar command posts that could identify practically anything that moved through the air and in some cases while still on the ground. In the Gulf waters, the ships of the Middle East Force were constantly on patrol.

The MEF operated out of Bahrain, where a permanent dock space was alloted to the white-painted command ship, USS *La Salle*. But the overall operation was so low-key that many inhabitants of the small island nation off the Saudi coast were unaware of the American presence, or assumed it was British. Some prepositioned logistics vessels were also operating from Diego Garcia, a British-held atoll some 2,500 miles south of the Gulf. The United States had kept at least one aircraft carrier group, and sometimes two, on duty in the Indian Ocean since the early 1980s.

In early 1987, as the war in the Gulf itself escalated ever more dangerously, the tiny Middle East Force found itself sailing in harm's way—without no more of a mandate than to show the flag, and with rules of engagement that, some said, were anything but clear.

On the night of May 17, 1987, an Iraqi F-1 Mirage on a mission to attack Iranian shipping hit the missile frigate USS *Stark* with two French-made Exocet missiles, killing 37 crewmen and nearly sinking the ship. The Baghdad government apologized, saying the attack had been a mistake—an explanation officially accepted by the Reagan administration but regarded by some American naval officers then, and to the present day, with some suspicion.

After an investigation, the Pentagon found the *Stark*'s commanding officer and a second officer at fault for failing to have their anti-missile defense system fully activated at the time of the incident. The skipper was not court-martialed but retired from the Navy.

Admiral Lyons, meanwhile, cited the *Stark* affair to buttress his argument that a military bureaucracy in Florida could not run a military operation in the Persian Gulf. He said this "eleven thousand mile chain of command" had left the ship's officers confused about their rules of engagement—the actions they were authorized to take if threatened. Specifically, his argument went, they did not know that the ROE allowed them to "lock on" to the Iraqi jet with fire-control radar, an action that would have alerted the Iraqi pilot that he was about to be fired on if he did not alter course.

If Saddam Hussein had intended to draw the United States into the war that he was then losing badly, he partly succeeded. The Kuwait government, which was quietly contributing millions to the support of Iraq's war effort, found its oil shipping the target of Iranian retaliation and asked for the United States to help by "reflagging" eleven of its state-owned tankers with the Stars and Stripes, entitling them to U.S. naval escort.

The scheme drew strong opposition in Congress, especially among Democrats. Some argued that any such move would indeed draw the United States into the war, to defend an oil state that was not, after all, a direct major supplier of the United States. Only about 15 to 20 percent of the U.S. petroleum supply came from the Persian Gulf. But proponents pointed out that Kuwait was a principal supplier to U.S. allies in Europe and Japan, and any cutoff would affect the Western alliance, with immediate repercussions for the United States.

In the end, the Reagan administration went ahead with the plan, with enough support that it resisted Congressional efforts to invoke the War Powers Act, which requires the White House to obtain Congressional approval for continuing an operation after the first sixty days.

The Middle East Force was doubled, then tripled, in size. A battleship group was added to the two carrier groups in the Arabian Sea, just outside the Gulf. Oceangoing minesweepers and an assault carrier with helicopter minesweepers were dispatched to the Gulf. To help with the crisis, the British also bolstered their naval force in the Gulf, and warships and mine hunters were sent from France, Italy, the Netherlands, and Belgium. At its peak, there were some seventy to eighty ships in the region, about half of them American.

The reflagging and escort of Kuwaiti oil tankers by the United States, code-named Operation Earnest Will, began in July 1987 and achieved its purpose over the year or so that it was in full effect. An Iranian mine damaged a Kuwaiti supertanker, the *Bridgeton*, on its first upbound trip, and a Chinese-made Silkworm missile fired from occupied territory in Iraq's Fao peninsula badly damaged another of the ships, blinding its American master, while the vessel prepared to load cargo at Kuwait's main oil terminal. But the reflagged tankers made scores of trips the 600-mile length of the Gulf under U.S. naval escort without being molested by Iranian gunboats.

The "tanker war" and Operation Earnest Will served as a laboratory for updating naval methodology and for testing innovative ideas. For the first time since World War II the Navy had been called on to use convoy navigation techniques, and its thirty-year-old mine-sweepers had their first work ever with mines laid by an enemy. It also was the first test in combat of numerous weapons systems, including the Aegis cruisers.

Even the U.S. commitment to defend Kuwaiti shipping was not enough to induce the Kuwaitis—or the Saudis—to allow the United States to have a land base near the Gulf coast, so General Crist improvised by leasing two huge construction barges. Fortified with guns, surrounded by anti-missile decoy shields, the barges were anchored off the Saudi coast in the northern Gulf, serving as bases for Navy patrol boats and highly secret Army helicopters that flew only at night on patrol of the sea-lanes. Other Army helicopters operated from Navy warships, scoring their biggest coup in September 1987 when they disabled an Iranian vessel, the *Iran Ajr*, as it laid mines in the Gulf.

Ever mindful of the *Stark* tragedy, U.S. commanders were vigilant against the Iraqi threat as well. And given Iraq pilots' penchant for reckless flying, it was a wonder that none were ever shot down by an American warship. The closest call was on Thanksgiving Day, 1987, when the missile cruiser USS *Richmond K. Turner* came within a hair's breadth of shooting three Iraqi Mirages armed with Exocet missiles coming directly at it. They were eight miles out and Captain John Luke had his hand on the firing button when the Iraqis finally responded to warnings and veered away.

On April 14, 1988, the missile frigate USS *Samuel B. Roberts*, a sister ship of the *Stark*, stumbled into a newly laid Iranian mine field in the central Gulf, and while she was backing out, she was nearly ripped in half by a submerged mine. Eleven crewmen were hurt but by some miracle none were killed, as the blast hurled the ship's huge turbine engines off their mounts and sent a fireball up the stack two hundred feet in the air.

Navy officials credited strong leadership by the captain, Commander Paul X. Rinn, and a well-drilled crew for saving the ship to fight another day. Thirty months later, it was back on duty in the Red Sea, helping to enforce the United Nations-mandated embargo on cargo shipments to Iraq after its invasion of Kuwait.

Divers clearing the underwater mines from the waters where the *Roberts* was hit found one scrawled with large white letters, USA. Four days later, the United States retaliated against Iran for the *Roberts* mining with a multipronged operation code-named Praying Mantis. The *New York Times* quoted military analysts as calling it the most significant naval action involving U.S. forces since the battle of Leyte Gulf in the Philippines in late 1944.

While six warships attacked and destroyed two major Iran-owned oil platforms in the southern Gulf, three others went after an Iranian warship whose attacks on commercial shipping had earned it the nickname the "frigate Nasty." In a daylong series of clashes, the American ships and attack bombers from the carrier USS *Enterprise* sank two large Iranian gunboats and several smaller craft and left the "frigate Nasty" dead in the water, its notorious skipper screaming for help on the radio. The only U.S. loss in the operation came hours after the shooting stopped. A Cobra helicopter gunship crashed on a night patrol mission, apparently while taking evasive action after being tracked by Iranian radar. The two pilots were listed as killed in action.

One of the American SAGs, or three-ship surface-action groups, reported coming under fire from Iran's

shore-based Silkworm missile batteries in the Strait of
Hormuz. The missile frigate USS *Jack Williams*, command ship for SAG Delta, fired all its anti-missile chaff,
and several crewmen on the fantail claimed to have
seen one of the lumbering missiles pass behind the
ship and hit a distant oil rig. A second ship in the
group also reported Silkworm firings; the third, the
destroyer USS *O'Brien*, did not support the claim.

Although some officers aboard the *Jack Williams*
remained convinced still that the Silkworms had been
fired, General Crist and the Pentagon later asserted
that analysis of computer tapes showed no evidence
that any missiles had been fired from shore, and that
radar operators had misidentified the signals on their
screens in the *Jack Williams'* combat information center. The Iranians never commented one way or the
other.

On the same Monday that the Iranian navy was being
pummeled in the southern Gulf, six hundred miles to
the north, Iraq's Republican Guard troops were recap-
turing territory in the Faw peninsula that the Iranians
had held for the previous two years. It was the first in a
series of stunning rollbacks that by midsummer had
the Iranians on the ropes for the first time in the eight-
year war. Battering of Tehran by long-range Scud missiles in the "war of the cities," the erosion of the
Iranian Air Force through attrition and parts shortages,
and a general flagging of enthusiasm for the conflict
were suddenly tipping the advantage sharply in Saddam's favor.

On July 3, the American missile cruiser USS *Vincennes* shot down an Iranair A-300 Airbus on a commercial flight from Bandar Abbas to Dubai in the
United Arab Emirates. All 290 aboard the plane per-
ished when it was hit by two Standard missiles from
the Aegis-type cruiser. The ship was involved at the
time in a running scrap with some Iranian gunboats,
and in the heat of battle had mistaken the plane taking

off from Bandar Abbas for an F-14 fighter coming its way with the possible intent of attacking the ship.

Though some critics wondered what a powerhouse ship like the billion-dollar *Vincennes* was doing in the narrow confines of the Gulf in the first place, Crist took full responsibility for the decision to fire. He said it had been the right weapon to defend against the fixed Silkworm missile installation that the Iranians had completed at Kuhestak, in the Hormuz strait. Left unclear was what made that threat more significant than any of the other Silkworm sites, fixed or mobile, that had been in place along the strategic waterway for more than a year.

Meanwhile, an investigation by a team of Central Command officers showed that the *Vincennes'* radar, a super-sophisticated system that could locate, identify, and prioritize targets at 200 miles, had worked perfectly. But it had not been able to correctly identify the aircraft at ten miles, or indicate whether it was climbing or descending. For that, Captain Will C. Rogers III had depended on a separate system, which once again had been misread by the responsible operators.

The investigators found that the stress of first-time combat was a major factor in the faulty performance. Their heavily censored final report said nothing about why the *Vincennes* apparently was in Iranian waters, where it was not supposed to be, or why there was no air cover for the ship while it was involved in the clash with Iranian gunboats, although the carrier USS *Forrestal* was in the north Arabian Sea, ostensibly within reach with its aircraft.

The impression of an official whitewash was reinforced by the fact that neither Rogers nor the subordinate officer who had relayed the wrong information to him were disciplined. Rogers was reassigned to shore duty at San Diego, and according to Navy tradition, he is unlikely to get another command. General Crist, in approving the investigators' report, recommended a letter of reprimand for the junior officer. But when the report reached the Pentagon, Admiral William Crowe, chairman of the Joint Chiefs, and Defense Secretary Frank C. Carlucci decided against even that mild punishment. In the end, the officer was given a new assignment as the executive officer of a brand-new Aegis cruiser.

About three weeks after the Airbus was shot down, Iran announced that it was prepared to accept a United Nations-sponsored cease-fire to end the war with Iraq. The official announcement cited the *Vincennes* incident as one factor in the decision. On August 20, the war ended in a truce, and United Nations peace-keeping troops were deployed along the border where most of the land battles had been fought.

The embarrassment of the *Vincennes* affair aside, the end of the Iraq–Iran war, and especially the success of Operation Earnest Will, had left the United States in its strongest position ever in the Persian Gulf region. The doubts about American resolve that had deepened after the Marines pulled out of Lebanon were largely dispelled by its defending the oil sea-lanes and protecting shipping despite fears in Washington of becoming caught up in another Beirut, or even another Vietnam.

U.S. diplomats, and the top military officers who had to double as diplomats, believed, as Schwarzkopf had suggested in his remarks aboard the *La Salle*, that Washington now enjoyed an unprecedented credibility with the Gulf Arab leaders. "All the skepticism we'd felt for years was gone," said one senior officer. "You could tell not just by what they said, but the way they said it."

7

★ ★ ★ ★

A Dangerous Scenario

When General Schwarz-kopf took charge at Central Command in November 1988, he had already done some thinking about how the world had changed since the 1970s, when President Carter spelled out his doctrine asserting that the United States viewed the Persian Gulf and its resources as important enough to be defended with military force. That concept had been forged partly in response to the Soviet invasion of Afghanistan, which by demonstrating the aggressive nature of Moscow's policy had underscored the Soviet threat to the Gulf as well.

During the "tanker war" the Soviets maintained their own fleet of warships in the region—usually anywhere from five to ten ships. But they kept to themselves, escorting Soviet and eastern bloc shipping through the troubled waters in much the same way that Americans protected the reflagged Kuwaiti tankers. From a purely naval standpoint, the Russians behaved impeccably, keeping a correct distance from the American and other allied warships that plied the Gulf during the explosive fifteen months from May 1987 to August 1988.

Now, with the Soviet government beginning to focus its concern more and more on internal unrest and domestic problems, it was the right time for a new look. Schwarzkopf found that his predecessor, General Crist, had already begun to address the question of whether the gospel that had stood for forty years was still valid. In an interview with the *New York Times*, Crist has said the situation had changed. He argued that the threat of a land attack by the Soviets southward through Iran, to be met in the Zagros Mountains, was an outmoded concept and that the United States needed a new, flexible strategy that could deal not only with the Soviet threat but with threats of regional origin, such as the dangers generated by the Iraq–Iran war. Crist said that as long as there were no U.S. bases in the region, any such strategy would have to be based primarily on naval forces.

Schwarzkopf evidently did not share Crist's views. In the interview aboard USS *La Salle*, he said that the plan as outlined by his predecessor "probably would" constitute a dramatic shift in U.S. policy. "But I will tell you there hasn't been any dramatic change in strategy," he added. "I think the strategy for the United States in this area has been the same for some time and will continue to be the same."

Nor did he acknowledge any reduction in the Soviet threat itself. Rather, he suggested that all signs pointed to it worsening. Noting that Foreign Minister Eduard Shevardnadze had recently suggested that all foreign powers should leave the Persian Gulf, he said, "I think it's important not to think in terms of the Gulf, but in terms of the entire geostrategic region we have out here. First of all, the Soviets have a permanent presence in the Arabian Gulf that they've never had before. And they are continuing very close escort mission with the reflagged tankers, unlike ours, which has been pulled back to monitoring.

"Second, they have a heavy presence of naval forces in the Red Sea, which of course Mr. Shevardnadze didn't mention. They have an overwhelming number of military advisers and military men in many countries in this area, starting with the People's Democratic Republic of Yemen, of course, and we can't ignore Ethiopia, Iraq, and many, many other countries.

"Finally, they have a large troop presence immediately to the north of the Iranian border. So I would say that when they talk about the Soviet presence in the Middle East, they are very much present here. I have seen no indication of withdrawals. As a matter of fact, what we've seen is an increase. And any consideration of any sort of withdrawal from this area has to be viewed in terms of the entire area and not just exclusively the Arabian Gulf."

In March 1989, in his first appearance as CentCom commander before the Senate Armed Services Committee, Schwarzkopf still laid stress on the Soviets as posing the major threat. Noting that the command's area of concern had been marked by constant political turmoil, religious dissension, insurrection, and war, he said this had provided "fertile ground for the expansion of Soviet influence.

"The Soviets are steadily increasing their presence and gaining influence in the region by providing any willing recipient state with not only political support but also arms, equipment, military training, and technical advice," he testified. "In far too many instances, the United States has proved a reluctant suitor in responding to needs and requests of our friends in the region, and the Soviets were on the spot, ready to step forward in our place. It is to this latter threat that we must respond if we are to maintain our position in the area."

The testimony included brief comments on each of the countries in the region. Of Iraq, Schwarzkopf then said: "Iraq poses a potential threat to the weaker and more conservative Gulf Cooperation Council states, despite their extensive support for Iraq against Iran. Iraq's persistent claims to strategic portions of north-

eastern Kuwait could be a problem in the future. As is
the case with Iran, the United States must seek to
assert a moderating influence in Iraq."

Despite his ringing public reaffirmation of the Soviet
threat, Schwarzkopf has suggested since that he was
looking harder at the regionally based threat, particularly that presented by Saddam Hussein. In an interview in March 1991, Schwarzkopf said he recalled
telling his newly acquired staff at Central Command
that it was time to "change the focus of this headquarters to a more realistic scenario" than that which had
existed for so long.

"We had just gone through the Gulf war. We had
gotten in a tanker war, a big shooting match with the
Iranians. Why? It was a local conflict that overflowed
its boundaries. It impacted upon the Free World, and
therefore the Free World got involved," he said.

According to the article, in *Insight* magazine, he
then formulated a worst-case scenario for the region,
figuring that would cover any situation that arose.
"The worst case was this tremendous military machine
that Iraq had. . . . We came to the conclusion that one
of the things that would threaten Free World interests
more than anything else was if Iraq decided it was
going to come down here and take over the oil fields.
That's the one we developed a plan for."

By the spring of 1990, when Schwarzkopf returned
to Capitol Hill for the annual threat-assessment hear-
ings, he told the same Senate committee that the
picture had changed:

"The dramatic events of the past year have given rise
to high expectations that the Cold War is over. While
we at CentCom still believe that the Soviet Union
remains the most dangerous military threat, we also
believe that their setback in Afghanistan and the
changes in Eastern Europe have rendered Soviet intent
to use their power remote, at least for now.

"As a result, we in Central Command now consider
our most dangerous scenario to be the spillover of some

local conflict leading to a regional war which would threaten American lives and vital U.S. interests."

He did not pinpoint any single country as the most likely potential source of such trouble, but in a more detailed comment concerning Iraq, he said the cease-fire with Iran had allowed it to "resume its bid for leadership within the Arab world," and build "one of the largest and best-equipped military forces in the world." Schwarzkopf said Baghdad "continues to import arms," had "the most advanced domestic arms industry in the region," and was capable of producing chemical munitions and medium-range missiles. He added that the recent test of a three-stage missile with a range of over 1,500 miles "will further complicate the existing problem of missile proliferation by other regional states."

Concerning U.S. policy toward Iraq, he told the lawmakers: "Although generally mistrustful of the U.S., Iraq would welcome measured U.S. participation in its economic development. Currently, oil exports make it America's second largest Middle East trading partner. The U.S. should continue to develop its contacts with Iraq by building selectively on existing political and economic relationships. We should also encourage and reinforce those other states in the region that act as a moderating influence."

In the last week of July 1990, Central Command scheduled one of its periodic war games for the staff. Three hundred fifty of CentCom's officers assembled at Hurlburt Field and Elgin Air Base, in northern Florida, on July 23 to take part in the five-day "command post exercise" with the mystical code name Internal Look '90. The exercise, largely written by Schwarzkopf himself, postulated a crisis in which acts of aggression by a regional dictator endangered the oil fields. The officers were asked to explain how they would prepare for such a situation—how to make sure that U.S. forces were combat ready to respond, how they would be deployed, how would air and sea lines of communication be safeguarded, how command and control of such a massive operation would be exercised.

Participants in Internal Look '90 had no problem identifying Iraq as the hypothetical aggressor nation. The only other visible belligerent, Iran, had already wound up the loser in the war with Iraq. Tehran was trying to rebuild its shattered, depleted military and was, in any case, preoccupied with internal power struggles between fundamentalist hard-liners, who wanted to retain the rigid precepts of the late Ayatollah Khomeini, and the so-called pragmatists rallied around President Hashemi Rafsanjani.

As for the possible victims of Iraqi aggression, who better than Kuwait? Along with the Saudis, the Kuwaitis had poured billions of dollars—the Kuwaitis alone an estimated fifteen billion—into Baghdad's coffers during the eight-year war with Iran. That had been to help a brother Arab nation defend itself against a non-Arab threat; never mind that the Arab brother had started the fight in the first place. Neither of the benefactors was pressing for repayment of the debt. Nor were they expecting any show of gratitude from Saddam Hussein. This was especially true of the Kuwaitis, who knew their neighbor to the north all too well.

Despite their remarkable prosperity and seemingly untroubled society, the Kuwaitis seemed forever caught in the middle. From the time of its founding by desert tribesmen in the mid-eighteenth century, Kuwait has been menaced by tribes from Saudi Arabia, by the Ottoman Turks, and most often by Iraq, who contended that part, if not all, of Kuwait belonged to its southernmost Basra province.

Kuwait became a British protectorate in 1897 to avoid being taken over by the Turks. The British withdrew in 1961, but soon returned with troops to block a move by Iraq to take over the sheikdom. On at least three later occasions the Iraqis seized small parts of Kuwait, only to withdraw soon after.

In recent times, the country has ridden a tide of oil to become the world's richest, per capita, with a population of 1.6 million, of which more than half have been imported workers from Jordan, Egypt, India, Pakistan, Bangladesh, the Philippines, and other countries. It was a self-indulgent, consumer-oriented society, a wealthy welfare state that hired other people to do the work.

The ruling family, headed by the emir, Sheik Jaber al-Ahmed al-Sabah, was generally exempt from public criticism, although many other Kuwaitis with the Sabah surname were accused of abusing the special privileges it bestowed.

During the Iraq–Iran war, Kuwait was in peril again. Of the six Gulf states, it was the closest to the fighting. The gun flashes in the Fao peninsula of southern Iraq occasionally could be seen at night from Kuwait City. Also, the Iranians fired Silkworm missiles that hit two ships and an offshore tanker loading dock at al Ahmadi. The attack would have hit Kuwait City itself had not a missile decoy on an offshore barge not diverted the projectile.

In July 1990, Saddam Hussein complained that Kuwait was infringing on the Iraqi portion of the huge Ramallah oil field that straddles the border between the two countries. He threatened military action if Kuwait did not desist, and added that he no longer felt bound to repay the money that Kuwait had funneled into his war chest.

Although questions remain unresolved about whether the United States, through its ambassador, unwittingly encouraged Saddam to take over Kuwait by indicating that Washington would not interfere, and whether the White House failed to heed warnings by the Central Intelligence Agency that an attack was certain, the fact was that Schwarzkopf's war-game exercise proved chillingly prophetic.

Less than a week after Internal Look '90 ended—the date was August 2—Iraq did exactly what the scenario had foretold.

Schwarzkopf had just returned from a round of physical exercise at his Tampa home when he learned in a telephone call from General Colin Powell, the chairman of the U.S. Joint Chiefs of Staff, that the Iraqi forces that had been marshaling for days in southern Iraq and along the border with Kuwait had invaded. "Well, you were right. They've crossed the border," to which Schwarzkopf has said he replied, "I'm not surprised. Now it's going to be interesting to see what they do."

He told TV interviewer David Frost that he had anticipated that if the Iraqis did invade Kuwait, they would go only as far as the Ramallah oil field north of Kuwait City and then stop, to use the field itself as a bargaining chip for further negotiations.

Not much time elapsed before Powell called again. "Now we're getting reports that they're in downtown Kuwait," Schwarzkopf recalls Powell saying. "That made an entirely different situation," Schwarzkopf said.

In the *La Salle* interview nearly two years earlier, Schwarzkopf had said his role as a military man "is not to think about people's intentions, it's to look strictly at their capabilities." He could not be sure of Saddam Hussein's intentions, but the conquest of Kuwait seemed a foregone conclusion. What's more, nothing prevented his forces from rumbling down the coastal highway to capture the oil fields in Saudi Arabia's Eastern province. Such a maneuver, if successful, would give the Iraqi dictator control over forty percent of the world's oil reserves, according to some estimates.

Schwarzkopf knew that Saudi Arabia's forces—an army of some 65,000 troops and 500 tanks, and an air force of 180 combat planes—were outnumbered, outgunned, scattered about the country, and, in any case, untested in battle. They stood no more chance of fighting off Iraq than had their Kuwaiti cousins to the north.

No time was lost in putting things together. The Saudis at first seemed disbelieving that Saddam had invaded Kuwait, especially after giving assurances to them, and to Egyptian President Hosni Mubarak just days earlier, that he had no such intention. The Saudi press, tightly controlled by the government, contained no word of the invasion for the first few days, while King Fahd and his key advisers mulled their best course of action—and specifically whether to call for foreign help.

In Tampa, Schwarzkopf ordered contingency plans put in motion, then boarded a jet for Washington, where he personally briefed President George Bush on the military aspects of the situation, including the capability of the United States to respond in force if need be.

Internal Look '90 was moving from the exercise table to the planning conference. Military units predesignated as most likely to be called in a crisis were advised to go on preliminary alert: the 82nd Airborne Division at Fort Bragg, North Carolina; the 24th Infantry Division (Mechanized) at Fort Stewart, Georgia; and the 101st Airborne Division (Air Assault) at Fort Campbell, Kentucky.

All were elite divisions, with long traditions. The 82nd had been the Army's quick-reaction force for years, and always had one division ready brigade on call to go anywhere in a crisis. The 24th was Schwarzkopf's own former command, a division equipped with M-1 tanks, the U.S. Army's best, and the Bradley fighting vehicle.

These were among several new weapons systems that had been controversial in development and never put to a major battlefield test. But the division was tailored especially to the task that American forces would face in a desert conflict. The Screaming Eagles of the 101st, a famed paratroop division in World War II, had been reconstituted since Vietnam, from a helicopter-borne "airmobile" infantry to a new and more streamlined air-assault force whose principal firepower was the AH-64 Apache helicopter gunship, another trouble-plagued weapon that had yet to prove itself in battle.

Sunday, August 5, was a critical day. As the United Nations Security Council prepared to vote on economic sanctions against Iraq, Arab governments scrambled to determine where they stood in a world suddenly in political disarray.

Saudi Arabia and Egypt called for a summit of top Arab leaders at the Red Sea port city of Jiddah, ostensibly to condemn the invasion of Kuwait. U.S. officials fretted that it might instead result in a statement by the nervous Arabs accepting Iraq's takeover of Kuwait in exchange for a promise from Saddam not to go any farther. The summit, however, fell apart before the first meeting—scuttled mainly by Yasser Arafat, chairman of the Palestine Liberation Organization, who passed through Egypt en route to Baghdad with what he called a peace plan supported by Libyan leader Moammar Ghadafi.

Jordan's King Hussein, caught between neighboring Iraq and his long-standing friendships with Western governments, tilted toward Saddam, as did most Palestinians in his country, following the lead of the PLO. This move would have terrible repercussions for both—for the king, vilification and a cold shoulder from many friendly governments; for the Palestinians, vengeance and retribution from other Arabs.

Returning from three days at Camp David, where he had heard, among other expert opinions, General Schwarzkopf's views on the situation, President Bush virtually committed the United States to taking military action if Iraq did not withdraw from Kuwait voluntarily. Declaring that "this aggression will not stand," Bush told reporters he was finding many other governments who felt the same way. "Nobody is willing to accept anything less than total withdrawal of the Iraqi forces and no puppet regime," he said.

Bush also disclosed that he was sending Secretary of Defense Dick Cheney to Saudi Arabia to seek King Fahd's approval for a massive U.S. military intervention, should that become necessary. He had already spoken with Fahd at least twice by phone, finding him uncertain about the gravity of the threat and unwilling to commit himself to asking for American help.

Few decisions were more sensitive for the Saudi monarch than to invite foreign military forces from non-Islamic countries onto the sacred soil. It would require ironclad assurances from the United States that once the problem was resolved, those forces would withdraw quickly and completely.

The White House announcement briefly noted that General Schwarzkopf, the commander-in-chief of Central Command, would accompany Cheney. This evidently meant little to the Washington-based news media and was skipped over in most press reports. In fact, however, the general's role was critical to the success of the mission. Not only had he dealt personally with King Fahd and other top Saudi leaders before, he knew thoroughly Iraq's military capabilities. Finally, if there was a major military operation as a result of the talks, he would be running it.

The American group, which also included Paul Wolfowitz, a Pentagon undersecretary for policy, left the United States on Sunday night, arriving in Jiddah the next day for meetings with the king, Crown Prince Abdullah, and Prince Sultan, the Saudi defense minister, the next day.

Since any deployment of U.S. forces required the use of Saudi air bases and other facilities in that country and the nearby Gulf states, they carried fresh intelligence data that the White House hoped would persuade the cautious Saudi monarch both of the seriousness of

the threat to his country and of the resolve of the
United States to come to its aid.

"This is what all our interaction, all our friendship,
all our cooperation, has led up to—this moment of
crisis," an unnamed State Department official told the
New York Times.

The message about American resolve was, of course,
was one that General Schwarzkopf and his immediate
predecessor at Central Command had worked relentlessly to get across to the reluctant and skeptical Saudis, as well as the other oil oligarchs. In endless cere-
monial meetings in the gilded palaces of the Gulf, with
their plush rugs and armchairs, over endless cups of
cardamon-laced Arab coffee, the American generals
had stressed that the United States was fully committed to the defense of the Gulf region against outside
aggression, but would need their help and facilities
should that time ever come. Now, it appeared, that
time was at hand.

The Middle Eastern political landscape was already
being altered dramatically; taking the easy way out by
appeasing Saddam might alter it permanently to the
disadvantage of Saudi Arabia and its allies. But to side
with a Western power against Arab brothers was a risky
undertaking, sure to feed the deepest feelings of fundamentalist xenophobia and resentment.

Events continued to move at a dizzying pace on many
fronts. In a dramatic meeting at the United Nations,
the Security Council voted unanimously, 13 to 0, to
impose economic sanctions on the Baghdad government. The United States and Britain then indicated
they were considering a naval blockade to back up the
embargo.

The resolution's declared aim was "to bring the
invasion and occupation of Kuwait by Iraq to an end
and to restore the sovereignty, independence, and territorial integrity of Kuwait." To do this it prohibited all
trade and commercial dealings with the Baghdad government, including debt payments and monetary trans-

fers. It specifically exempted transactions for humanitarian purposes and the delivery of medical supplies or food for famine relief.

The Pentagon announced that the aircraft carrier USS *Saratoga*, which was to have departed within days for a scheduled Mediterranean deployment, would leave immediately from Mayport, Florida, rendezvousing at sea with the battleship USS *Wisconsin*, out of Norfolk, Virginia, and head for the Gulf region. The carriers USS *Dwight D. Eisenhower* and USS *Independence* were already on station there. Britain and France announced that they, too, were bolstering their naval forces in the Gulf.

In Baghdad, Saddam summoned Joseph C. Wilson, the American chargé d'affaires, to his palace, the first direct contact by an American official with the Iraqi leader since the invasion. In a two-hour harangue that U.S. officials later characterized as "very difficult and very negative," Saddam made clear to Wilson that he had no intention of pulling his forces out of Kuwait.

Typically, Iraq at the same time was claiming for international public consumption that its forces were withdrawing from Kuwait, and that they would be replaced by a "popular army" of Arab soldiers organized from within the country. Iraq already had announced the creation of a provisional government, ostensibly made up of Kuwaiti military officers but in reality a group of Iraqis, according to Kuwait diplomats watching the developments from outside.

Photographs showed Iraqi armored personnel carriers loaded with troops appearing to head northward on a highway, passing the turnoff to Kuwait City. But whatever movements toward the north were actually made meant nothing. Satellite photos and what on-the-ground intelligence was available told U.S. officials that Iraq, having moved an estimated 100,000 troops into Kuwait in the first week after the invasion, were now digging in. What's more, as many as 20,000 troops were massing along the border in southern Kuwait.

Reports from the occupied land also said that Iraqi soldiers were rounding up foreigners from hotels and taking them away for purposes unknown. These were said to include more than 300 people from a British Airways 747 jumbo jet that had had the misfortune to land at Kuwait's airport the day of the invasion, and at least 28 Americans. In all, the State Department said, there were 3,800 Americans in the country. Fear was expressed that these people would become hostages, possibly even "human shields" to protect vital Iraqi military and industrial installations from attack.

Although news accounts at the time depicted King Fahd debating with his council of advisers on what action to take after hearing Cheney's and Schwarzkopf's presentations, the general has said since that the Saudi monarch made the decision to invite the Americans in without hesitation. He told TV interviewer David Frost: "My expectations were that we'd brief King Fahd and tell him what the situation was, and the real danger to Saudi Arabia. The President's message was very clear, that if asked to defend Saudi Arabia, we would. We would also leave when asked to leave, and we wouldn't establish any permanent bases. And I think that based upon the decision-making processes we've seen over here before, I was quite sure in my own mind that we would be told, 'Thank you very much, I now need to confer with my advisers.'

"Instead, after discussion, the king said, 'Fine, we want you to come.' And at that moment I knew that we were more than involved, we were committed."

Cheney, sharing the podium with Powell at a Pentagon news conference on his return from Saudi Arabia, described the meeting with King Fahd as "a significant moment." He said the monarch had listened to briefings by himself and Schwarzkopf on "the situation in Saudi Arabia, Kuwait and Iraq, and was also briefed on our military capabilities."

Fahd, he said, cited the security of Saudi Arabia's people as his first priority. "Based upon that, based

upon the historic relationship of the United States and
the government of Saudi Arabia, and based on their
fundamental trust of the United States, they were prepared to ask for our assistance." Fahd had added a
historical note by recalling the first high-level meeting
of American and Saudi leaders forty-five years earlier,
when President Franklin Roosevelt welcomed Fahd's
father, King Abdul Aziz al-Saud, who forged modern
Saudi Arabia out of warring desert tribes, aboard the
cruiser USS *Quincy*.

Although it was not emphasized in the early reporting on the Cheney–Schwarzkopf trip, U.S. officials said
the visitors had given King Fahd the necessary assurances that the American forces would stay only as long
as needed—and would leave whenever the Saudis re-
quested them to do so. No consideration was being
given, they said, to a permanent base or United States
headquarters in the kingdom.

Cheney, speaking later before an audience of American veterans, quoted King Fahd as having said, "I trust
the United States of America. I know that when you
say you will be committed, you are, in fact, committed.
I know that you will stay as long as is necessary to do
what has to be done, and I know you will leave when
you are asked to leave, that you have no ulterior mo-
tives."

On Tuesday, August 7, Bush ordered the first contin-
gents of American troops to leave immediately for the
desert. As many as 15,000 were slated for the first
wave, with the 82nd Airborne in the lead, as usual,
followed by the advance elements of the 24th Mech
and the 101st Airborne. In addition, Bush ordered two
squadrons of Air Force F-15's, 48 planes in all, and two
AWACS radar surveillance planes to fly to Saudi Arabia.

Bush also announced that Egypt had agreed to commit troops to the cause—the Egyptians officially denied it, though it was true—and said discussions had
been held with other member states of the Gulf Cooperation Council and with Morocco and Pakistan. Over-

looking no possibilities, Washington also approached Syria and Iran—no friends of the United States, to be sure, but bitter enemies of Baghdad—to sign on. Soon, all except Iran would declare themselves part of the growing coalition.

In the search for a solid front, the United States also gained Turkey's consent to shut down the oil pipeline from Iraq, one of two that carried Iraqi crude in lieu of a fleet of tankers. That the other pipeline, carrying oil from Iraq across the Saudi desert to the Red Sea port of Yanbu, would be closed as well was a foregone conclusion. Turkey, the easternmost member of the NATO alliance, also indicated that it would allow U.S. bombers to operate against Iraqi targets from Turkish bases.

The initial statements from the White House stressed that the purpose of deploying troops was limited in scope—to protect Saudi Arabia from further aggression by Iraq. They said nothing about liberating Kuwait, even though Bush himself had already said that the aggression "will not stand." The implication of action beyond the simple protection of Saudi Arabia's borders was implicit in the commitment. But as the White House knew, and General Schwarzkopf would later acknowledge, the first U.S. troops on the ground would have had great difficulty in stemming any major move southward by Saddam's armor-heavy forces.

"A brigade of three thousand men is not going to hold the line against the Iraqi Republican Guard force of seven divisions," said Representative Les Aspin, the Wisconsin Democrat who heads the House Armed Services Committee. "But it establishes a presence across the line in Kuwait. If Iraq attacks across that line now, it is at war with the United States, and that is a different story."

If the decision to go to war in the Arabian desert was happening too fast for most Americans to absorb, it was of momentous importance in Jiddah, where Cheney and Schwarzkopf had met with King Fahd and the princes. The country that had publicly rejected all non-Arab alliances, and had not allowed the United States to have land bases even to help protect Saudi Arabia's oil shipping from Iranian attacks in the "tanker war," was now openly declaring itself allied with that same Western power—and against another Arab nation.

The rationale for this action seemed easy enough: Iraq itself had broken the rules first by becoming the first Arab nation in modern history to invade another Arab nation. But clearly the Americans' evidence of the Iraqi threat had deeply impressed the Saudi officials as well. "We are at the point where we have no choice but to stand up to Saddam," a senior government official, speaking anonymously as usual, told the *New York Times.* "If we were to allow the status quo to remain, there is little question that we would be next on Iraq's list."

As if to underscore Bush's declaration on August 8 that "a line has been drawn in the sand," Saddam's government announced that it had annexed Kuwait as the nineteenth province of Iraq. "Thank God that we are now one people, one state that will now be the pride of the Arabs," the Iraqi leader said while presiding over a televised meeting of top Baath party officials. The announcement was followed by martial music and repeated statements on Baghdad radio that Iraq and Kuwait were now "one nation, one fate."

Within a day the U.N. had passed another resolution rejecting the annexation of Kuwait. It would adopt ten more in the course of the next few weeks, including one authorizing the use of armed force. This show of solidarity was unprecedented in the memory of most United Nations delegates—especially on an initiative sponsored by the United States—and clearly showed that the act of aggression by a powerful country against a weaker neighbor had struck a chord with many Third World members.

Equally remarkable, in the view of some U.N. observers, was the fact that the Soviet Union was joining with the U.S.-led group in condemnation of Iraq, which, along with Syria, was one of Moscow's two major client states in the Middle East. The United States, whose policy for the Gulf region was predicated heavily on keeping the Soviets from gaining influence in the oil-rich region, was now making gestures toward inviting them to join the building anti-Baghdad military coalition. Moscow's spokesmen indicated that they might do so, provided such an effort had full United Nations endorsement. But in the end, even after the Security Council sanctioned the use of force, the Soviets declined to commit forces.

In Saudi Arabia, where the government had hesitated for several days before disclosing to its people the details of the Iraq invasion of Kuwait, King Fahd issued a lengthy statement to the nation that was read on Saudi television. In it he stressed that there had been Arab solidarity against Baghdad's action, "the most vile aggression known to the Arab nation in its modern history."

While holding out hope that an Arab summit called again by Egyptian President Mubarak would solve the crisis, he said that Saudi Arabia was forced to look to its own defenses, and that the American and British governments "took the initiative, on the basis of the relations of friendship which link the Kingdom of Saudi Arabia and these states, to send air and land forces in order to back the Saudi armed forces in performing their duty to defend the homeland and the citizens against any aggression."

The king added, "It is worth mentioning here that the forces which will participate in the joint training between them and the Saudi armed forces will be present temporarily in the kingdom's territory and will leave it immediately when the Kingdom of Saudi Arabia wishes so."

They Are a Bunch of Thugs

For a brief time it looked as if H. Norman Schwarzkopf might lead the biggest U.S. military operation since Vietnam without anybody knowing he had anything to do with it. Not until August 13, six days after President Bush announced the dispatch of troops to Saudi Arabia, did the news media finally begin to ask who would be in charge. The *New York Times*, in a story on page ten, described the general as an "old desert hand" and veteran of Vietnam and Grenada who found himself now "playing a pivotal role" in the Gulf operation. It further noted that he was a tall, burly man nicknamed "the Bear." "Stormin' Norman" was not mentioned, perhaps because the reporter had not heard that name applied to his subject, or the *Times* decided in its wisdom that such a nickname would be altogether too obvious for anyone named Norman, who also happened to be a four-star general.

Except for that, and a brief reference to his testimony

before Congressional committees six months earlier, in which he had said the biggest threat in the Gulf was a "spillover of a regional conflict" that could threaten U.S. interests, the story appeared to have been written from the official Army résumé.

The *Times* said that Schwarzkopf would coordinate all planning for the Gulf deployment from U.S. Central Command headquarters, which had been regarded as "something of a misfit" because it had no physical presence in its area of responsibility and no forces of its own, only what it could call on from other areas in time of crisis. Like most articles, it failed to mention that the Tampa headquarters had for two years run the U.S. naval escort operation in the Persian Gulf, an endeavor that at its peak had cost the government an estimated twenty million dollars a month, and had by and large achieved its objective, marred only at the end by the *Vincennes* tragedy.

During these early days Schwarzkopf remained in Tampa while Lieutenant General Charles Horner ran the new headquarters in Riyadh. Horner was a veteran of 112 combat missions in Vietnam, flying the F-105 Thunderchief (better known to pilots as the Thud). The Iowa-born Horner, who doubled as commander of the 9th Air Force and Central Command Air Forces, would later be credited as the guiding genius behind the highly successful air war against Iraq.

One of the early tasks was figuring out how the multi-national forces would fit into a command structure. U.S. officials conceded privately that the organizational problems of getting the Saudis, Egyptians, Syrians, Moroccans, and other Arab forces, along with the Americans, British, and French, all "singing from the same sheet of music" were considerable. Inevitably, the historically minded among them compared the situation to that facing Lawrence of Arabia more than seventy years earlier, when he forged a coalition of mutually hostile Saudi desert tribes to overthrow Turkish Ottoman rule during World War I. A major concern always lurking in the background was what might happen to this tenuous Arab arrangement if Saddam suddenly provoked Israel enough to invite an armed response. Which way would the Syrians swivel their tank turrets then?

But the biggest task by far was supply. Even as the first American troops were deploying to forward positions in the Saudi desert, officials in Washington said the original estimate of 50,000 would fall short by at least half of what was required. The big C-5 Galaxy transports and smaller C-141 Starlifters were landing at the Dhahran air base every ten minutes, disgorging their loads of troops and material, and as soon as possible they were airborne again. Meanwhile, the first ships were arriving at the port of Dammam, offloading supplies for the Marine Corps units that were being assigned to Jubail, an oil port on the road north toward Kuwait.

Schwarzkopf's supply expert was Major General William G. Pagonis, a short, energetic Greek-American known as Gus. He had been one of the first Americans in Saudi Arabia, arriving literally hours after the decision to send troops was announced, and lacking a hotel room, he had slept the first two nights in the back of his rented Chevrolet near the port.

Pagonis had been amazed at the facilities at his disposal. Dammam was a shipper's dream, with modern pier facilities and enough docking space for several ships to offload simultaneously. Dhahran air base had equally sumptuous facilities; in fact, arriving Air Force officers said the hangars and maintenance bays were far superior to anything back in the States. And best of all was the road system, a network of modern expressways that led directly from the ports and the air bases to the forward areas.

Right from the beginning, the American commitment was massive, fast, and efficient. Major General Don Kaufman, the acting chief of staff for Central Command Forward, told members of an early Pentagon

news media pool that the Saudis had seemed surprised
at its size, as if they had not anticipated what inviting
the United States to come to their rescue really meant.

The question of how many troops would eventually
be needed was one that the Bush administration did
not want to discuss, though, for fear of encouraging the
Iraqis to attack while they still had an overwhelming
advantage in manpower and armored forces.

In Congress, Democrats Les Aspin of Wisconsin and
John Martha of Pennsylvania urged still faster deployment of troops on the ground, but some advocates of
air power argued that a full-scale bombing campaign
could stop the Iraqis without committing large numbers of troops.

Even as the Pentagon was doubling its estimate of
the force needed from fifty to a hundred thousand, it
was putting more than twice that figure on alert for
possible deployment. Officials called that only a contingency, and one senior administration official said
the idea that 200,000 or more troops might be sent to
Saudi Arabia was "preposterous." Nobody in Washington appeared to envision that more than a half million
eventually would be arrayed against the Iraqis.

On August 12, Bush made the first overt military
move against Iraq, ordering Navy warships to use minimum force to stop all vessels carrying Iraqi oil prod-
ucts and all imports to the country except some food.
Saying the action was in response to a request from the
deposed emir of Kuwait, Bush called it an interdiction
rather than a blockade, on the advice of legal experts
who said the latter term referred to an act of war and
might clash with the intent of the embargo imposed
by the United Nations. Already some U.N. delegates
had expressed concern about the United States going it
alone with naval action.

In apparent response, the Iraqi tanker *Al Qadisiyah*
weighed anchor at the Saudi Red Sea oil port of Yanbu
and left empty. It had been waiting for a load of oil

from the Iraqi pipeline that terminates at Yanbu. The next day, Bush warned in a Washington news conference that ship traffic to and from the Jordanian port of Aqaba, at the northern end of the Red Sea, might be sealed off because it was serving as a funnel for cargos to and from Iraq, in violation of the U.N. embargo.

Bush's warning was thoughtfully timed. King Hussein of Jordan, who had sided with Saddam, was due to meet Bush in Kennebunkport, Maine, the next day, seeking an agreement on resolving the crisis short of war.

Saddam Hussein, who repeatedly declared his intention to stand fast on Kuwait but at times also seemed to be casting about for an escape hatch, stunned the world by offering to concede virtually all of Iran's demands still unresolved from their eight-year war. In effect, he would give up everything that Iraq had gained in a conflict that cost an estimated half million lives on each side. In the major concession Saddam said he would given back to Iran control of its side of the Shatt-al-Arab waterway. The dispute over this narrow estuary, the outlet of the Tigris and Euphrates rivers into the northern Gulf, had led to the war in the first place.

American officials worried that a friendship pact between Baghdad and Tehran would undercut the U.N. embargo by allowing goods to flow across the border dividing the two countries and would also enable Saddam to move troops from that border into Kuwait. Like many other concerns that flowed to the surface in the whirlpool of events, it came to nothing.

Pundits, think-tank experts, and Congressional skeptics began to refine their assessments of the Bush policy. Nobody came out in support of Saddam Hussein, but many were critical of Kuwait's rulers and of an American commitment to "make the world safe for feudalism," as one popular catch-phrase put it. "Once people in the United States find out what we're defending, they will revolt against it," said Edward Luttwak, an expert on military issues at the Center for Strategic and International Studies.

Criticism came from all sides. In New York, outside the United Nations, peace-oriented church groups demonstrated against the troop deployment and its supporters in Congress. On the right, former U.N. Ambassador Jeanne Kirkpatrick said the United States had taken on a responsibility "larger than the national interest."

Some urged that economic sanctions be given months, or a year, to work against Iraq. Others dismissed the sanctions, saying similar embargos had failed to work and urged immediate military action. Still others warned that the country was being led into another Vietnam.

Senate Minority Leader Bob Dole said public support for the troops was certain to erode if they stayed in Saudi Arabia for a long time. Gene LaRocque, a retired rear admiral and director of a privately funded military watchdog organization in Washington, said Bush in his public statements had provided no more "clarity of purpose" for the Gulf commitment than there had been for the war in Indochina.

Spokesmen for Arab–American groups in the United States complained about the negative image of Arabs perpetuated by the government and the news media. Israeli-born Leon Hadar, a professor of international studies at American University, predicted that a military clash between the United States and Iraq could drag Israel into a war with Syria. Further, anti-American sentiment in the Arab world could topple King Hussein and moderate Arab governments in Egypt, Morocco, Tunisia, and perhaps even Saudi Arabia.

Of growing concern to the United States and its allies were some 10,000 foreign citizens, including 3,000 Americans, who were being held virtual prisoners in Iraq, with the clear implication that they would be used as human shields to discourage allied bombing of key military and industrial installations.

The Iraqis called them guests and said they would suffer the same deprivations of food and other comforts as ordinary Iraqsi if the U.N. boycott continued. "The people of Iraq have decided to play host to the citizens of these aggressive nations as long as Iraq remains threatened with an aggressive war," Saadi Mahdi Saleh, the speaker of the rubber-stamp Baghdad parliament, said on August 18.

While responding that holding people against their will was totally unacceptable and "contrary to international law and to all accepted norms of international conduct," the White House sought to soft-pedal this element of the crisis as best it could, even to the point of avoiding the use of the word *hostage* to describe the captives. Clearly the Bush administration was determined to avoid a repeat of the unhappy experience of the Carter administration a decade earlier, when the 55 American hostages held at the U.S. embassy in Tehran became the main factor that drove policy, leading to the humiliation of Desert One.

On August 23, Saddam held a bizarre personal meeting with some of the British hostages, asking them questions about how well they were doing and patting one evidently frightened boy on the head for the benefit of television cameras. The Iraqi leader went to some lengths to explain that his communiqués had not used the term *human shields* to refer to the foreigners. The Arabic word *dher*, meaning to prevent war, had been mistranslated as *dhar*, or shield. Despite the attempt at niceties, the veiled menace to the safety of the detained foreigners was inescapable, and the British government denounced the televised affair as "a repulsive charade."

Eventually the hostages would be released by Saddam, ending a pointless but agonizing sideshow to the main event in Kuwait.

As Defense Secretary Cheney landed aboard the carrier USS *Dwight D. Eisenhower* in the Red Sea, beginning his second trip in ten days to the region, there came the first report of shots fired in anger since the crisis began sixteen days earlier. In the Gulf of Oman, the missile frigate USS *Reid* had fired warning shots to induce an Iraqi tanker to stop for inspection. In a separate incident, the *Reid*'s sister ship, USS *Thomas G. Bradley*, also opened fire to stop a second Iraqi tanker that was sailing toward the Strait of Hormuz. Both ships refused to stop, but instead of taking more severe action, the American warships continued to shadow them.

A third warship, the missile cruiser USS *England*, stopped and boarded a Chinese cargo ship, the *Heng Chun Hai*, carrying a load of fertilizer from Iraq, and persuaded its master to put in at Dubai in the southern Gulf.

The incidents spurred the Bush administration to ask the United Nations for further authority to exercise military power to enforce the embargo, a request that was ultimately approved after overcoming Soviet objections. Some analysts saw the Soviet reluctance to endorse the use of force as reflecting internal differences in Moscow between the Gorbachev–Shevardnadze faction, which was willing to go along with the Bush administration on the use of force, and the Soviet generals, who had spent their entire careers opposing American military policy in whatever form.

Each passing day brought more troops to the desert. By August 20 the unofficial total of forces committed to Operation Desert Shield passed the 20,000 mark, with 80,000 more on the way. On the 22nd—as General Schwarzkopf marked his fifty-sixth birthday in Tampa—Bush announced plans to mobilize 40,000 Army, Air Force, and medical reservists to augment the combat forces, the first call-up of reserves since the Vietnam War. Some reservists already at work would become casualties within the week, as a C-5 transport carrying supplies for Desert Storm crashed on takeoff in Germany, killing 14 people on board.

Although Schwarzkopf and many of his key advisers

remained in Florida for the time being, the new head-quarters of Central Command Forward was taking shape in Riyadh. The Hyatt Regency Hotel, on Abdul-Aziz street, overflowed with American military person-nel in combat garb—the brown, tan, and white desert camouflage pattern that had been dubbed "chocolate chip cookie." On the fourth floor, the Joint Information Bureau—*joint* meaning U.S. and Saudi—with desks, telephones, and copying machines, filled two large rooms. The hotel was opposite the Saudi Ministry of Defense and Aviation, known as MODA, where office and living space for Schwarzkopf's operational head-quarters was being set aside, five stories below street level.

The sudden influx of foreigners was having its im-pact on the Saudi capital. Riyadh—the word means *garden* in Arabic—had been only a cluster of mud-walled buildings in the middle of nowhere when the man who would become the founder of Saudi Arabia, King Abdul Aziz al-Saud, better known to the world as Ibn Saud, was born there around 1875. Fifteen years later, the al-Saud tribe was driven from the city by a rival clan, the Rashid—to return again in 1902 when Ibn Saud, now a dynamic, swashbuckling figure leading a hardy band of fewer than a hundred desert warriors, captured the Mismak, the Rashid's mud fortress that still stands in the center of the old city.

Though transformed into a modern city by the post-World War II oil boom, Riyadh's isolation and the conservatism of Saudi Islamic society discouraged for-eign influences to a greater extent than in the Red Sea port of Jiddah or the petroleum center around Dhahran, Dammam, and al-Khobar on the Persian Gulf coast, where foreigners on the streets were more common.

Thus Saudi men in desert robes stood agape, with disbelieving eyes, at the sight of Americans in uniform, and in particular the women members of the Air Force cargo crews who thronged the lobby of the Interconti-

nental Hotel, arriving and leaving at all hours in their
green uniforms and military gear.

Schwarzkopf and his tight group of aides finally flew
to Saudi Arabia over the weekend of August 25. Before
leaving Tampa, he would recall in a television interview months later, he called the family together for a
last council. "They didn't have any idea I would be
leaving as soon as I did," he said. "As a matter of fact,
I think they really thought, because Central Command
had been run from Tampa that I would be running this
whole thing from Florida. So a couple of days before, I
got the whole family together, and I told them what
was going to happen. I told them it was my job, that I
was proud to be doing it."

The day he left was the day he was to have driven his
younger daughter, Jessica, to her first day of college. He
had to pass that up. The deployment also meant he
would have to forgo, at least for a while, a hunting trip
with son Chris, thirteen, and the usual autumn hunting and fishing forays with friends in the Tampa area.

In Riyadh, the staff moved into the Hyatt, which had
metal filigree screens covering all the windows and
now appeared even more fortress-like, with concrete
barriers blocking the driveway and armed Saudi and
Americans guarding the doorway and checking visitors. Eventually most of the Americans would move
out to well-guarded compounds borrowed from private
companies, but the top command trust, including
Schwarzkopf himself, would take quarters deep inside
the MODA building, close to their war room.

Four days after his arrival, Schwarzkopf went to the
field for an inspection tour and met with the news
media for the first time. Accompanied by a small group
of Pentagon pool reporters, he made a helicopter tour
of the potential combat zone, talking with soldiers,
Marines, and Air Force personnel. It was the first
glimpse the troops had of the man who would lead
them—a tall, hulking figure in combat fatigues, standard Army web gear, and a soft cap with visor rather

than the floppy-brimmed "boonie hat" that had become military issue in Vietnam and was now part of the desert uniform for most.

The general, walking fast, talking faster, shook hands with Marines digging in at an outpost near Jubail, at that time the northernmost position of American forces. He strode through a large warehouse that had been converted into a barracks for arriving Army troops, and discussed the situation with the maintenance crews working on Air Force A-10 "Warthogs," the slow-flying, heavily armored jets that would later live up to notices as the killers of Iraqi tanks.

Clearly in his element among the troops, the general paused to answer questions at several points on the tour. He told a Marine who asked about the C-5 crash in Germany that the victims were "just thirteen more counts against Saddam Hussein." He told the A-10 mechanics he was "completely confident" that the Americans had the strength already in the country to repel any attack by Saddam's armored forces.

Then he turned up at the Dhahran International Hotel, where Central Command had set up another Joint Information Bureau to handle the reporters flocking to Saudi Arabia to cover the war. After decades of barring foreign correspondents for all but the rarest of government-sponsored events, the Saudis had suddenly opened the gates—and got a flood. More than 600 journalists from some 30 countries were in Saudi Arabia, more than had ever visited the country since its founding as a modern country in 1932.

Perhaps 200 of them were assembled in the third-floor ballroom of the hotel when Schwarzkopf arrived, a flurry of aides and junior officers preceding him. The threat of terrorism against top American officials was taken seriously, and the general himself was always ringed by a coterie of bodyguards—hard-faced, unsmiling soldiers in civilian clothes and vests jammed with extra ammo clips for their automatic rifles. The bodyguards, though all members of the military, were trained in martial arts. They dressed in mufti rather than in uniform to avoid any "misunderstandings," as an officer phrased it, should they have to push a general, a foreign dignitary, or even a president out of the way in order to protect Schwarzkopf.

As for the troops, this was the first opportunity for the press to see the mystery man who would lead Desert Shield. Most of the reporters present had never seen a four-star general in the flesh and especially in combat clothing. They found an imposing figure, easily fulfilling the image conjured up by his nickname, the "Bear." He was a man who talked rapidly, the words sometimes tumbling and falling as the thought process raced on to the next idea. In trying to be accommodating, he sometimes used many more words than needed to answer most questions, yet could be abrupt when the question did not please him.

The first question to Schwarzkopf was the obvious one: would there be war? "There is not going to be any war unless the Iraqis attack," he retorted. The reply reflected the then current mission of the U.S. forces—strictly to defend Saudi Arabia against further incursions by Iraq.

But what of Bush's repeated promises that the takeover of Kuwait would not be allowed to stand? "The force that I am assembling here is exactly the force that was briefed to the President of the United States as necessary for the defense of Saudi Arabia," said Schwarzkopf. Anything beyond that, he added, was hypothetical.

At this first meeting with journalists, Schwarzkopf dealt with a number of themes that he would return to again and again over the next few months. One was his utter contempt for Iraq's president and his generals. "They are a bunch of thugs," he said. "If the Iraqis are dumb enough to attack, they're going to pay a price."

Bush and Secretary of State Baker, recalling that Iraq had used chemical weapons against the Iranians and rebellious factions of its own Kurdish population, had already warned that any use of such weapons against American forces would trigger massive, but unspecified, retaliation by the United States. When the question came to him, Schwarzkopf chose the blunt parlance of the field troops to make the point. "They will pay for it, big time," he said.

The general also said the civilian hostages held by the Iraqis would not affect his decisions in mapping the campaign. "I would tell you that I am just as concerned as anyone else about every single human life. But what I have to do is plan the military component and not concern myself with the hostages."

One question that Schwarzkopf did not answer—and one that would dog him throughout the months to come—concerned the way in which the United States forces could coordinate their actions with the disparate group of allies. He himself faced a pandora's box of questions.

In a sense it was the joint-command concept carried to a new and seemingly impossible extreme. In addition to the language barriers—with various components relying on English, Arabic, and French—there were touchy political considerations. No Western army agreed to risk the lives of its troops under an Arab commander. For the Saudis, it was at the very least a matter of pride: what army could permit its soldiers, in its own country, to be subservient to the orders of a foreign army on that soil? And while the Gulf states, and probably the Egyptians, would be willing to operate under Saudi command, would the Syrians?

Schwarzkopf had said before leaving the United States that "the Saudis have made it clear that they are going to command the Arab forces," but the question of where his own, and the other non-Arabs, fit in was anything but clear. Now the question rose through press reports saying Lieutenant General Khalid bin-Sultan, the commander of the Saudi forces, had said that King Fahd and President Bush would have to con-

sult before any decision committing American forces
to offensive combat operations from Saudi soil.

According to the *Washington Post*, Schwarzkopf "objected strenuously" to the statement and complained
to Washington that it would undercut the ability of
U.S. forces to react properly to some contingencies.
Bush was said to have personally called in Prince Bandar bin-Sultan, the Saudi ambassador to Washington
and brother of General Khalid, to resolve the dispute,
only to be told that the Saudis, by virtue of having
invited the Americans in, indeed felt they should have
a voice in the process of making war from their own
territory. Since nobody at this point was talking in
terms of offense—the mission was still to defend Saudi
Arabia against attack—the matter was left unsettled
for the time being.

In Saudi Arabia, neither American nor Saudi officials
were willing to discuss the subject on the record. The
two Saudis, Khalid and Bandar, were sons of the powerful Saudi defense minister, Prince Sultan bin-Abdul
Aziz, the king's brother. But privately the officials
scoffed at the story. If war came, said one senior American officer, U.S. forces would not be paralyzed by
"sheer, unadulterated bullshit."

Schwarzkopf was furious over the story, and when
the reporter who had written it arrived later to cover
Desert Shield, Schwarzkopf let it be known that he had
no chance of getting a private interview. Schwarzkopf
"wouldn't have minded if the story had been true, but
it just never happened," said one source who was close
to the general. "Other than that, he had no strong
feelings about it."

Weeks after the war ended, the *New York Times*
reported that there had indeed been many problems in
coordinating forces. It cited as examples the British,
deciding they preferred to operate with U.S. Army
forces rather than the Marines, to which they had been
originally "op-conned." The French refused to supply
technical data about the radar-jamming equipment

aboard the F-1 Mirage fighters they had sold to the Iraqi Air Force. And the Syrians, who could not decide whether to join the attack into Kuwait, in the end were placed in a reserve role.

The *Times* said the allies had managed to overcome these differences and avoid public feuding. Of Schwarzkopf, it said, he "exercised diplomatic skills worthy of a statesman to persuade the Arabs that Washington was not dictating the war plan."

Every Waking and Sleeping Moment

Schwarzkopf was putting in eighteen-hour days in the planning of the intricate military operation. Every night he returned to a small room deep in the MODA complex. It was spartan, cramped, almost a monk's quarters. A large bed filled a sizable portion of the room and was covered with a military-issue camouflage poncho liner. There was a television set, rarely used, as Schwarzkopf paid as little attention as possible to what was being reported on CNN (and asked that his staff, to avoid confusing the decision-making process, do the same).

A desk held pictures of his family, papers and writing materials, mementoes and souvenirs that people had sent to him. Next to the telephone, a clutch of feathers sent by a member of the Osage Indian tribe from Joplin, Missouri, honoring him as Big Chief White Bear. Later, the collection would include a double-barreled shotgun, a personal gift from his Saudi counterpart, Lieutenant General Khalid.

100

The room, though cramped, offered its occupant a few hours of privacy, which he used to read a succession of books, mostly on military topics, answer letters—he received scores every week and replied to them all—talk with his family by telephone, and listen to music tapes. In the latter, his taste was eclectic. The one-time tenor in the West Point choir had a deep appreciation for Luciano Pavarotti. As an American of unabashed patriotism, he found a favorite in country singer Lee Greenwood's song, "God Bless the U.S.A." As an outdoorsman—fisherman, duck hunter, climber of mountains in Alaska—he liked falling asleep to the sounds of nature: rushing water, honking Canada geese, loons crying across a lonely lake.

Even after the long days, the weight of responsibility often intruded on his sleep, the general said. "The most difficult decisions are the ones that involve human life. I agonize over it. I wake up several times a night, and my brain is just in turmoil over some of these difficult decisions that I have to make," he admitted to several journalists in one of his frequent interviews.

"Every waking and sleeping moment, my nightmare is the fact that I will give an order that will cause countless numbers of human beings to lose their lives. I don't want my troops to die. I don't want my troops to be maimed. It's an intensely personal, emotional thing for me. Any decision that you have to make that involves the loss of human life is nothing you do lightly. I agonize over it."

Aides, while accustomed to the candor displayed by the CINC in talking with reporters, were dismayed by that particular interview, fearing that it might erode public confidence by leaving a false impression of mental anguish, hardly what the American people were looking for in their Gulf commander. Evidently, Colin Powell thought so, too, for in a subsequent telephone conversation the Joint Chiefs chairman suggested to Schwarzkopf that he try to avoid being so forthright about personal matters.

Schwarzkopf, for his part, saw talking with the news media as an essential part of his role as commander-in-chief. After all, he had not forgotten Vietnam, when soldiers returning home—himself included—found a country that seemed either to detest the military or care nothing about its sacrifices. After wavering, he had elected to stay in uniform to try to do something to make things right.

He also had memories of Grenada, when the uproar over the imposed news blockout had led eventually to the establishment of the Pentagon's media pool system. Although that decision had been taken ostensibly in the interests of "op sec"—operational security—it had outraged the media, who argued that the United States military had a clear obligation to keep the American people informed as to what it was doing in their name. Never, not even in Vietnam, had the news media and the military been at such odds.

In the media pool system, small groups of designated journalists from each medium—wire services, newspapers, magazines, radio, and television—were designated as members of rotating pools, based in Washington. If the balloon went up, those in the pool rotation at the time were notified, and within hours were flown to the scene of the story, wherever in the world that might be. Their written reports, photographs, videotape, and audiotape, after being cleared for security, were sent back via military channels to the Pentagon for distribution to the rest of the news media.

The pool system was not regarded as satisfactory by either side, although the military preferred its controls to having journalists roaming at will over a battlefield. The news media accepted it grudgingly as better than no coverage at all, which, judging by Grenada, could be the alternative.

The media pools had been activated several times during the 1980s, always on military exercises, until the "tanker war" in the Gulf in 1987–88. There it received its first test under actual combat conditions, aboard Navy ships. The convoy-escort operations produced little in the way of hard news, at least until Operation Praying Mantis in April 1988, when a media pool was able to report from shipboard the U.S. attacks on the Iranian navy.

The Gulf pools also had educated some journalists on the way the Navy operated, and in turn enabled some Navy officers to learn how to deal with the media. Many who took part thought the experience was beneficial to both sides.

The public information office at Central Command, which had run the Gulf media pools, prepared a report on them for future reference. But by the time the invasion of Panama occurred two years later, the Pentagon ignored it. The media pools were flown to Panama hours after the invasion began, but instead of being placed with units in the field, the journalists were confined to a headquarters building where they, like everybody else, were forced to rely on independent television reports to find out what was going on. Panama, from a media-pool standpoint, was another fiasco.

Schwarzkopf, familiar with all this, was determined from the start that Operation Desert Shield would not be another Grenada or Panama. He professed to feel strongly that the American people deserved to know the truth, and he scheduled interviews several times a week with journalists, either individually or in small groups. In one interview, on September 13, he defined his views with typically Schwarzkopfian candor:

"Listen," he said, "I ain't no dummy when it comes to dealing with the press. And I fully understand that when you try to stonewall the press, and don't give them anything to do, then before long the press turns ugly, and I would just as soon not have an ugly press. I don't care if they report the truth, I just want them to be correct. Not everything is going to be right. Every time there is something new for the press to look at, I want them to see it. I want to create opportunities for them so they are kept informed."

In October, after a team of officers had visited Saudi
Arabia to study ways of organizing war news coverage,
the Pentagon issued an elaborate plan. In addition to
setting up the media pool structure, it provided that
once the shooting began, the authority for releasing
information would shift from the Pentagon to Schwarzkopf's headquarters in Riyadh. It also stipulated that
concern for the safety of correspondents would not be
used, as it had been in Panama, as a rationale for
keeping them away from the fighting. Schwarzkopf had
approved the document, officers said. The news media
was only one of many questions—peripheral yet crucial—that occupied Schwarzkopf's time amid the planning of the military operation.

As Operation Desert Shield entered its second
month, Schwarzkopf's officers were grappling not with
the enemy, but with the myriad details of providing
troop facilities and comforts. For instance, plane loads
of mail, six tons of it a day, were arriving at Riyadh;
the problem was getting it to the troops in the desert,
especially the ones whose units were changing positions, deploying farther north toward the potential battle zone or out into isolated areas where they could
conduct line firing and other training exercises. Other
trucks rolling north carried field toilets, showers, and
washstands. Some units were providing facilities for
laundry and setting up small PXs and tents where the
troops could watch videotaped movies.

The mail system was far from perfect, but the sheer
volume was overwhelming. At one point, forty tons of
mail was backed up at Heathrow Airport outside London because there was not enough space on aircraft to
the gulf to handle it.

Dan Rather had seen the situation, and the CBS
anchorman was convinced that it should be improved.
In a radio commentary tacked on to the end of a CBS
evening news broadcast on September 6, he commented:

"The troops don't complain. From one reporter's

observation, at sea and in the field, here are some things they have to complain about: Mail delivery. Coming and going, in and out, has been inexcusably slow. If Defense Secretary Richard Cheney and Chairman of the Joint Chiefs Colin Powell were half as good as I think they are, they will raise Cain, take names, and kick fanny in this department. Poor planning, lousy execution, slow reaction and correction. If the rest of this operation had been handled as poorly as the mail, Saddam Hussein would be in the Hamptons by now.

"Laundry facilities. Even rudimentary ones, are non-existent to terrible. The U.S. Army general in charge of this theater, H. Norman 'Stormin' Norman' Schwarzkopf, has been quoted as saying, 'This isn't important.' I hope he has been misquoted, because that is dead wrong and a dangerous thing for a general to think. Especially for infantrymen, who win and lose wars, laundry is important.

"Infantrymen, perhaps the general needs to be reminded, walk—filthy, sweat-permeated, and salted fatigues cut and chafe. The troops can't say it, but others can and perhaps should. Stormin' Norman needs to storm less, battle less, think and do more. Like fix the darn mail and get infantrymen in forward positions a way to launder their fatigues.

"And while General Stormin' Norman is at it, he can check into foul-ups in hospital and medical supplies. There are a lot of them—most of them appear to be inexcusable—and he can work on getting our best tanks, not our next best, into Saudi Arabia. Dan Rather reporting, with the troops, in Saudi Arabia."

Needless to say, the Rather commentary was not well received at Central Command. Some staff officers laughed at the idea of a TV anchorman lecturing a professional infantry commander—one who had won three Silver Stars and had been wounded five times in Vietnam, each time while saving the lives of his men—on how to take care of his troops.

Schwarzkopf was considerably annoyed by the Rather report but rejected staff suggestions that he invite Rather for an interview to set the record straight. Publicly he fumed over the incident.

"I don't mind getting bad press when we deserve it, but when it's not a correct story, that absolutely drives me up the wall," he said. "Dan Rather's telling me how to do it? From the Intercontinental Hotel in Abu Dhabi, he's gonna let me know how to be an infantryman?"

Five months later, when Schwarzkopf flew to an airstrip in southern Iraq for a dramatic confrontation with defeated Iraqi commanders, both Rather and his NBC competitor, Tom Brokaw, happened to be at Dhahran. But only Brokaw made the trip to Safwan. CBS sources said Schwarzkopf had intervened personally to make sure that the CBS correspondent and crew who regularly covered his headquarters in Riyadh were part of the media pool not going to cover the meeting in Iraq. Was there a connection? Schwarzkopf, as far as is known, never said, and his top aides merely shrugged when asked that question. But as one had said, in another context: "The CINC has a photographic memory. He never forgets anything you tell him—unfortunately."

From Day One of Operation Desert Shield, Schwarzkopf also was forced to worry about the cultural clash that a massive infusion of American and other foreign troops was likely to have, not just on the Saudi leaders but on the country itself.

Saudi Arabia was unlike any place that most Americans had ever seen or lived. It was old world in the purest sense—some would say medieval. The country was governed by Sharia, or Islamic law. Though the rigidity of this varies from one Muslim country to another, Saudi Arabia set the standard for many of the Gulf states.

Liquor was banned. Women could not drive cars or

ride in them with men other than a husband or immediate relative. Saudi women were required to cover
their faces and bodies completely in public, and foreign
women, while not similarly obligated, were expected
to observe standards of dress and decorum that in no
way offended the Saudi code of public behavior.

The idea of a woman jogging in the streets was out
of the question. Hotel coffee shops had family sections
set aside where the women and children ate separately
from the men. And the swimming pools maintained
certain hours during which only women could swim.

There were no movie theaters. Pornography was
strictly banned. Foreign movies and television series
were shown on the Saudi English-language channel,
but censored to eliminate all scenes in which people of
opposite sexes embraced, kissed, or shook hands. On
Saudi television a boy could not even kiss his mother.

Magazines considered only mildly racy in the West
were subject to confiscation by Saudi customs authorities, who also went so far as to rip out pages with
liquor advertisements or to black out photos of well-
known movie stars in magazines like *Time* and *News-
week*. Anything that referred to Israel was likely to be
confiscated or censored if the inspectors happened to
spot it.

These rules were annoying to many Americans arriving in Saudi Arabia. To others, they were merely quaint
or amusing. But some were offended by the idea that
they were being sent to defend a country which banned
the practice of all religions except for Islam. This, in
particular, provided something for politicians and cler-
ical leaders back in the States to rail against.

H. Norman Schwarzkopf had experience in the Islamic world, but as the build-up continued he found
problems coming at him from all directions. "Every
day we run into a new aspects of cultural differences,"
he said at one point. "We then sit down and work with
our Saudi friends and try to work out a common-sense,
intelligent way to solve the problem, without offending

anyone and at the same time without depriving our troops of what we think they should have. And I'm convinced it's gonna be that way until the day we leave. There's no magic solution out there."

Fortunately, most of his troops were arriving and heading straight into the desert, where they lived in military encampments and rarely came in contact with the local populace, except perhaps for the occasional Bedouin, who were themselves desert nomads tending their goats and camels.

As the general was aware, many of the thousands of foreign civilians residing in Saudi Arabia lived in private compounds provided by the oil companies or other employers. Behind those walls, away from Saudi society at large, they lived somewhat as they had at home. People actually made wine and other alcoholic drinks in their bathtubs. They practiced their religions in what were known simply as "meetings." As long as discretion was observed, they had no real difficulty with the authorities.

Thus Schwarzkopf believed that religious practices could be observed by the troops as long as they were kept quiet. This meant, for example, that Christian chaplains and Jewish rabbis had to be careful not to display their crosses or other trappings of religion. What's more, out in the desert, there was little chance that a native would see a group of soldiers gathered around a chaplain for a religious lesson or service. For all anyone could tell, they could be holding a training class in infantry and squad tactics.

The approach of Christmas brought a new problem for Schwarzkopf to worry about: Christmas cards. Thousands and thousands of Christmas cards would be mailed. Families back home were counseled against sending cards or gifts with strong religious themes, but in the end, the Saudis proved to be understanding. And Norman Schwarzkopf himself spent Christmas Eve with his troops, sharing the holiday spirit of brotherhood in a tent full of soldiers where, he would admit

later in an interview, it was all he could do to keep
from shedding tears.

"I was going to take a seat way in the back where
nobody could see me, so that if I did get overcome by
emotion, there would be just me. But when I walked
into the tent where the service was being held, they
had found out I was coming. Of course there was a seat
reserved, absolutely right square in the middle of the
tent, under all the lights in the front row, and so I just
had to control it. Because all the troops were there, and
because I had ordered the troops not to do that, and so
I didn't. And it was a blessing that I was in the front
row."

After all the worry, the troops had their Christmas
in the desert. So did Norman Schwarzkopf. And as far
as the Saudis were concerned, Santa Claus was just
another foreigner in a strange uniform.

★ ★ |10| ★ ★

They Never Thought
the Free World
Would Care

On August 25, on the same weekend that Schwarzkopf arrived in Riyadh to take personal command of the troop build-up, the United Nations Security Council had met in the pre-dawn hours to approve another resolution condemning the Iraqi takeover of Kuwait. It was the fifth such resolution in three weeks. And this one George Bush had wanted most—giving Washington and its allies the right to use military action to enforce the economic embargo against Baghdad.

Voting 13 to 0, with two abstentions, the council approved a draft document stipulating that the allied forces were free to use "measures commensurate to the specific circumstances as may be necessary" to blockade shipping bound to and from Iraq.

The United States had argued for even stronger language, specifically endorsing the use of "minimal force." But even though the council was not prepared to go that far, diplomats widely agreed that the wording approving measures "as may be necessary," by its very ambiguity, was broad enough for the purpose. U.N. historians noted that it was the first time since the Korean War in 1950 that the Security Council had endorsed the use of force to solve an international crisis. Not in decades had there been such unanimity on a proposition put forth by one of the superpowers at the organization long dominated by its Third World members.

Iraqi diplomats warned, as they had since the beginning, that any military action against Iraq would be met in kind. "The use of force by the United States or any of its allies or puppets will lead inevitably to a number of explosions which will burn all in their path," declared Abdul Amir al-Anbari, Baghdad's ambassador to the world body. But Baghdad could not escape the hard truth—that on this most crucial of votes, it had been deserted by its usual allies. Not only had the smaller nations who normally opposed virtually any controversial initiative of the United States fallen into line. Not only had Yemen and Cuba, both outspoken apologists for Saddam's takeover of Kuwait, abstained. The Soviet Union and China, both major arms suppliers to Saddam Hussein's military powerhouse, had voted with the West.

As the weeks wore on, so did the international debate over whether the sanctions were having the desired effect in bringing Saddam Hussein to his senses. Critics of the embargo argued that such measures historically had failed to achieve their purpose, and pointed to evidence of leakage through Iraq's borders with Turkey, Iran, and Jordan.

The interdiction-at-sea campaign was working in the Persian Gulf, by now a lake filled with patrolling ships from a half dozen countries. U.S. Coast Guardsmen, experienced in chasing drug runners in the Caribbean, had arrived to bolster the boarding teams operating from aboard Navy ships.

The Red Sea was another matter. U.S. officers conceded that some war-oriented material was almost certainly filtering through the Jordanian port of Aqaba, simply because ships' manifests designated Jordan itself as their designation. If the papers appeared to be in order, there was no way that the boarding officers could prove otherwise. One example they cited was a ship's deck filled with Land Rovers painted in desert colors, marked for Jordan but in the Coast Guard's opinion almost surely destined for Iraq.

Advocates of the embargo counseled patience. If ever a situation existed where economic sanctions might work, they said, this was it. Iraq was not South Africa. The country was self-sufficient only in some forms of agriculture and otherwise heavily dependent on imported food, costing some two to three billion dollars a year. Indeed, it needed to import almost everything else to maintain its economy, including more than one million foreign workers, mainly from Egypt, Jordan, and India. And without oil revenues to pay for vitally needed goods, it would be even more difficult for Iraq to circumvent the embargo.

Although history may prove that the size of the Iraqi forces was exaggerated by the U.S., Schwarzkopf was not taking any chances. His planning was already well along. If the war came, it would be a winter war. The *shamal*, the sandstorms out of the northwest, and the seasonal rains might cause difficulties, but they were deemed less serious than a protracted conflict in the searing, energy-sapping, equipment-savaging heat of the desert summer.

Schwarzkopf had even decided on how he would change the name of the operation to reflect its purpose. When the moment arrived, Desert Shield would become Desert Storm.

From the first days Schwarzkopf and his officers had watched as the Iraqis moved their tanks into Kuwait and proceeded to spread them around the desert, digging them into revetments that in some cases left only the turrets showing. In this way they became pillboxes—fixed-gun positions rather than tanks. Armored personnel carriers and artillery pieces also went into revetments.

Concealing such equipment in the middle of a desert might have seemed impossible but the Iraqis had maintained a generally static defensive posture during the long war with Iran, and in so doing had become adept at camouflaging large pieces of equipment in the open. U.S. intelligence also said they were making extensive use of decoy tanks, which from the air were often impossible to distinguish from the real thing.

Schwarzkopf's concept of desert warfare was decidedly different. Tanks, he said, had wheels on them. "Look at Rommel. Look at North Africa, the Arab–Israeli wars, and all the rest of them," he said. "A war in the desert is a war of mobility and lethality. It's not a war where straight lines are drawn in the sand and say, 'I will defend here or die.' Most people who do that, die."

As planning for the war intensified, Schwarzkopf rarely left the war rooms deep in the MODA complex, except to make trips to the field to inspect troops or confer with his field commanders. His closest associates included his deputy and long-time friend, Lieutenant General Calvin Waller, Major General Robert Johnston, his chief of staff, and Major General Burton R. Moore, chief of operations.

Johnston was a Marine Corps officer who emigrated to the United States from his native Scotland at age eighteen, but he could still turn on the brogue at will. Moore was Air Force, having flown more than 100 combat missions in Vietnam. He also held a college degree in radio-TV journalism, but bombed out in a couple of tries as Central Command's daily news briefer in Riyadh.

Schwarzkopf's eighteen-hour days were consumed by

morning and evening staff briefings, plus meetings and
conferences in between. He met daily with Prince
Khalid and often with the commanders of other allied
forces. He conferred constantly with Lieutenant General Charles Horner, the Central Command air chief,
who, operating in a stronghold at a nearby airbase, had
his own staff at work planning the air war.

Schwarzkopf used the red phone on his desk in the
U.S. war room to confer several times a day with
General Colin Powell. The phone also connected him
with the White House, but he did not regularly call
there. Aides to the general said during Operation Desert Storm that he had not talked with the President
directly since his White House briefing on the second
day after the invasion of Kuwait, but Schwarzkopf
himself told interviewers later that he had spoken with
Bush on three occasions during the six-month period.

Later, Schwarzkopf would tell interviewers that he
believed Saddam Hussein's original intent was to go
beyond Kuwait, a judgment based partly on the discovery of vast amounts of pre-positioned supplies found
by the allied forces in Kuwait. It was, he said, "far in
excess of anything anyone would need either to attack
Kuwait or defend Kuwait. So I think we're all pretty
well convinced that he had greater ambitions than just
taking Kuwait."

He suggested that Saddam had sealed his own fate by
failing to stop once he got into the Ramallah oil fields
of northern Kuwait. "Militarily, that would have been
the course of action," Schwarzkopf said. "The major
miscalculation on the part of Saddam and his military
is that they never thought that the Free World would
care if Kuwait was taken. They thought the timetable
was of their choosing, and they thought they could
take Kuwait and subsequently the oil fields of Saudi
Arabia without anyone ever caring."

Had Saddam halted his forces in northern Kuwait,
Schwarzkopf theorized, the outside world could have
done little about it. Moreover, "many people in the

Gulf might have thought it was the right thing to do, because Kuwait was really almost by itself as far as OPEC was concerned, regarding the price of oil. So if he had done that, I think we would see him today with his entire armed forces intact. More important, having taken that slight aggressive step, he would really be a major threatening power for the entire rest of the Gulf. From a political–military standpoint, he would have been able to dominate the Gulf for many, many years to come. So he made a strategic miscalculation of a major order."

Schwarzkopf and his generals also came to believe that Saddam had made another gross error. Although he was reputed to be full of surprises, they found him quite predictable. In deploying his forces, he was doing everything they expected. "We studied the Iraq–Iran campaign very carefully, and based upon that war we came up with a lot of assumptions about what he would do, and we weren't wrong a single time," he said.

At the time, however, the prudent approach was to plan for the worst case. As the Central Command staff did, they found some things to be discomforting. What troubled Schwarzkopf the most—or so he frequently said—was the difference in the estimated size of the forces. Iraq was referred to constantly by military experts and in the press as having a million-man army and the fourth largest army in the world. It had poured about 200,000 of these troops into Kuwait and the adjoining border areas.

Iraq, according to the most authoritative analysts, possessed more than 6,000 tanks, including many of the Soviets' latest, the T-72, which came equipped with a powerful 125mm main gun that supposedly could outshoot the Americans' latest, the yet to be blooded M-1A1 Abrams main battle tank, with its 120mm gun. Central Command estimates would eventually show that about 4,700 of the Iraqi tanks were stationed in Kuwait, along with 4,000 armored personnel carriers and 3,200 artillery guns.

The Iraqis gained a reputation in the war with Iran for skillful use of their artillery. Their tutors in this military art were the Soviets, who had a formidable reputation of their own in the use of the long guns, dating back to World War II. In addition to the Soviet-built artillery that constituted the bulk of its arsenal, Baghdad also had acquired some of the so-called G-5's, the enhanced-range 155mm guns designed and built in South Africa. These guns could fire 39,000 meters, about 23 miles—half again as far as the best artillery piece owned by the United States.

The single most formidable element of Hussein's army, according to experts, was the Republican Guard. Estimated at 150,000 troops, the Guard had distinguished itself in the latter months of the war with Iran. They were better trained and paid than other Iraqi soldiers, and as a result were politically reliable, serving as Saddam's palace guard against any internal conspiracies as well as external threats.

Against all this, the Americans and their allies would have some 2,000 tanks, hundreds of APCs and artillery guns. Though outnumbered in these categories, the Americans could depend on the latest night-fighting technology, helicopter gunships, and other advanced weaponry. Once the ground war began, the by-word for the Americans would be, as Schwarzkopf had said, "mobility and lethality." If all the new high-tech weapons worked, the U.S. forces would be able to pick off the Iraqi armor at "stand-off" range, inflicting losses on the enemy while holding their own casualties to a minimum.

The big edge for the allied side, however, was in the air. The Iraq Air Force, about 800 combat aircraft of varying types, mostly fighters and close-air support bombers, would be outnumbered by the allies—and clearly overmatched in every other way.

The U.S. Air Force's F-15 Eagle, F-16 Falcon, and

F-111 Aardvark, and the Navy's carrier-based F/A-18 Hornet and F-14 Tomcat, were superior to virtually every plane in the Iraqi lineup. Iraq had nothing comparable to the Air Force's AWACS planes, which could see everything that moved in the air as well as most aircraft on the ground up to 200 miles away. Also outclassing them was the clumsy-looking but sturdy A-10 anti-tank aircraft, widely known among pilots as the "Warthog," or the radar-dodging F-117 Stealth fighter, a plane so oddly configured that it was almost impossible to tell from photos what it really looked like.

The American inventory also included some aging but still able veterans: the B-52 bombers, last used in Indochina, the Air Force F-4 Phantom, now converted to service as radar-busting "Wild Weasels," and the venerable naval workhorse, the A-6 Intruder attack bomber.

Nor were the Iraqi pilots any match for their adversaries. Americans had observed Iraq F-1 Mirage pilots in action against Iranian targets, and noted that they fired their Exocet missiles at long distance—even maximum range of 40 miles—rather than come too close to Iranian antiaircraft batteries.

At sea, Schwarzkopf could call on not only the naval air arm but the big guns and long-range missiles of the battleships USS *Missouri* and USS *Wisconsin*. A dozen or so cruisers, destroyers, and missile frigates provided air defense. And he had nearly 20,000 Marines aboard amphibious assault ships in the Persian Gulf, prepared to assault the beaches of Kuwait if it became necessary.

Given the powerful forces at his disposal, Schwarzkopf went on record several times as saying that given enough forces and enough time to prepare, he would guarantee a victory. But at the same time, he noted that a wise field general never assumes weaknesses on the part of his adversary. That was a lesson he had learned in Grenada, where the resistance of Cuban troops had been stiffer than anticipated. He was planning for that worst case—and hoping for the best.

Schwarzkopf was quoted as saying he had based his plan for Desert Storm on British General Bernard Montgomery's scheme for defeating the German "Desert Fox," General Erwin Rommel, at the battle of El Alamein in 1942. "I figured that if Montgomery could make it work, I certainly could," he reportedly said.

The plan had not sprung full-blown from a textbook on armored tactics, however. As the troop strength increased, the plan evolved. Schwarzkopf told interviewer David Frost that he had initially briefed President Bush on a contingency that CentCom had put together months earlier for the defense of Saudi Arabia.

At the Camp David briefing three days after the invasion, he said, he tacked on slides explaining the structure and strength of the Iraqi military. "We said, 'Oh, by the way, if we should happen to change our objective from defending Saudi Arabia to taking him on offensively, here is his offensive capability, and it will take many, many more troops than we currently plan to deploy, and it will take a lot longer.' "

Bush did not respond immediately, but shortly thereafter, Schwarzkopf said, he was asked to assemble a plan for ejecting Saddam from Kuwait with the limited forces already at hand. He prepared "one we would go with if we had to do it." But he stressed in presenting it: "This plan is not what the commander-in-chief of Central Command is recommending. It is a weak plan, it is not the plan we choose to execute, and here are all the things that are wrong with it. If in fact we are serious about ejecting them from Kuwait, what we need is more forces to be able to execute a proper campaign."

Some critics compared Schwarzkopf to the Civil War Union General George B. McClellan, who postponed a much ballyhooed offensive for a year while constantly badgering President Lincoln for more troops. Schwarzkopf had a history lesson ready. "McClellan had four or five times as many forces as Lee, and McClellan wouldn't attack," he told an interviewer. "I had one fifth of the forces of the enemy, and I alluded as how I could probably use a little bit more force."

At a White House news conference on November 8, President Bush announced his intention to double the size of the American commitment in Saudi Arabia to nearly 400,000. The newly organized VII Corps was heavy with tanks and armored vehicles, drawn from forces assigned to NATO as well as from the United States. It was an election year, and the President had waited until that political hurdle was out of the way before announcing a decision that would change the entire complexion of the allied commitment against Iraq.

Bush said the move was "to insure that the coalition has an adequate offensive military option, should that become necessary to achieve our common goals." He reiterated the demand that Saddam get out of Kuwait, adding, "If this movement of force is what convinces him, so much the better."

It meant there would be no ground war before New Year's unless Saddam himself started it. It also meant that Schwarzkopf and his staff could get to work refining their plan for Desert Storm.

Whatever the inspiration, the overall scheme was textbook simple. It would commence with a strategic bombing campaign aimed at knocking out Iraq's capacity to make war: its airfields, communications, utilities, nuclear and chemical weapons potential, antiaircraft defenses and command structure, with the concurrent aim of achieving air supremacy. As that progressed, the attacks would shift as well to the Kuwait theater of operations, striking the entrenched armored and artillery forces and supply dumps, at the same time "isolating the battlefield" by severing supply and communications lines, highways, and bridges. The objectives were to seal off the Iraqi forces in Kuwait from their own rear, demoralize them, and leave them blind to what the adversary in front might do next.

Once the bombing had achieved a certain level of disruption, there would be the option to send in the ground forces. And at this point the plan became an intricate web. The allies would not mount a massed frontal assault against the defensive barriers in southern Kuwait as Saddam and much of the news media seemed to anticipate.

American and European publications offered their readers elaborate charts and graphics explaining precisely what Stormin' Norman intended to do. Some claimed even to have gotten the information from top military sources, as if anyone with access to such closely held information would just give it out. Most of this was regarded by the CentCom staff as useful propaganda to confuse the Iraqis. But Schwarzkopf would admit later that one magazine's version of how Desert Storm would play out was dangerously close to the plan then being assembled.

He also had scorn for civilian experts and analysts. "The analysts write about war as if it's a ballet," he said in one interview. "Like it's choreographed ahead of time, and when the orchestra strikes up and starts playing, everyone goes out and plays a set piece.

"But what I always say to those folks is 'Yes, it's choreographed, and what happens is that the orchestra starts playing and some son of a bitch climbs out of the orchestra pit with a bayonet and starts chasing you around the stage."

Later, in a postwar interview with ABC's Barbara Walters, Schwarzkopf came down even harder on the hired experts. "Most of them were a joke. And a lot of them are my friends, so I don't want to give the wrong impression. But you know, some of the analysis you heard was ludicrous. They didn't know what was going on, they didn't have facts at hand, and they were talking about stuff that didn't make any sense.

"Some of them I resented. I resented the fact that they had served our military and received military training for a great number of years, and now they were using it to guess openly on television what I was going to do over here, on a program that they knew very well was being monitored by the enemy. That's difficult for me to reconcile with my sense of values. Why would anyone do that?

"I don't want to get into names, but there were some that I thought were very helpful in their analysis and careful to explain to the American public what was going on. They were not going beyond that point to predict what was going to happen, or to predict reasons why."

The world watched as the two sides moved ever closer to war. Diplomatic efforts fell to the wayside. Bush stood firm. The amazing coalition he had cobbled together stayed united. The United Nations Security Council passed another resolution, setting January 15, 1991, as the date after which the allied side would be free to take whatever action was required to enforce the previous resolutions.

In Baghdad, Saddam Hussein again rejected the demand that he leave Kuwait, replying with bombastic pronouncements about the coming "mother of all battles" that would cause "rivers of blood" to flow in the desert.

Schwarzkopf and his brain trust in the depths of MODA studied carefully the daily satellite maps and other intelligence material for evidence of change in the disposition of Iraqi forces in Kuwait. In particular, they looked for signs of movement to protect their right flank, which incredibly was exposed from north to south, the length of Kuwait. Schwarzkopf knew that if Saddam did not shore up this glaring weakness before the bombs started falling, it would then be too late.

Meanwhile he proceeded with his battle plan, which would combine surprise, speed, power, and high technology with deception, diversions, and false clues. If all worked as intended, the Iraqis would never know from where the next blow was coming. But as a student of military history, Schwarzkopf knew well the adage that the plan ends when the first shot is fired.

Gotcha

At 12:50 A.M. on January 17, the Hyatt Hotel in downtown Riyadh shook to the vibrations of jet aircraft roaring overhead. One, two, three. Then four more, at one- to two-minute intervals. The noise was deafening, almost unearthly, and very unlike the normal sounds of planes taking off from the airbase about two miles away. "Tankers," said an Air Force officer in the public affairs office on the eleventh floor. "If you've heard it before, you can't mistake it. Nothing else sounds like that."

The KC-135s were en route to a rendezvous near the Saudi–Iraq border 300 miles to the north. At the same moment, swarms of Air Force F-15E Eagles were lifting off at al Kharj airbase south of the Saudi capital. F-117 Stealth fighters raced into the night sky from a base near Taif. Steam catapults hurled Navy F/A-18 Hornets and A-6E Intruders from a standing start to flying speed in three seconds from the decks of the carriers SS *Saratoga* and USS *Dwight D. Eisenhower* in the Red Sea, USS *Midway* and USS *Ranger* in the Persian Gulf.

Once airborne, the planes regrouped and turned north, missiles and bombs slung beneath their wings.

Desert Shield was no more. It was now Desert Storm.
After 139 days of planning and waiting, the war was on.

The approach of the January 15 deadline set by the
U.N. Security Council had set off a furious last round
of diplomatic maneuvering to head off the conflict.
None of it was getting anywhere. Saddam was still
trying to link any agreement to the resolution of the
Palestinian problem. Bush rejected that out of hand,
repeating that Saddam must simply comply with the
dozen resolutions adopted by the U.N., all aimed at
getting his forces out of Kuwait. If he did not, Bush
said in a January 5 radio address, Iraq would "face
destruction."

Saddam replied the next day, using the celebration
of Iraq's annual Army Day for a televised pep talk to
his forces. "The battle in which you are locked today
is the mother of all battles," he declared. "Our rendezvous with victory is very near, *Inshallah* [God will-
ing]."

Secretary of State James Baker met in Geneva with
his Iraqi counterpart, Foreign Minister Tariq Aziz.
Their meeting had finally been arranged after a break-
down in earlier efforts to have each of the two officials
meet directly with the leader of the other's country. In
lieu of that, Bush had sent a personal videotaped message to the Iraqi people, stressing that the allied argument was not with them but with their leaders. The
Iraqi government allowed it to be shown, but did not
respond to its message.

Many on the American side saw the Baker–Aziz
meeting in Geneva as the last chance for any Iraqi
signal of willingness to compromise. But nothing in
Aziz's position offered hope. Baker had brought a letter
from Bush for the Iraqi official to take to Saddam.
When Aziz refused even to pick it up from the table,
Baker said, "I have said everything I have come to say."
Aziz replied that he, too, had nothing left to say.

On Capitol Hill, where going to war in the Gulf had
been debated, sometimes bitterly, since the first troops

had been dispatched to the Gulf five months earlier, Congress met at last to vote on a resolution authorizing the use of force in keeping with the U.N. resolutions. The split had been largely, though by no means entirely, along party lines, with Democrats urging that the economic sanctions be allowed more time to take hold, and Republicans backing Bush's threats to attack if the U.N. deadline was not met.

Although the White House took the position that Bush did not need Congress to declare war, he wanted badly to have a resolution that would remove any doubt—especially where the Saudis and other coalition members were concerned—that the American people were willing to fight for Kuwait's liberation. Meeting over the weekend, the lawmakers on January 12 ended three days of impassioned debate by voting to support Bush. The Senate vote was a narrow 52 to 47. Ten Democrats sided with the administration, two Republicans against. In the House, 86 Democrats and 164 Republicans backed Bush. He said the outcome "unmistakably demonstrates" the U.S. determination to oust the Iraqis from Kuwait.

In direct response, amid chants for a holy war, Iraq's rubber-stamp parliament voted the next day to endorse Saddam's rejection of the U.N. deadline, then just forty-eight hours away. On the same day U.N. Secretary General Javier Perez de Cuellar, who had made a last-gasp flight to Baghdad to appeal to Saddam, emerged from a meeting with the Iraqi leader, conceding that his mission had failed. On the 15th, the twelve-nation European Community admitted that their last-minute initiative also had collapsed. France then said it had a plan, but it faded quickly as Americans contended there was no point in trying to keep peace hopes alive in the face of Iraq's unbending defiance.

For Schwarzkopf, the diplomatic flurry mattered little. His only concern at this point was a go—no go order from the White House. Should it come, it was his job, and that of his air commander, General Chuck Horner, to make sure that the planes got to their targets and home again.

Bush was ready. On Tuesday, January 15, he signed the National Security Directive that formally authorized military action. But, according to the *New York Times*, he instructed Cheney to wait at least until the end of the next day before issuing the order. That would give Saddam time to demonstrate to his people that he could defy the U.N. deadline before making any eleventh-hour deal. When no such feeler came from Baghdad, Cheney instructed Schwarzkopf, late on the 16th, to execute the order.

In the war room five floors below the street, General Schwarzkopf gathered with his top aides. As the order went out to the fleet and the air force bases, he asked the chaplain, Colonel Carl Peterson, to say a prayer for the safety of all the American forces. Then he put on a tape of Lee Greenwood's song, "God Bless the U.S.A." "Anybody who knows me knows how much I love that song," he would later tell a television interviewer.

Although the war in this opening stage consisted only of air attacks and long-range naval missiles fired from ships at sea, Schwarzkopf issued a prepared statement to all his forces. It said in part: "The President, the Congress, the American people, and indeed the world stand united in their support for your actions. Our cause is just! Now you must be the thunder and lightning of Desert Storm. May God be with you, your loved ones at home, and our country."

The war room was tense. The attackers were on their way, and there was nothing to do but wait. "We knew exactly what time the first shot would be fired, and we knew who would fire it," said Schwarzkopf. The first bomb was to hit its target in Baghdad—specifically a laser-guided "smart bomb" delivered by a F-111 Stealth fighter on a government air-defense complex—at 2:40 A.M. local time, Thursday. That would be 6:40 P.M. Wednesday night in New York and Washington, just as the network news programs were about to go on the air.

The planes streaked northward.

The primary concern for Schwarzkopf and his staff was Iraq's formidable antiaircraft defenses—a mixture of rapid-firing guns and missile launchers of several kinds. On paper, this system could throw up a curtain of fire exceeding that faced even by pilots in Indochina. Most of these guns and missiles were of the same types that the Americans had encountered over North Vietnam, and since the Iraqi gunners were also Soviet-trained, the American planners were braced for what one officer would later call "some pretty bad numbers" in aircraft losses.

Air Force F-4 Phantom Wild Weasels loaded with radar-jamming gear and HARM anti-radiation missiles led the way, clearing a corridor for the attackers by picking up radar emissions from the Iraqi missile batteries, locking on, and firing their own missiles, which followed the radar beams unerringly to their source, destroying the ground radar and blinding the Iraqi gunners to their targets. The F-4s were hoary campaigners, predating even Vietnam, but the gear they carried was ultra high tech. Before this war ended, Iraq would be subjected to a stunning array of such weaponry from air, land, and sea.

At the al-Rashid Hotel in Baghdad, a handful of American television reporters watched and listened as explosions boomed and flashed on the horizon, and antiaircraft fire floated upward, streams of orange balloons crisscrossing the night sky above the city. The first Stealth fighters had slipped undetected through the radar screen, exactly on schedule, and the gunners were firing randomly in hopes of hitting aircraft that they could not see. Other aircraft were homing in on airfields, command centers, and other key targets north, south, and west of the capital. Farther south, bombs exploded in military installations in Kuwait, and waves of lumbering B-52 Stratofortresses, almost every one older than the pilots at the controls, prepared to unleash their payloads on the desert where Saddam's vaunted Republican Guards were entrenched in bunkers and tank revetments.

Within minutes after the first GBU-15 laser-guided bomb from an F-117 zipped through the airshaft of a building housing the nerve center of the Iraqi air-defense system, and another blasted through roof vents of the air force headquarters, the word was received in the Riyadh war room. "There was elation, but it was really kind of subdued," one officer said later. "The best thing about it was that after all the publicity and the whole world expecting it to happen, we apparently had achieved complete tactical surprise."

Having anticipated the worst case, Schwarzkopf and his staff were surprised by the near total lack of response by the Iraq Air Force. Even the antiaircraft missile batteries were erratic. In the first 36 hours, the allied side would lose seven aircraft—three American, two British, one Kuwaiti, and one Italian, all to ground fire. Those losses, about a third of what pre-battle estimates had anticipated, symbolically reflected the multinational character of the forces committed. Eventually, about a dozen air forces would be flying missions of one kind or another.

On Thursday night, even as the bombs continued to fall, President Bush went on television in the United States to announce personally the start of Desert Storm. He restated the goals of the offensive—to force Iraq's withdrawal from Kuwait in compliance with the U.N. resolutions and to restore Kuwait's legitimate government—and praised the dedication of the American forces and their coalition partners to that cause.

At 9:30 P.M., reporters assembled in the Pentagon briefing room to hear Cheney and Powell deliver the first preliminary briefing on the war. Their assessment was understandably cautious—the first reports on the air campaign were favorable, Cheney said, but it was too soon to know how many allied aircraft might have been lost.

The two officials stressed that the aircraft were concentrating on strategic targets in Iraq. Great care would be taken, they said, to avoid civilian casualties. Powell, in reply to a reporter's question, said that Saddam Hussein himself was not a target. "The purpose of our bombing facilities in the vicinity of Baghdad is essentially to go after the command and control system of the Iraqi armed forces," Powell said. "We're looking at principally military targets, command and control installations, air-defense sites that could put our planes at risk, but they are militarily oriented targets."

Had there been civilian casualties? Cheney was asked. "The best reporting that I've seen on what transpired in Baghdad was on CNN," Cheney said, drawing laughter from his audience of journalists. "It would appear, based on the comments that were coming in from the CNN crew in the hotel in Baghdad, that the operation was successful in striking targets with a high degree of precision."

At the al-Rashid in Baghdad, ABC's Gary Shepard and a trio of CNN reporters, Peter Arnett, Bernard Shaw, and John Holliman, had lost their live pictures in the first minutes when a laser-guided bomb hit the main telephone-exchange building, wiping out communications all over the city and destroying the satellite dishes on the roof. But the CNN crew, who had the foresight to arrange a separate telephone link through Jordan, continued to deliver voice reports on the battle through the pre-dawn hours.

In the United States, the U.S. Armed Forces Radio and Television Service was picking up the CNN feed and relaying it to, among others, the station serving the Americans in the Gulf. The CNN account of what was happening in Baghdad was on the screen in Schwarzkopf's war room, giving him and his officers the same information that the rest of the world was receiving. Never in history had a military commander enjoyed such access to his battlefield.

The recognition that Saddam himself might also be watching—the Americans assumed throughout the war that he had access to CNN as well—kept Cheney and Powell from divulging many details in their first news conference. That factor would continue to affect the way that U.S. military spokesmen, both in Washington and in Riyadh, would discuss the war, whether sending "messages" intended for Saddam's ears or refusing to divulge information on the grounds that it would help him.

Dawn Friday in Riyadh brought a clamor from reporters covering Schwarzkopf's headquarters for an update on the situation. Lieutenant Colonel Mike Gallagher, an Air Force officer who ran the news media operation in the Joint Information Bureau at the Hyatt, summoned the press to the fourth-floor briefing center, where he read a brief statement in front of the TV cameras that by now were permanently set up on a platform. Gallagher added little new information except the number of combat sorties that had been flown to that time—750—and the fact that in addition to the air strikes, long-range Tomahawk cruise missiles had been fired from Navy warships for the first time ever in combat.

By that afternoon, U.S. officials felt they had a good enough grip on the situation for Schwarzkopf himself to report to the media. He turned up at the briefing room with General Horner, who had brought along videotapes taken by aircraft gun cameras, showing something that had not been seen previously—the laser-guided smart bombs plunging down airshafts and cracking through doorways to blast their targets. One of the buildings seen exploding, Horner explained, was Iraq Air Force headquarters—"my counterpart's headquarters in Baghdad."

Schwarzkopf, assuming as always that the worldwide television audience probably included his adversary, said the war thus far had gone "just about exactly as we expected it to go," and the picture was far clearer and more detailed than he had experienced in any previous battle.

He said about two thousand sorties had been flown in each of the first two days. The number of allied planes lost was up to seven, all the pilots listed as missing in action, although Cheney had let slip at the first Pentagon briefing that one of them, a Navy F/A-18 Hornet pilot, was thought to have been killed. Eight Iraqi planes had been shot down, and two probables, all in air-to-air combat.

The significant news, Schwarzkopf said, was that the Iraqis had retaliated against the attacks by firing seven Scud missiles into Israel and one at Dhahran, the site of the biggest allied air base, in eastern Saudi Arabia. Scud was the NATO code name for the Soviet SS-10 surface-to-surface missile, a cumbersome but powerful projectile derived from Germany's V-2 rocket, which had caused widespread damage in London in the latter days of World War II. It had been used by both Iraq and Iran during their eight-year war, in an intermittent "war of the cities" against each other's capitals. The Iraqis, in order to reach Tehran, had modified the original Scud with boosters to more than double its 200-mile range. This had forced a significant reduction in the weight of the warhead, but the long-range version remained a potent weapon when fired into a populated area.

The Scud launched at Dhahran had been destroyed in the air by a U.S. Army air-defense missile called the Patriot. It was the first time that one of these weapons, whose years of development had been marked by controversy, had ever been fired in anger. As each one cost close to a million dollars, the story went, only one of them had ever been test fired.

The Scuds fired at Israel were another matter. One of the worst nightmares of American officials, from the very start of Desert Shield, was that Saddam would try to involve the Israelis in the war, and that the Israelis, who had always defended themselves with vigor against any Arab threat, would retaliate without regard to the effect that action might have on the Arab members of Bush's coalition.

Saddam's efforts to link the Kuwait crisis with the Palestinian question had fallen largely on death ears in the Arab world. Israel being under attack was a new and dangerous situation. It did not seem likely that Syria, for one, would allow itself to be even indirectly connected with Israel against an Arab state. Such a situation might even put intolerable pressure on the Saudis and the other Gulf Arab states. According to subsequent reports, Bush himself was forced to intervene with Israeli Prime Minister Yitzhak Shamir to keep Israel from launching a retaliatory strike.

Schwarzkopf conceded in the Frost interview that had Israel retaliated for the attacks, some of the coalition's Arab members—he did not say which—probably would have pulled out.

"I think we all expected the Scud attack on Israel," he said. "It became a question of how soon can we get it under control and would Israel be patient enough to let us get it under control before it entered into the fray. There's no question that if Israel had entered the fray at that moment, it would have put severe pressures on the entire coalition."

U.S. officials were reluctant at the time to say where in Israel the missiles had hit, for fear of giving the Iraqis information that would help them to correct their aim for the next time. It was apparent from news reports that at least one had hit in Tel Aviv, inflicting some damage. Schwarzkopf sought to minimize the whole issue, saying of the Scuds, saying, "I would characterize [them] as having yielded absolutely insignificant results. As a result, I think to date we can say that the enemy Scud campaign has been ineffective."

He said Air Force planes had scored a victory by finding 11 of Iraq's mobile missile launchers, a feat he described as "like finding a needle in a haystack, as you can well imagine," had destroyed six of them in two raids, and was going after the rest.

All of those launchers—videotape released later by the Air Force would show them being blown up by American cluster bombs while parked haphazardly at a road junction—were found in an area where they were clearly to be fired at Saudi Arabia. The ones destined to fire at Israel were in far western Iraq and harder to locate.

Israel had no Patriot missiles—although several batteries and Americans to operate them would be rushed to that country from the United States within two days—and something had to be done. The Air Force put a high priority on knocking out the Scud sites along both borders, but was stymied for a week by bad weather. Eventually, indications would reveal that the United States had grossly underestimated the numbers of mobile launchers that the Iraqis had available, but the air strikes did take effect. From 35 Scuds launched in the first week, the number would drop to 18 in the second week, and diminish still further as the campaign went on.

The Patriots were programmed to hit any Scud whose trajectory took it toward a worthwhile target. They proved their effectiveness by knocking those down, while numerous others fell harmlessly in empty desert or the waters of the Persian Gulf. But the unerring aim of the Patriots had an unexpected effect. As they were fitted with proximity fuses, causing them to detonate close enough to blow a Scud out of its trajectory, many Scud warheads escaped destruction and exploded on impact with the ground. In other instances, the huge 30-foot steel casings crashed in streets or residential areas, but in most cases did surprisingly little damage.

Later on, a Scud fired at Dhahran was knocked out by a Patriot, and by the cruelest turn of irony it fell on a building serving as a barracks for American service personnel, killing 28 and wounding about one hundred. Those casualties would prove to be the most inflicted on U.S. forces in any single incident of Desert Storm.

When Iraq displayed several captured pilots—four American, two British, and one Saudi—on national television, it evoked images of two decades earlier, when other fliers were paraded before hostile crowds and exploited for propaganda purposes at rigged "press conferences" in Hanoi. At first the pilots appeared to have been badly abused; this fear later would prove largely unfounded. But at the time, Schwarzkopf and his senior staff officers were furious over the pictures of the pilots forced to stand before the camera and mumble statements of apology that obviously had been written for them.

Schwarzkopf recalled later that he had felt "a combination of anger with the Iraqis for doing that, because it was such a blatant violation of the Geneva Convention, and at the same time, compassion, not only for the pilots but their families, because you just didn't know what the pilots were going to have to go through." He added, in the same postwar interview, that he felt CNN, by showing the Iraqi videotape of the POWs, was "aiding and abetting an enemy," a charge that the network naturally rejected. All of the prisoners who appeared in the videotape were eventually released, and for whatever reason, the Iraqis never again put any other POWs on display.

At the January 18 briefing, Schwarzkopf also mentioned, for the first time, his aversion to trying to count casualties on the other side. Asked for his "best estimate" of Iraqi military and civilian casualties, the general snapped that he had "absolutely no idea."

It was to become a recurring theme. Schwarzkopf still felt strongly from his Vietnam days about the American habit of measuring battle results by the "body count." According to him, the policy, foisted on field commanders by higher-ups, had undermined the integrity of American officers—himself included—by pressuring them to tell lies and falsify official reports.

"I don't think many of us came out of Vietnam and could hold our heads up and say my sense of integrity is still lily white, because we all know that we had lied about body counts. We all knew there had been a lot of other lies, and it did bad things to the officer corps," he said on one occasion. "But it's a different officer corps today, one that has learned from this experience. When we went into this thing, I was determined that we were going to tell it absolutely like it was."

Schwarzkopf's vehemence on the subject of body counts had a predictable effect on his staff. None would speculate, even privately, on the subject of Iraqi casualties. Day after day, the reports by Riyadh headquarters spoke of the number of tanks, armored personnel carriers, and artillery weapons destroyed by allied bombers, but briefers invariably skirted the issue of soldiers. Not until his final briefing weeks later, when the war had ended, did Schwarzkopf use what reporters had come to call the "d-word." In reply to a question about what had become of the thousands of Iraqi soldiers who had not been accounted for as prisoners or probable deserters, Schwarzkopf said American forces had found "very, very many dead" in the bunkers and destroyed vehicles in the Kuwaiti desert.

Twice more in the next few weeks, Schwarzkopf personally offered evidence of how effective the Air Force's smart weapons were proving to be. Inviting the chief targeting officer, Air Force Brigadier General Buster Glosson, to explain the technical details in a televised briefing, he revealed the use of a special 2,000-pound bomb that could punch through the walls of Iraq's specially hardened concrete aircraft shelters, wrecking whatever was inside. Another time he showed how two precision-guided bombs from an F-111 had disabled underground pump manifolds in a Kuwaiti oil field, shutting off the hemorrhaging of oil into the Gulf from an offshore loading terminal sabotaged by the Iraqis.

Central Command spokesmen said the accuracy of the bombs was responsible for holding "collateral damage" and civilian casualties in Iraq to a minimum. Iraqi officials countered with allegations that many civilians were being killed by U.S. bombs, and they began taking Western reporters around Baghdad and beyond the city to show the damage inflicted. The fact that the news reports were strictly controlled by the Iraqis did not help their cause with Schwarzkopf's people. A great deal of resentment built within the Riyadh headquarters over the reports, especially those of CNN reporter Peter Arnett, who for a time was the only American reporter in the Iraq capital.

Schwarzkopf said later that although the Baghdad reports did not bother him at the start, he, too, became resentful. "That was when the Iraqis ran the team out, showing them a civilian target that had been heavily bombed and said, 'You see there?' The implication was almost that we were lying to the American people. Of course, they didn't run out and say, 'Here's military targets that have been totally destroyed.'

"The implication was that we were deliberately doing that kind of thing, and that was resented by every member of my headquarters because it simply was not a true picture."

The strain became greater in the fourth week of the war, when on February 12, U.S. bombers struck a reinforced bunker in Baghdad that Schwarzkopf's meticulous targeting process had identified as a military-communications center, but turned out to be in use at the time as a civilian air-raid shelter.

The Iraqis gave reporters a tour of the wrecked facility, claiming that more than 400 innocents had been killed. The final figure would be considerably less, but that did little to ease the shock felt by U.S. officers over this apparent failure of intelligence.

Pressed for evidence to back up their insistence that

the bunker was a command and control center, Brigadier General Richard "Butch" Neal, Schwarzkopf's deputy chief of operations and senior spokesman, refused to do so on grounds of operational security. Privately he told a reporter, "Look, you can be absolutely sure that we knew what it was. Otherwise it would not have been on the target list. That's the best I can do."

Neal, a pugnacious Marine from Massachusetts who had survived a winnowing process to become the daily press-briefing officer, bristled when a reporter asked whether the command regretted the incident. "Well, you're damn right," said Neal. "If four hundred civilians, as reported, were killed, then logic would tell you that of course the American people and the coalition forces are saddened by that fact."

Three days before the bunker incident, Cheney and Powell had arrived in Riyadh, where they met with King Fahd, Kuwait's exiled ruler, Sheik Jaber al-Ahmed al-Sabah, and spent an entire day with Schwarzkopf and his senior Army, Navy, Air Force, and Marine commanders. The purpose of the meeting was clear. Desert Storm was moving along on schedule, and they would take back to Washington the views and recommendations of Schwarzkopf on if and when the ground war should commence.

At a pre-departure news conference in Riyadh, Cheney was asked whether Bush would "accept the military judgments of General Schwarzkopf and his staff as to the timing of the ground assault, or perhaps accelerate the timetable on his own."

In response, Cheney noted, "The President will place very significant emphasis upon the military advice he receives with respect to this decision. He has done that from the very beginning of the campaign. He has established goals and objectives for us, he has signed off on the broad outlines of the strategy and reviewed the overall plan, but he has then left it up to our military commander in the field, General Schwarzkopf and

General Powell, to decide exactly how the campaign ought to be prosecuted."

The visit from Washington was the occasion for Schwarzkopf and his team to take complete stock of the situation as it stood after 25 days of a round-the-clock air campaign. What they found was nearly 70,000 aerial sorties flown since the start, about half of them combat; 25 allied aircraft lost, 18 of them American. The allies had acquired unquestioned air supremacy through the destruction inflicted on Iraq's air defenses and the disintegration of its air force. Of the nearly 800 combat planes it was known to have had at the start of the war, 40 had been shot down, dozens more destroyed on the ground, and nearly 140 had mysteriously fled to Iran, where the Tehran government said they would be impounded for the duration of the war. Anything that moved in the air over Iraq was instantly pounced on and shot down by American fighters.

Iraq's power plants, communications centers, its means of production including chemical and nuclear plants, were in ruins, as were virtually all of the Euphrates River bridges that linked Baghdad with the Kuwaiti war zone. The anti-bridge campaign by American and British planes had forced the Iraqis into using pontoon bridges to move supplies southward, and these as well as the convoys themselves were under constant attack.

The focus of the bombing campaign, the Kuwaiti theater of operations, as Schwarzkopf's headquarters defined it, had been increasingly "isolated." Stockpiled supplies and munitions that had been brought there before the war began had been severely depleted. Schwarzkopf said that one secondary explosion triggered by a bomb hit on a fuel-and-ammunition dump had been "on a scale of one to ten . . . a twelve," and the Iraqis were virtually unable to replenish their forces.

The armor and artillery dug in across the desert had become sitting ducks for allied planes. Almost 1,000

tanks, 700 guns, and hundreds of armored personnel
carriers were gone. Three times those numbers would
be wiped out in the next two weeks as the campaign
intensified, and U.S. pilots used infra-red sighting to
pinpoint the heat radiated by the sand-covered weaponry.

Although U.S. officials did not publicly estimate the
number of Iraqi casualties, it was obvious that thousands had died in the raids. What appeared to be mass
graves were spotted in aerial-surveillance photos. In an
ever increasing flow, at least one thousand Iraqi soldiers had made their way through their own mine fields
and defensive barriers to surrender to allied troops
along the Saudi border. They brought tales of sparse
rations, low morale, desertions on a major scale, and
"execution battalions" from the hard-core Republican
Guards roaming the rear areas, tracking down and
killing soldiers trying to escape toward home.

The Iraqis had attempted some armored thrusts
along the border with Saudi Arabia. All failed except
one, in which an armored column of tanks and APCs
from Iraq's highly rated 5th Division had crossed into
Saudi Arabia and seized the Gulf resort town of Khafji
for some 36 hours. In the end, however, that foray
ended in defeat for the Iraqis, as Saudi troops backed
by U.S. Marine artillery and allied air strikes destroyed
the attackers. Some 500 Iraqis had surrendered, and
Schwarzkopf, who described the affair as "about as
important as a mosquito on an elephant," concluded
that if that was the best the Iraqis had to offer, the task
of driving them from Kuwait was likely to be easier
than anyone had hoped.

In the same way that it had blinded Iraq's air defenses
and neutralized its air force, the allied air campaign
appeared to have achieved the disabling of its military
communications network. Saddam's generals were
forced to rely on slow, circuitous means to send and
receive messages from their field units; those units
could not readily communicate among themselves.

Lacking the aerial observation that could locate and track their enemy, unable to anticipate his movements or coordinate their own maneuvers with each other, the Iraqi armored forces would be fighting blind. In the end, every tank commander could be fighting for himself.

Taking all these factors into account, Schwarzkopf felt reasonably confident of success. But there was yet one more factor—the most important of all.

For months the constant surveillance of the desert along the Kuwait border with Iraq, marked by a dry riverbed called the Wadi al-Batin, had revealed no sign of Iraqi military movements toward the west. Although Saddam and his generals were looking at maps very much like Schwarzkopf's, there was no indication that they saw what they saw—their right flank, exposed and ignored, while they reinforced their defenses along the Saudi–Kuwait border to the south and built elaborate beach defenses along the coast of the Persian Gulf, where Schwarzkopf's invasion fleet of 30 ships and some 18,000 Marines lurked, they knew, just beyond the horizon.

Even as Saddam's high command was committing this most crucial of tactical blunders, Schwarzkopf was exploiting it. In a massive movement of forces that the American general himself said later was probably unprecedented in military history, he managed to shift 100,000 troops, mostly armored forces, as far as 300 miles to the west, along with supplies for a 60-day campaign.

Once the bombing began, it was too late for Saddam's high command to do anything about the exposed flank. Pulling large numbers of tanks out of their sand revetments and moving them westward across open desert would have been suicidal.

In one of his postwar interviews, Schwarzkopf said he had told his component commanders in a meeting on November 10, two days after Bush announced he was doubling the size of the forces in the Gulf, that—

barring some change in the Iraqi disposition of forces—
his plan would be to move the forces to the west and
launch a flanking attack.

"We still kept all our forces over to the east, and they
had reacted beautifully to that. And now I knew that,
number one, I could move the forces without him
being able to see them, and more important, even if he
saw them, he couldn't do anything about it. Because
we were going to control the air, and had he tried to go
out there, we could have gone ahead.

"So that's when I knew—we gotcha!"

I'm Not Here to Give Them Anything

Everything was ready. The Saudi-led Arab forces were in position to drive up the coastal highway into Kuwait City. Two divisions of U.S. Marines, already blooded in a series of skirmishes and armored clashes along the border, were primed to drive the center, through the oil fields. The three divisions of the Army's XVIII Corps, already veterans of six months in the desert, and the more recently arrived armored juggernauts of VII Corps, were deployed along the western flank, ready to plunge northward in a lightning dash that would bypass many of the Iraqi forces and hook around behind the Republican Guards, cutting off their escape. The French, with elements of the 82nd Airborne Division, awaited the orders that would take them northward to al-Salman, sealing the allied left flank from being blindsided, just as Saddam had failed to do on his right.

Then came the Russians. As if suddenly realizing that his chief client state in the Middle East was in

dire straits, Soviet President Mikhail Gorbachev
mounted a fresh diplomatic offensive, proposing a plan
under which Iraqi forces could withdraw from Kuwait
within an unspecified period and the U.N. sanctions
would be lifted in stages.

On February 22, as the forces of the American-led
coalition continued their final preparations for combat,
Moscow announced that Saddam Hussein's government had accepted the plan. "My God, he's surrendering to the Russians," exclaimed U.S. Navy Captain
Mike Doubleday as the story came across CNN.

Within hours, Bush appeared in the White House
Rose Garden to say that although he "frankly appreci-
ated" the Gorbachev effort, it would permit a condi-
tional withdrawal, failed to guarantee Iraqi adherence
to all U.N. resolutions, and was therefore unacceptable.
He proposed a counterplan giving Iraq a week to get
out of Kuwait and meet a host of other demands. It
gave Iraq until noon Saturday, February 23, New York
time, to begin its withdrawal.

When Iraq did not reply, even the Soviets threw in
the towel. Hours before the deadline, a Gorbachev
spokesman said Saddam had lost the chance offered by
the Soviet plan and should "have the guts" to begin
pulling out of Kuwait voluntarily.

Schwarzkopf, meanwhile, had been authorized in a
message from Bush to commence his attack at a time
of his choosing after the noon deadline, which was 8
P.M. in Riyadh. In fact, the presidential approval had
been in his hands for over a month, with a tentative
window of February 21 to 25, unless Iraq capitulated
beforehand.

Returning to the White House from Camp David to
make the announcement himself, a somber Bush told
the nation, "I have directed General Norman Schwarzkopf, in conjunction with coalition forces, to use all
forces available, including ground forces, to eject the
Iraqi army from Kuwait. The liberation of Kuwait has
now entered a final phase. I have complete confidence

in the ability of the coalition forces swiftly and decisively to accomplish their mission."

In his underground headquarters at MODA, Schwarzkopf had notified his component commanders to launch the first attacks at 4 A.M., Riyadh time. The scene there, as the hour came, was much like it had been 38 days earlier when Desert Storm began with the air strikes on Baghdad. But there was none of the ceremony.

Schwarzkopf, examining all the factors, had estimated that the war would last as long as two to three weeks. "I thought we would probably gain initial surprise," he said afterward. "Had they chosen to stand and fight, I'm sure it would have taken longer, but my initial estimate was about two to three weeks."

Two unexpected factors had intruded on the plans in the final hours before the attack. The weather had turned bad; cloud cover obscured much of the western desert along the Iraq border and rain was beginning to fall in some areas. Worse, in an orgy of sabotage over two days, Iraqi soldiers had blown up and set fire to more than 200 of Iraq's approximately 900 oil wells. Unceasing fireballs leaped into the sky from the damaged wellheads, creating a vast blanket of black smoke that drifted across the desert and out into the Gulf. The combination of weather and smoke was sure to put a crimp in air support for the ground forces.

Schwarzkopf's other big worry, one he had had from the start, was whether the Iraqis would use chemical weapons. Great effort had been put into preparing the troops to deal with this threat. The Iraqis had used nerve gas and mustard gas in the war with Iran and on their own rebellious Kurds, and although the fear of chemical warheads on the Scud missiles had not materialized, it had to be assumed that they would use chemicals against the coalition forces on the battlefield.

In the initial stages of the assault into Kuwait, the allied forces found a number of pleasant surprises. The vaunted defensive barriers of sand berms, mine fields, and trenches filled with flaming oil proved far less formidable in most areas than had been expected.

There was no sign of the Iraq Air Force. The planes that had fled to Iran weeks earlier remained on the ground there. Those left in Iraq, whether fighters or helicopters, risked almost certain destruction by taking off.

On the ground, armed resistance was light. Incredible as it seemed, Schwarzkopf had caught his adversaries flat-footed again. Tactical surprise was nearly complete.

As allied troops rolled north through the eerily blazing oil fields, they found Iraqi soldiers surrendering by the thousands. Schwarzkopf had anticipated this, but so many were giving up that the special details of troops assigned to handle them were being overwhelmed by numbers, and some of the advancing forces simply passed many of them by. By the third day, the numbers of EPWs, as the command called them, had swelled to 50,000 and the U.S. headquarters gave up trying to keep track.

Nor did the allied troops encounter gas attacks. Although the Iraqis had stockpiled the chemicals for battlefield use, they apparently feared the reprisal it would engender. Leaflets dropped by allied planes warned the Iraqis that they would be held accountable as war criminals for using gas. In addition, many senior officers who had the authority to order such attacks evidently had abandoned their posts ahead of the invasion, leaving their troops to fend for themselves.

Cheney, making a brief appearance at the Pentagon on Saturday night as the assault was in its early stages, announced a blackout on news coverage, saying it was needed to protect the attacking forces' operational security. Although nearly two hundred accredited journalists were in the field with the troops, their "pooled" reports were to be held up—forty-eight hours was the time frame officers mentioned—and the regular daily briefings in Washington and Riyadh were suspended until further notice.

The blackout naturally prompted outcries from the news media. Schwarzkopf, who had repeatedly assured journalists in Saudi Arabia that he wanted them to have as much access as possible, obtained Cheney's approval to make a statement to the news media on Sunday afternoon in Riyadh, thirteen hours after the start of the ground war.

In a succinct statement Schwarzkopf disclosed that the initial assault had begun at 4 A.M., armored forces on the far west flank had joined in about eight hours later, and "are moving north with great speed." He said Iraqi resistance "can best be characterized as light," and friendly casualties were "extremely light." Were the Iraqis retreating, simply not engaging, or surrendering? he was asked. "All of the above," Schwarzkopf said.

Would he pursue the Iraqis into their own country or stop at the Kuwaiti border? "I'm not going to answer that question," retorted the general, then did. "We're going to pursue them in any way it takes to get them to get out of Kuwait."

By Wednesday, 90 hours after the start of the ground war, the coalition forces were in total control of the battlefield and mopping up. A total of 42 Iraq divisions, out of more than 50 that had made up the world's fourth largest army, had been "captured, destroyed, or rendered combat ineffective," according to Butch Neal, the command spokesman. American casualties were listed as 79 killed in action, 212 wounded, and 45 missing. The KIA numbers would climb gradually to about 125 on the basis of later reports. Iraqi dead were in the uncounted thousands.

Kuwait was liberated, its citizens hugging and kissing the Americans who had entered the shattered city after pausing at the outskirts to make sure that Arab forces, with Kuwaitis in the lead, symbolically got there first. After a final outburst of murder, rape, curbstone executions, and other atrocities, the Iraqis had fled. Hundreds of them—in tanks, APCs, and stolen cars and trucks—had been caught by U.S. planes on the wide superhighway that led north toward the border and the city of Basra. U.S. pilots called it a "turkey shoot." Journalists dubbed it the "highway of death." Despite the shocking pictures of the carnage, few protested that the action was excessive. Most of those in the exodus had been soldiers, and their vehicles were loaded with stolen goods, a final footnote to months of wholesale rape and pillage in Kuwait.

On Wednesday evening, February 27, Schwarzkopf appeared before live cameras to explain the plan that he had devised and used to destroy the Iraqis in four days—not the two to three weeks that he had anticipated it would take.

He confirmed for the first time what some, though not the Iraqis, had long suspected—that the huge amphibious assault force in the Persian Gulf had been largely a diversion to preoccupy the Iraqis and force them to build defenses against it.

If the Marines, who spent six months at sea in the Gulf, were unhappy at being ultimately cut out of the action, Schwarzkopf noted that the amphibious operation, which had its own code name of Imminent Thunder, had been more than simply deception: "We had every intention of carrying out amphibious operations if they were necessary." He also lavished praise on the shore-based Marines, calling their assault on Iraqi barriers in Kuwait an "absolutely superb operation, and I think it will be studied for many, many years to come as the way to do it."

Schwarzkopf outlined for the first time in detail his grand flanking movement that had sent several American divisions and one British northward and then east to encircle and cut off the Iraqis from escaping north.

"Once we had taken out his eyes, we did what could best be described as the Hail Mary play in football. I think you recall that when the quarterback is desperate for a touchdown at the very end, what he does is he sets up behind the center, and all of a sudden, every single one of his receivers goes way out to one flank, and they all run down the field as fast as they possibly can, and into the end zone, and he lobs the ball. In essence, that's what we did."

It seemed an odd analogy, Desert Storm and Hail Mary. If anyone had been desperate for a touchdown, it was hardly H. Norman Schwarzkopf. But nobody was prepared to argue semantics with the former star tackle from Valley Forge Military Academy. And the evidence, in any event, showed how well his plan had worked. American troops arriving in Kuwait City discovered an Iraqi headquarters with a sand-table model of the battle zone, complete with miniature tanks, guns, and flags marking the Iraqi and allied positions. The toy guns all pointed south and east toward the Persian Gulf.

Bush, after consultations with his military commanders, prepared to announce a cessation of hostilities at midnight Wednesday, New York time, ending what he called "the hundred-hour war." It was a one-sided cease-fire that could be rescinded at any time, with the stipulation that American and coalition forces would use force against any suspicious moves by the enemy.

Schwarzkopf, though basking in a victory that some military experts were already calling one of the most brilliant in history, was anything but finished with the Iraqis. Among pressing business at hand, he had to get back the prisoners of war held by the Iraqis, along with the bodies of any coalition service members in their possession, and exchange the more than 50,000 Iraqis being held in Saudi custody. In addition, the Iraqis had to give up the thousands of Kuwaitis who had been abducted, many of them in the days just prior to the fall of Kuwait City.

On Sunday, March 3, an airplane descended through layers of black smoke as it approached for a landing at Kuwait's devastated airport. As it burst into the clear,

Norman Schwarzkopf as a West Point cadet in 1956 (top). (*Sygma*) Stormin' Norman in charge, 1991. (*AP/Wide World*)

Saudi Arabia's King Fahd stands at attention with Schwarzkopf during the king's review of allied troops. (*AP/Wide World*)

Iraq President Saddam Hussein shortly after the bombing raids on his country (right). Schwarzkopf points to a row of photos of Kuwait's Ahmadi Sea Island terminal that caught fire after being struck in a U.S. air strike. (*AP/Wide World*)

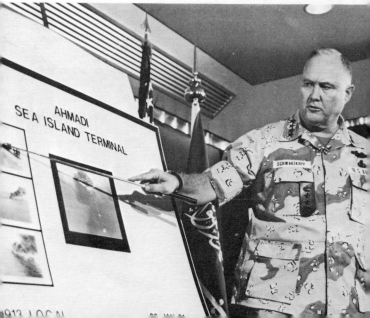

AHMADI
SEA ISLAND TERMINAL

SCHWARZKOPF

Schwarzkopf confers with General Colin Powell, chairman of the Joint Chiefs of Staff, and Defense Secretary Dick Cheney in the war room of the U.S. Central Command in Saudi Arabia (top). (*AP/Wide World*) Schwarzkopf at the French Embassy in Saudi Arabia with French generals Roquejoffre (left) and Schmitt. (*Sygma*)

Schwarzkopf stoops to talk to a U.S. Army service-woman (right). The six-foot-three, 230-pound Schwarzkopf stands out among soldiers of the 1st Infantry Division. (*AP/Wide World*)

The Bear gives a thumbs-up sign to the crowd along the beach at Kuwait City shortly after liberation (top). Brenda Schwarzkopf (center) with Barbara Bush and Marlin Fitzwater. (*AP/Wide World*)

General Jaber al-Sabah, commander of the Kuwaiti forces, poses with Schwarzkopf on the beach at Kuwait City with Kuwaiti flags and a bottle of sand from the beach (top). A young Kuwaiti girl performs a traditional Arab dance in Kuwait City in celebration of the liberation. (*AP/Wide World*)

Schwarzkopf cracks a smile as he talks about the success of coalition forces liberating Kuwait. (*AP/Wide World*)

General Schwarzkopf saw the balls of fire roiling upward from the oil wells not far from the runway. "I was totally unprepared for the scene, and the first thing that flashed through my mind was that if I ever visualized what hell would look like, this was it," he later told Barbara Walters. "It was so senseless, absolutely senseless destruction, because by every definition it would accomplish nothing."

At the airport, Schwarzkopf switched to a helicopter, which joined with eight others on a short flight that took them over the former stronghold of Iraq's Republican Guard. The flower of the Iraq Army had been hammered to pieces by the air campaign and American and British armor, suffering the same ignominious fate as the rest of Saddam's forces and performing with no more distinction. From the air, the Guard's tanks were smashed lumps of metal, some with gun barrels pointing askew, others with turrets laying several yards from the main hulk. Trucks, vans, and other flotsam of the war littered the desert. Brass artillery shells were scattered randomly near a gaping hole that had been a storage bunker.

The helicopters landed at a small airstrip at Safwan, where a hint of green marks the end of the desert and the beginning of the Euphrates Valley. A wooden sign read, "Welcome to Iraq. Courtesy of the 1st Infantry Division." Hundreds of American troops in full battle dress watched as Schwarzkopf, surrounded by his bodyguards, military police, and a swarm of photographers, strode up the tarmac toward a cluster of tents where he was to meet with a delegation of Iraqi generals to discuss terms for a permanent cease-fire. But it was not a negotiation. "I'm not here to give them anything," Schwarzkopf said in answer to a reporter's question. "I'm here to tell them exactly what we expect them to do."

Schwarzkopf embraced Major General Jabir al-Sabah, commander of the Kuwait forces, and Lieutenant General Khalid bin-Sultan, his Saudi counterpart, and entered his private tent, marked by a red flag with four white stars on a pole near the entrance, to await the defeated enemy.

The historic meeting already had been postponed one day. Schwarzkopf's standing order that anything flying in Iraqi airspace was to be shot down had obligated Iraqi officials to come by car, which meant they had to travel around or through one or more of the southern Iraqi towns where civil order had broken down in the wake of the defeat. The streets were full of angry citizens and rival factions of soldiers supporting or opposing Saddam Hussein.

Eventually the Iraq delegation—eight officers headed by a pair of lieutenant generals—arrived at the designated rendezvous, a highway intersection about a mile from the airstrip. There the Iraqis boarded U.S. Army Humvee utility vehicles, escorted by several Bradley fighting vehicles, two M-1A1 tanks, and a brace of AH-1 Apache helicopter gunships, which hovered low overhead as the caravan drove to the airstrip. If awed by this unsubtle display of hardware that had helped to destroy their army, the Iraqi officers did their best to conceal it.

The Iraqis, wearing dark green winter-dress uniforms, were required, like everyone else who would be inside the main tent, to undergo a body check with a metal-detection scanner. Schwarzkopf, who said later he was still fuming over the sight of the blazing oil wells, nevertheless gave instructions to permit no pictures because "I don't want to humiliate them."

He later said in the Walters interview that the senior Iraqi officer balked at being searched. "The general didn't think too much of that idea, and I told the interpreter to tell him that I would be the first one to be searched.

"Then he looked at me and said, 'Well, the only person that's going to search me is my counterpart,' and we said, 'What do you mean by your counterpart?' He said, 'The person that's going to negotiate,' and the guy kind of looked me up and down and said, 'Who are you?' I said, 'I'm General Schwarzkopf,' and he said, 'Oh, all right.'

"I don't know whether he'd seen my picture or not. Apparently, I'm not that famous there, but it was sort of funny. He didn't expect the general to be out there in the same uniform that all the rest of the troops were in."

Once inside the tent, Schwarzkopf and Prince Khalid sat at a main table, facing the two senior Iraqis. Allied commanders, including Lieutenant General Sir Peter de la Billiere, head of the British forces, French Lieutenant General Michel Rocquejeoffre and representatives from ten other coalition member countries sat behind Schwarzkopf. Carafes of water, note pads, and other items lay on the table. A can of Diet Pepsi was at Schwarzkopf's place.

The American general, dressed as usual in desert battle fatigues, looked stern. The two senior Iraqis, who identified themselves as Sultan Hasheem Ahmad, Saddam's deputy chief of staff, and Salah Abbud Mahmud, commander of the Iraq 3rd Corps, appeared uncomfortable. Their subordinates sat in chairs behind them.

Schwarzkopf said an Iraqi spokesman had reported that his country had 41 POWs and had asked how many the allied side was holding. " 'As of last night we had 60,000, but we're still counting.' And the entire delegation, they all kept a poker face, but you could tell that every one of them tensed." He said he rejected Iraq's claim that their forces had voluntarily withdrawn.

"I wasn't about to accept that at that point. I just said, 'You know, we could probably argue here until sunset as to whether or not what you were doing was withdrawing. Therefore, what we're going to discuss is the arrangements that will make sure that we continue to cease the offensive."

After two hours, Schwarzkopf and Prince Khalid saw

their guests off in the Humvee caravan—this time without the Apache escort—and stepped before a microphone to tell the assemblage of several hundred soldiers and journalists that they had obtained Iraq's agreement on all demands. Schwarzkopf said a symbolic release of prisoners would occur immediately to show good faith.

A handful of the allied POWs were released the next day, followed by the rest within days. Schwarzkopf was among those who greeted them on arrival at the airbase in Riyadh.

PART TWO

SCHWARZKOPF IN HIS OWN WORDS

★ ★ ★ ★

General H. Norman Schwarzkopf
Interview
SEPTEMBER 13, 1990

Q: We are now six weeks in a defensive posture, and Saddam Hussein hasn't done anything to challenge it. President Bush said again that aggression against Kuwait will not stand. What's the next move, General, and whose move is it?

A: One next move is when Saddam Hussein picks up and gets out of Kuwait. I think the President clearly announced his next move. He's going to wait for a while to see if the sanctions—which are already having some effect in Iraq, from everything we've heard—will continue to have that sort of effect.

If we figure, as has already been announced, that Iraq is losing one billion in revenues every day the sanctions are in effect, then it's going to be interesting to see how much loyalty he has in his armed forces when he's unable to pay their salaries, feed them, and resupply them with fuel and spare parts and ammunition. So I think that's the next move right now.

Some other possible moves are that the Iraqis will get desperate and as a result attack to accomplish some objective. So we have to be prepared for that. And we are. He could also perpetrate some other outrageous act, with regard to the hostages or terrorist activity, and we have to be prepared for that.

Right now, as I have said, my orders are to deter, and if attacked, to defend. I know a lot of people look at the size of this build-up and say, gosh, this has to be something more than defense, but it really isn't. Every force coming into the country I told the President would be required if Iraq launched a full-scale attack into Saudi Arabia.

Obviously we can defend effectively today. But on the other hand, he has a 1,500,000-man army, 5,000 tanks, and 1,000 aircraft, and if he choses to, he could bring a tremendous amount of military might to bear in an attack on Saudi Arabia.

My philosophy as military commander is, when the President of the United States tells me to defend Saudi Arabia, I'm going to guarantee him that I can.

Q: How far away are we now from the build-up? I believe you said two months?

A: That was quoted out of context. What I said was that as far as the build-up is concerned, we are only six days behind, and that does not disturb me at all because the vast preponderance of the combat force was front-loaded. What I needed to do was get the immediate defense forces in the country, and we have succeeded in doing that. Now what I'm doing is bringing in follow-on forces. I'm bringing in robustness, bringing in infrastructure to support the deployment, and, obviously, more armored forces to back up the light forces. I think that's pretty obvious to anybody.

What I really said was, give me a couple of months and I will be able to stand up to the President of the United States and the King of Saudi Arabia and say, there is absolutely no question, whatever he chooses to throw against you, and whatever form he chooses to throw against you, you have a one hundred percent chance of Saudi Arabia being defended. But I am certainly not saying I'm not competent for two more months, because I'm competent now and getting more so every day.

Q: If he were to attack now?

A: If he were to attack now, I feel confident that we could handle the problem. He would suffer extraordinary losses. But I still do not have the ground forces of choice that I'd like to have to fight a mobile war in the desert.

Q: Armor?

A: Sure. Obviously, look at Rommel. Look at North Africa, the Arab-Israeli wars and all the rest of them. A war in the desert is a war of mobility and lethality. It's not a war of straight lines drawn in the sand, where you dig in and say, I will defend here or die.

It is a highly mobile war where there is no front to speak of, and it's a war of attrition. I don't think any military commander will ever tell you that you can win a mobile war with air forces alone. I'm very confident that we will inflict very high casualties on the enemy if he comes at us with our air forces.

The same goes for our attack-helicopter forces. It is entirely conceivable that we will inflict so many casualties on him with these two forces that it will, in fact, stop his attack.

As a prudent military commander, that is not the way you plan a defense on the ground, though. You plan to use a combo of your air forces, sea forces, and land forces. And you want to make sure all of them are capable of doing everything you think they need to do to have a rock-solid defense, and that is what we are in the process of doing.

Q: What if nothing happens? Will that affect troop morale or cause an erosion of confidence, especially with the holidays coming on?

A: This is something that we are very much aware of, but we are not concerned. I have great confidence in

our American fighting men and women out there. I
think they understand their job calls for them to be
away from home. I think, particularly in this case, they
know they have the support of the vast amount of the
American people and also, in this case, the support of
the world. I think that is going to help them a great
deal with the separation.

That American service person wants action and the
more action the happier they are. So, lacking Saddam
Hussein giving them any action, we have got to give
them action in the form of good training rather than
just sitting around in a foxhole in the sand. We have to
rotate them back to the rear where they can watch a
football game. We have already put in a radio station
for them. My orders were very specific. We have a
different type of service person out there. They were
asking me some questions about the world in regard to
this situation. They want information. Their second
strongest interest is in sports. This radio station is
going to broadcast news, sports, and music.

I made the first priority radio, handing out 5,000
radios, and I said those radios had better wind up in
the hands of the troops. I don't want to find them in
the rear headquarters. We're also putting in TV so that
when these folks do rotate out to the rear areas, they'll
be able to watch football games. The TVs have already
been put in out in some rather austere locations where
we set up tents and put air conditioning in the tents
and where they're playing twenty-four-hour movies
and videotapes. They are putting up large screens and
running regular movie schedules in at least four or five
locations. I told all my commanders I want them to do
something like that.

Now we have a shortage of videotapes over here and
what we really need to come up with are a lot more
videotapes so I can put them in locations so all the
troops can see them.

Q: I don't mean to be a spoil sport, but we're in

Saudi Arabia, and you are aware, sir, the Saudis are tough on things they allow to be shown in the country. Are you going to want to view all that stuff and take out whatever may be objectionable, such as sex and violence?

A: The Saudis have their customs regulations and they are going to be inspecting things that come in from a customs standpoint. It is their law, just as we have customs regulations that do not allow outsiders to bring certain things into the United States. So if they deem it objectionable and confiscate it, that's okay. I am sure there are plenty of other videotapes out there will not be deemed objectionable and will come into the hands of the troops.

Q: A lot of stuff you get will be objectionable. There will be more videotapes in the confiscation warehouse than out in the field.

A: We are carefully controlling what we are doing and where we are doing it. We are trying in every way possible to be culturally sensitive, recognizing that two months ago, Saudi Arabia did not have any concentration of foreigners to speak of and now, of course, they have this huge United States presence.

Movies are being shown in closed tents, exclusively for the troops. We will have USO shows over here before long—that's an aspect of our planning, how we are going to conduct these shows. For many reasons, not the least of which is that I do not want a lot of advertising and have a huge audience watching one of these shows, and then being targeted by some terrorist to blow up a bomb. So we have to think of that aspect, too.

What we are doing every day is that we are running into a new aspect of cultural differences. We then sit down with our Saudi friends and try to figure out a common-sense, intelligent way to solve the problem without either offending anyone or depriving our troops of what we think they should have. And I am

convinced that it is going to be that way until the day
we leave. There is no magic solution out here.

Q: Back to the question of protracted presence.
What is going to be the effect of this on the equipment?
A: Hopefully it is not that sensitive. We build our
equipment to military specs that are pretty tough.
Sure, we have to change filters on engines. Sure, there
will be a certain amount of corruption on helicopter
blades. Yes, we will have to change engines on aircraft
more often, but we know how to do all that. We know
how to maintain our equipment. I absolutely do not
expect to see huge breakdowns of equipment all over
the kingdom.

My aide-de-camp said it is like flossing your teeth. If
you forget it once, your teeth are not going to fall out.
If we are smart about it, we are not going to have that
sort of problem.

Q: What can you say about the Iraqi order of battle?
Is it what you had expected?
A: They have done pretty much what we expected
them to do, in a basically defensive formation. They
have pushed their infantry up to the front, regular
infantry in defensive positions. They have pulled back
their mechanized infantry into a second line of defense, and they have pulled their strike forces back into
assembly areas, as basically counterattack forces. This
is what I would expect them to do in going into a
defense. The problem with that is that strike forces in
assembly areas can also pass through the forward infantry and quickly go on the attack. Is it a Russian tactic?
Sure.

So we are saying that they are basically in a defensive
posture, but capable of attacking, within *x* amount of
time, and that time varies from estimate to estimate.
As a military commander, I am not going to ignore any
capability that they have.

Q: Can you give any numbers and locations?

A: They are predominantly in Kuwait, but they are in Iraq also. I won't give any numbers, but I can tell you that their numbers have increased considerably over what they originally had. They went into Kuwait with, I think the number was given out as 100,000, 200,000, or so, and they have continued to reinforce those forces. So they are considerably bigger than that now.

Q: There have been some questions about the multinational forces. The officers in the desert say there are 2,000 Egyptians total. Other reports say 3,500. There seems to be mass confusion on this point. Also, U.S. officers have said they saw Syrian T-72s on flatbed trailers. Is this true?

A: The Saudis are in charge of the multinational forces, so why don't you ask them.

Q: We did.

A: Okay, this is strictly on background. There are Syrian and Egyptian forces here already. They were the forces that could be immediately deployed and I would say that in the future you are going to be seeing more Syrian and Egyptian forces.

Q: Do the Syrians have tanks here already?

A: I find that very hard to believe. As a matter of fact, I would be willing to bet you that they don't. Why are the Egyptian commando forces here? Same reason the 82nd is here. Because they are the ones who can fly and get their equipment in. Anything else that comes in here is going to have to come by sea. So if those other forces are going to be introduced, an alert reporter could probably figure out when their equipment is coming.

Q: If the war spreads to Kuwait by way of Iraqi aggression, what kind of a war is it going to be? Kuwait is a city of masonry, high rises, traffic circles—what kind of a war is that going to be?

A: That is a highly hypothetical question. I would just like to go back to what I said before. In desert warfare you do not necessarily go after a terrain objective. What you do is seek to destroy the enemy's center of gravity. And there are a lot of ways you can do that without ever having to worry about house-to-house, dig-'em-out fighting.

Q: The Iranian religious leader Ali Khamenei made a statement calling for holy war against America. What is the effect of this statement on the Arab forces that you have as partners?

A: The answer to that is that today I read in a Saudi paper that a religious leader in charge of 50–100,000 Shi'ites in Saudi Arabia made a statement that Shi'ites should be allowed to join the armed forces to fight against Iraq. Also, the leading religious Islamic scholars in Cairo, which has long been recognized as the center of Islamic scholarship, have loudly proclaimed that what Iraq is doing has nothing to do with Islam.

When Saddam Hussein was fighting Iran, he said he was fighting as a secularist to eliminate the spread of Islamic fundamentalism. Now all of a sudden he is an Islamic fundamentalist. So I say there are just as many religious leaders, even more, who are saying that Iraq is completely in the wrong. I think the bottom line is that it is typical of the enigma of Iran these days. You have several different voices speaking at the same time, which is one of the reasons we haven't been able to restore our relations with Iran.

Frankly, I find it very hard to believe that many people in Iran are ready to throw their arms around the Iraqis and embrace them as brothers. Remember that Saddam is saying that everything that he is doing is in the name of pan-Arabism. The Iranians are not Arabs.

Q: Would you please clarify what Secretary of Defense Cheney said the other day about a permanent U.S. presence?

A: Cheney said after the commitment of forces was announced that the military-to-military relationships in the Middle East had fundamentally changed and would never go back.

I do not think any of us knows after the determination of the crisis what military posture in this part of the world will be. That is very much open to negotiation. It depends not only upon what the U.S. would want to do, but obviously upon the willingness of the Gulf nations. The one constant is that we have told King Fahd we would come when asked and we would leave when asked. And we are seeking no permanent bases in the area.

When you stop and think about it, I would rather you not write this now. If you had asked me at Central Command two months ago what I would like to have in Saudi Arabia, I probably would have said I would like to have bilateral planning, combined exercises, and prepositioning. We are doing bilateral planning right now. We are doing combined exercises, and we're sure as hell putting an awful lot of equipment into this country.

Why weren't we doing it two months ago? Because the Saudis wouldn't have anything to do with it. So Cheney is absolutely right. When this is all over, I would imagine there will be any number of combinations of long-term military-to-military arrangements that didn't exist before we came here.

Q: We have Saddam Hussein to thank?

A: The ultimate arrangement over here is very much dependent on the outcome of this crisis. Obviously, if Saddam Hussein is still in power with his military one hundred percent intact and he continues to develop chemical and nuclear weapons, the military arrangements in this part of the world would be considerably different than they would be if there were some lesser threat over here. The perceived threat is going to drive what the military arrangements are.

Q: Will there be other units coming in? What about the 1st Cav?

A: Who is releasing these numerical designations of U.S. units? That really pisses me off because those guys at the Pentagon pouring that stuff out are supposed to be keeping their mouths shut. We have adopted a standard policy in building up your forces. When you start saying it's the umpteenth unit, you are giving information to the enemy.

I want to use my strength against his weakness. That's what you do, particularly when you are fighting against a guy who outnumbers you. One of the greatest advantages we have over Saddam Hussein is that from an intelligence standpoint, we know almost everything he is doing, and he knows almost nothing that we are doing.

I can tell you where every single one of his units are located on the ground. I can tell you what his troop disposition is, where his reserves are. I can tell you a great deal of information about him. He does not know any of that about us. So why should I, as a military man, volunteer anything to the open press that would assist him in his analysis of what we are doing? That's the sole reason for it. It's not to preclude you having information. It is because when it gets in the open press, he watches CNN religiously, the Iraqi military ambassador in Washington cuts articles from the *Post* and sends them home every day, and I don't want to give him one damn thing that will help his military analysis if I can prevent it.

Now to get back to your question. I am building up my heavy forces, bringing in the force of choice to fight in this environment. And I will continue to build up those forces until I can say beyond a shadow of a doubt—on land, in the air, and on the sea—we'll still clean his clock.

There was an article by one of our brilliant military analysts back in Washington, someone who has never spent the first day in uniform, but he spelled out the entire offensive campaign that's being planned against Iraq. He laid out amphibious invasions, air strikes, which would be the first step, which would be the next. And one of the Saudis came to me and said, What is this doing published in the paper? And I said, Hey, this is somebody who made it all up, but he is trying to make it look like he knows what is going on. And that works both ways. There were some reports that came out in the early days that were not exactly accurate, but they played very much to our advantage.

Somebody came to me and said, You ought to tell them the correct story. And I said, The hell with that, I love what's going out. It wasn't anything that we were orchestrating, but it was happening and I was delighted that it was.

Q: What about the problem with the ships breaking down? Was that a critical problem?

A: No. It would have been critical in the early days of the build-up, but we have significant force on the ground right now. It's a concern only because I want to have 100 percent of the unit together. I don't want to have 90 percent of the unit together and the other 10 percent floating around out in the ocean somewhere. But as far as a serious erosion of the fighting strength involved, it is not that. We are six days behind. During the first week or two, this was a dicey situation because we had minimal force on the ground.

And those troops that were deployed the quickest are not the most capable of fighting armored forces, so I felt it important to get the type of forces over here that could act as a protective umbrella for the ground forces. If at that point something had happened, I could have flat been very nervous and upset. Now it is the other way around. We can afford it now because we have a considerable capability built up.

Q: We've heard intelligence reports about Saddam Hussein executing some of his own officers and Republican Guards. Is there any indication his own people are wavering?

A: Iraq is one of the most closed societies, similar to North Korea. So you hear stories, you even get corroboration, but you still cannot be sure if there is anything to it.

As far as the Iraqi generals who are shot if they fail and shot if they succeed, I think it is one of those things where they're surviving. They know if they are unsuccessful, they get bumped off and they also can't afford to get too popular.

Q: What about R&R in this country and out of it?

A: One proposal has been to somehow get a couple of cruise ships and maybe bring them back to a cruise ship that's floating offshore somewhere, where they can relax and dance and have music and air conditioning and swimming pools and just kind of live it up.

Q: What about a deal with Bahrain?

A: There's been no formal contacts, and obviously we've got to work it very carefully. We don't want to inundate them, but I know some entrepreneurial Bahrainis who wouldn't mind setting up a hotel at some location that wouldn't interfere with Bahraini life. I have to be very careful about the terrorist threat. I'm not going to set up another Beirut barracks to get blown up, either. Remember, we're five and a half weeks into this deployment and everybody forgets we started from zero base. So we're a long way from having any firm plan with regard to R&R. There's a DOD directive and I know they're looking at it along with a lot of other things. Free mail also had to be under hostile fire. John Glenn is proposing income-tax breaks, which I'm all in favor of. I think we ought to have huge income-tax breaks, particularly for general officers. Just joking, for the record.

The Saudis have been very forthcoming in understanding the problem. We have a huge military presence in downtown Riyadh, something the Saudis are very uncomfortable with, and so are we. I'm uncomfortable with it from a terrorist standpoint, from a concentrated target standpoint. And from the cultural sensitivity standpoint, we don't want this to be disruptive to Riyadhis.

The Saudis have given us a beautiful area, very safe, with wonderful facilities, removed from Riyadh. Within that compound Americans can live almost exactly as Americans live in the States. They would be removed from everyday public view for jogging, et cetera. You just don't see that in downtown Riyadh, and it would be terribly shocking to them if you did. We go out to this fenced compound exclusively for Americans, and people will be able to run around.

Of course, there are always going to be the lunatic fringes on both sides. Some Saudis will object to anything like that happening in their country, even though nobody is going to see it. And there is always going to be somebody in the U.S. who will say that's a violation of the Constitution of the United States of America because we can't allow freedom of speech and let 2 Live Crew some over here and do a stage performance in downtown Riyadh. But that ain't going to happen either. It's their country, and let's face it, we were invited in and we are here defending Saudi Arabia and a lot of other things, We are not just defending a monarchy.

General H. Norman Schwarzkopf
CENTCOM Briefing
Riyadh, Saudia Arabia
Friday, January 18, 1991—7:00 A.M. (EST)

GENERAL SCHWARZKOPF: Good afternoon. Let me just start by saying, as you all know, we are now thirty-six hours into Operation Desert Storm. I would tell you that to date, the campaign is going just about exactly as we expected it to go. As in the early days of any battle, the fog of war is present, but I would tell you, having been in the outset of several battles myself, and having been at the early hours of the Grenada campaign, I would tell you that we probably have a more accurate picture of what's going on in Operation Desert Storm than I have ever had before in the early hours of a battle. That picture is not perfect, but I think it's pretty good, and I want to bring you up to date on where we are at the present time.

As far as air operations are concerned, we are flying a total of about 2,000 air sorties of all types each day. More than 80 percent of all of those sorties have successfully engaged their targets. The sorties are being flown by United States Air Force, the Navy, the Marines, and some Army. We also have six other nations involved with us in this coalition—Saudi Arabia, Kuwait, the United Kingdom, the Canadians, the French, the Italians—and all participated in the air campaign to date. In addition to flying offensive operations, they are also flying defensive air operations over Saudi Arabia to protect the kingdom, and also to protect, naturally, our forces that are here.

To date, we have lost seven aircraft—two United States Navy aircraft, one F-18, and one A-6; one Air Force F-15; one Kuwaiti F-4; two British Tornadoes; and the most recent one was an Italian Tornado. With regard to the disposition of the pilots, we are carrying all of the pilots as missing in action. However, we now have pretty good information that the Kuwaiti pilot is probably safe in the hands of the Kuwaiti resistance.

At sea, of course in addition to flying against the targets that the Navy is taking on, the Navy is also in the business of protecting the fleet—both with their ships and with their aircraft aloft. We're tracking any potential adversaries that look like they're coming out to threaten ships, and we're engaging those as required. This morning the Navy has engaged three enemy patrol boats and either disabled them or sunk them. In addition to that, we have increasing numbers of amphibious ships moving into the Gulf area at this time.

From the ground, of course the United States Army and Marine Corps are continuing to defend Saudi Arabia. We're also repositioning our forces for further action. To date, there has been no direct hostile confrontation on the ground. However, yesterday there was a slight artillery duel, artillery on the part of the enemy that was immediately reacted to by our air, and the artillery was silenced. During that duel we had two Marines that were lightly wounded in action.

Of course the significant news today, I'm sure you all know about, was the seven Scuds fired early this morning against Israel, and there was one Scud missile fired against Dhahran. The one Scud missile fired against Dhahran was destroyed by a United States Army Patriot missile. Fortunately, the seven missiles that were fired against Israel I would characterize as having yielded absolutely insignificant results. As a result, I think to date we can say that the enemy Scud campaign has been ineffective.

Now for the good news. As you know, finding fixed missile launchers is a relatively easy business, but finding the mobile launchers is like finding a needle in a haystack, as you can well imagine. This morning United States Air Force found three mobile Iraqi launchers, with missiles on board, inside Iraq. Thes launchers were obviously aimed at Saudi Arabia given their positions. Those three mobile erector launchers have been destroyed. In addition to that, at the same time we found eight more mobile erector launchers in the same location. We are currently attacking those launchers, and we have confirmed the destruction of three more of those mobile erector launchers. We are continuing to attack the others, and, I assure you, we will attack them relentlessly until either we are prevented from attacking them any further by weather or we have destroyed them all.

In concluding my remarks, I want to make just two points. The first is the one that you've heard from the Secretary of Defense and the Chairman of the Joint Chiefs of Staff, but I think it bears repeating. That is, that we are only thirty-six hours into what is a campaign. The President of the United States said this is not Panama, it will not be over in a day, and it certainly won't. So we are just continuing on in this campaign, and the campaign will continue until we have accomplished our objectives.

The second point I'd like to make is that we're doing absolutely everything we possibly can in this campaign to avoid injuring or hurting or destroying innocent people. We have said all along that this is not a war against the Iraqi people. I think very shortly you're going to hear a little bit more about what we're doing to avoid hurting innocent people.

At this point, I'd like to introduce to you Lieutenant General Chuck Horner. He is the commander of the United States Central Command Air Forces. Since August we have been planning this campaign, and I think the one person who should probably be considered the architect of the entire air campaign as it's being conducted today is Chuck Horner. He is certainly the one person, more than anyone else, who is responsible for the magnificent airmen who are out there conducting this campaign today. He's a superb leader. I'm very proud to have him as a member of my team. I'm exceptionally proud of the absolutely fantastic job he and the members of his staff and the people under his command have done today with their campaign. With that, I'd like to turn my podium over to Chuck Horner.

LIEUTENANT GENERAL HORNER: Thank you, General Schwarzkopf.

The objectives of the air campaign were set up by General Schwarzkopf in August. We've worked hard to bring together this very complex, very large campaign plan. We've been able to integrate all our forces because we all fly off a common air-tasking order. You heard that we have forces from all the services in the United States, plus many countries in the multinational force. We've been able to execute because we've trained very hard. You'll find sorties where a Saudi aircraft will be dropping bombs, will be escorted by an American fighter, provided support by other aircraft such as from the countries mentioned.

I can give you an excellent example that just happened the first day, where we had American F-15's escorting Saudi aircraft, the Navy was providing ECM jamming, and the Saudi airplane put four craters on the runway. I'll tell you right now, we couldn't have taken a pickup truck and laid those bombs out there any more accurately. So we've had some very good cooperation and integration of our forces.

The types of aircraft we have involved in this campaign have been key to its success. There's no doubt that our air defense and our awareness of what's going on in the air battlefield are a result, in large measure, because of what the AWACS provides us, and the defense that aircraft such as the F-14 and the F-15 provide our forces.

It has been, in some respects, a technology war, although fought by men and women. Certainly one of the strongest guidance we had from the very start was to avoid any damage to civilian targets and to the holy shrines that happen to be located in Iraq. We've looked at every target from the outset for avenues of approach, the exact type of weapon to cause damage to the target but preclude damage to the surrounding area, and precision delivery. I'll be showing you a film clip of the typical type of precision deliveries that we have come to expect.

Obviously, it has not been easy. I think you've seen on television the air defense in Baghdad, and you've seen interviews with the air crews that flew in Vietnam who say this is as tough or tougher than anything they've ever seen. I'm very proud of our air crews and the way they've shown tremendous discipline and tremendous courage. It is a long, hard task. We're very optimistic about what we do, but we're not overly confident.

What I have now to show you are some film clips of some actual weapons delivery. These first two will be F-111 deliveries using laser-guided bombs. This is a runway at an airfield halfway between Baghdad and Kuwait. The center of the runway is the end point. This is where the laser designator is pointed. This was taken at night with infrared sensors. There, the bomb goes off in the center of the runway. Heat shows up as white. Now you'll see the pilot switch to a higher magnification as he flies away from the target. The smoke plume from the bomb: there's the crater.

The next one is a Scud storage building in Kuwait. Keep your eye on the entrance to the storage. Again, the pilot has released the bombs about two miles away, he's banking away from the target, leaving the target area, lasing the target, and you'll see two bombs fly into the door of the storage bunker. You'll be able to count each bomb—one, two. Those are 2,000-pound bombs.

This is the air-defense headquarters in the vicinity of Baghdad. These are air shafts that provide best access into this concrete structure. Keep your eye on the front door, the air-locked door. The debris comes out the door, the bomb going in the air shaft.

Another air-defense sector over in the western part of Iraq. It's already been struck by a 117—this is a team effort. The second aircraft comes through, and this part of the building here provides some structural weakness that will be exploited in this impact. The bomb will hit this area here.

This is my counterpart's headquarters in Baghdad. This is the headquarters of their air force. Keep your eye on all sides of the building. The airplane overflies the building and drops the bomb down through the center of the building.

If we have any success in this air campaign, I can attribute it in large measure to the freedom with which we've been allowed to plan the campaign. We've had stringent guidance with regard to civilian damage and things of that nature, but the President down through the Secretary of Defense, Chairman Powell, General Schwarzkopf, have been the key reason we've been able to plan a very efficient military campaign with the guidelines they've set forth.

Thank you very much.

GENERAL SCHWARZKOPF: We'd be very happy to answer any questions anybody might have.

[*Some parts of the reporters' questions were inaudible.*]

Q: . . . possible entry of Israel into this campaign? If indeed Israel does get into this campaign, how will it be coordinated with the allied forces already in theater?

SCHWARZKOPF: I have no information at all about

any entry of Israel into the campaign. That's something that's being handled at the governmental level, and I really couldn't answer the question.

Q: Sir, does the Iraqi attack on Israel change at all the war aims of the United States in this campaign?

SCHWARZKOPF: Our objectives are exactly the same ones that were announced by the President of the United States quite some time ago. They were, in fact, the resolutions of the United Nations. Our objectives continue to remain exactly the same.

Q: A follow-up to Carol's question. Since the Scud attack on Tel Aviv yesterday, is there a change in the targeting of Saddam Hussein himself? Yesterday General Powell said he was not a specific target. Has that changed?

SCHWARZKOPF: We're not trying to kill any particular person. One of our aims all along has been to make sure that it's very difficult for the leadership to have any impact upon the decision-making process of the subordinate units, and there are several different ways we're going about doing that. We're not targeting any specific person to kill them.

Q: General, either one of you could say what kind of results you've gotten in air attacks on fuel dumps and ammo dumps and that kind of thing in Kuwait, the pre-positioned supplies that the Iraqis would use if there was going to be a ground attack. Have you had any success in destroying that materiel?

HORNER: The supply areas provide a very lucrative target. In many cases, though, when there are ground forces deployed, you have them deep in bunkers. I think you saw what we did to the Scud storage area. We're attempting to take out those key elements with strategic weapons. Then we will turn to individual attacks on the ground-based supplies in the Kuwait area.

Q: There have been reports that the B-52's were concentrating on the Republican Guards' location. Is that true? And to what extent have you allegedly decimated these Republican Guards' concentrations?

HORNER: The B-52's have been striking targets throughout the whole campaign, across both Kuwait and Iraq. I can't comment because I haven't seen the report.

SCHWARZKOPF: I think I know the report you're speaking of, and I think that report is certainly premature and, I believe, incorrect at the present time.

Q: You mentioned finding 11 mobile missile-launching sites. If you manage to destroy all of those sites, how much of the enemy's ability to launch these missiles will you have destroyed?

SCHWARZKOPF: That's a very tough question to answer because the estimates of the total number of mobile launchers he has has varied very widely, even within the intelligence community. But based upon the most recent numbers that we have, I would tell you that it is a rather considerable percentage of the launchers. I'd like to just leave it at that.

Q: The fact that the Scuds that were used against Israel didn't appear to be chemical or biological, does that tell you anything about the capacity of the Iraqis to use that kind of a warhead on a Scud?

SCHWARZKOPF: I think we could speculate about that all day long. I would say, frankly, that I'm quite encouraged by the fact that chemical weapons were not used, and I hope if he has the capability, he does not use them at all. That's the best I can say. I think anything else would be speculative at this point.

Q: General, do you have any theories about the subdued nature of the response of the Iraqis so far?

SCHWARZKOPF: I think General Powell has expressed it, first of all, in the fact that we probably achieved the degree of tactical surprise that we were trying to achieve. Second, once again, as Secretary Baker stated after his Geneva press conference, I think, quite frankly, that the Iraqis just had no concept whatsoever of what they were getting involved with when it comes to taking on the coalition forces.

Q: Have you detected any movement by the Iraqi armored forces?
SCHWARZKOPF: Nothing significant.

Q: I'm wondering, we hear varying degrees of percentages, that the planes hit 80 percent, some have said 50 percent. The targets we're talking about, I'm wondering, first of all, how many targets have we hit?
HORNER: The bombing percentages are a function of number of targets targeted versus numbers that were hit. The difference in those numbers are people who did not get to the target because of weather, enemy defenses caused them to miss the target, things of that nature. It was kind of relevant to this question about the subdued nature of the Iraqi response. I'd like to take him along on one of the sorties and it might change his opinion about the subdued nature.

Q: How many targets have we gone after?
HORNER: We've gone after quite a few targets.

Q: General Horner, can you give us some idea of what the state of the Iraqi Air Force is like right now? How many planes destroyed, how many immobilized because you've got runways destroyed, how many fled to the north—some general order of magnitude on it?
HORNER: It's obvious that I'd like to keep track of that. Unfortunately, a lot of their aircraft are in hardened shelters. We attacked the shelters, and we really don't know the results on the aircraft. What we have seen is when they've come up and engaged, we tend to shoot them down if they persist in the engagement.

Normally they break off when our fire-control radars lock onto them, and flee to the north.

Q: What were the targets in Saudi Arabia of the eight Scud missiles we discovered today?

SCHWARZKOPF: I have absolutely no idea. Given the positioning of the mobile launchers, the only territory they could have reached with those mobile launchers would have been into Saudi Arabia. It's an area that we've been watching, quite frankly, expecting something there, and we were delighted to see that they've done exactly what we thought they'd do.

Q: . . . oil refinery near Baghdad was hit, and one near Basrah was also rumored to be hit. Can you confirm that oil installations such as refineries and storage depots are military targets?

SCHWARZKOPF: Let me tell you that we have consistently, all along, made it a point of not going against targets that were not of a military nature or would not contribute to the military effort. So any targets that we do hit along those lines would be targets that we feel would contribute to the military effort, and not just simply done for the sake of destroying something.

Q: How about an Iraqi aircraft that's been shot down in air-to-air combat?

HORNER: Right now the figure looks like it's eight—six by the Air Force and two by the United States Navy. Then there are two probables we're looking into.

Q: General Horner, as you probably know, the Iraqis have been censoring and limiting the broadcasts of television reports from Baghdad. To what extent were those television reports beneficial to you in evaluating the success of the air campaign?

HORNER: I really don't know, because I don't have a TV set in my command center. But in retrospect, as we're getting a chance to look at some of the playbacks, I think I'm going to put a television set in.

Q: Have there been any reports of Iraqi desertions either along the occupied Kuwait border or the Iraqi–Saudi border? Are there any numbers available?

SCHWARZKOPF: I think that's a question that's better asked of the Saudis. They're the ones that are handling that, and I'd rather leave that in their hands.

Q: How far, roughly, are you into your aerial-bombardment campaign? And second, could you tell us how successful the British Tornadoes have been, and whether the JP-233 has come up to expectations?

SCHWARZKOPF: We're exactly as far as we expected to be thirty-six hours ago. (Laughter)

HORNER: The Tornado, obviously, is very important to the campaign. It's being flown by Saudi Arabia, Britain, and Italy. The reason it's so important is because it gives us the capability to penetrate the high, well-defended areas. You're absolutely right, the 233 has done very well on the airfield attack.

Q: . . . will be necessary to liberate Kuwait?

SCHWARZKOPF: I think it's far to early to speculate on anything in the future. We're going to continue to execute our campaign plan exactly as it's called out. If any unforeseen developments take place during the process of that campaign, we're completely prepared to react to them.

Q: What percentage of the ships that you had dedicated to the enforcement of the embargo against Iraq have you turned into battle-oriented ships?

SCHWARZKOPF: We're continuing to have a full-blown maritime-interception regime just as we did before. We have the same number of ships, and probably a few more now, involved in the maritime-interception regime. But there hasn't been any significant change.

Q: What your message is to the Kuwaiti people inside Kuwait?

SCHWARZKOPF: I think the message is very clear. It's the message that the President of the United States has stated, it's the message that the United Nations has stated, and it's the message that all of the forces that are involved in this coalition have stated, and that's the campaign has begun to eject Iraq from Kuwait and to restore the legitimate government to Kuwait.

Q: Do you know how long it takes us to . . . from the Gulf?

SCHWARZKOPF: That's an impossible question to answer. I would tell you that nobody is more dedicated to getting this over as quickly as possible than the President of the United States, than the people of the United States, and than I and all the other people involved in this thing. So we're going to do it as rapidly as we possibly can, but we're also going to do it in such a way that we try to minimize casualties. We don't want to have to pay a terrible price to get it over with quickly.

Q: There's been a report that 192 out of the first 1,000 air sorties were flown by Saudis. Can you confirm that?

SCHWARZKOPF: I can't confirm or deny that number, but that's approximately right.

Q: Can you tell us what proportion of your assets you've so far been able to devote to attacking Kuwaiti ground targets, as opposed to a mixture of targets in Iraq? And can you give me one technical answer—are the mobile launchers you're talking about all basic Scuds? Or are they the Iraqi developments of the Scud, the al Hussein and the Alabas?

SCHWARZKOPF: I don't think I'd like to get into the

first question. The second question, it's a combination of both.

Q: Can you tell us what the role of the Canadian planes were?

HORNER: The Canadian planes right now, the CF-18's, are flying counter-air defense—capping both over sea and over land. They've been in the operation from the start flying air defense for the coalition forces and the kingdom.

Q: In general terms, can you give us your impression of how the F-117 is performing? A follow-up question, were all the images we saw taken from F-111's using laser-guided bombs, or were they different platforms that were performing?

HORNER: The first two were 111's and the rest were 117's. I can tell you, the F-117 is doing great—you'd think I was a prejudiced witness. But quite frankly, you see the evidence of what it can do, and it's doing it day in and day out.

Q: General Horner, how many of the aircraft that we have lost have been lost to enemy fire? How many to missiles? What is the status of the Iraqi antiaircraft missile defenses now? This is supposedly a high-priority target system. Can you give us something on that?

HORNER: In terms of losses, we don't know. But we suspect one to SAMs and the rest to AAA. With regard to the air defenses, in some areas they're probably the most difficult air defenses assembled in the world. In other areas, they're not quite that difficult. Obviously, that's going to be a very strenuous campaign, achieving complete control of the air.

Q: How much of it have you destroyed so far?

HORNER: Quite a bit.

Q: Once you get on the ground, once you get forward, who is going to do the actual fighting on the allied side? Is there a special focus on the Arab units to do that?

SCHWARZKOPF: No, this is a coalition operation. Everybody that's involved in this coalition is planning to take part, just as it has been from the very beginning.

Q: Can you give us your best estimate of Iraqi casualties—military and civilian—at this point?

SCHWARZKOPF: I have absolutely no idea what the Iraqi casualties are. I tell you, if I have anything to say about it, we're never going to get into the body-count business. That's nothing more than rough, wild estimates, and it's ridiculous to do that. We couldn't do it even if we wanted to, but right now we have no estimate.

Q: . . . cooperation with the French Air Force?

SCHWARZKOPF: Cooperation with the French Air Force and the French Army is absolutely perfect.

Q: General Powell indicated yesterday that one of your principal objects was the destruction of the Iraqi command and control. Can you give us some estimate as to how far down that line you've gone?

SCHWARZKOPF: I think to date we have been quite successful.

Q: How is the coordination of the various forces actually working? Could you give us some insight into that?

SCHWARZKOPF: I think I'd let General Horner answer that from the standpoint of the air campaign because, as you can well imagine, coordinating the air strikes of seven different nations and the type of aircraft being used is a rather difficult proposition. Whether it's effective or not, I will leave to him.

HORNER: It's effective. (Laughter)

Q: My question, sir, was exactly how is it being done? It seems like an enormous effort.

HORNER: It is an enormous effort. Of course, now we have a lot of computers, and you can bring together the tens of thousands of minute details—radio frequencies, altitudes, tanker rendezvous, bomb configurations, who supports who, who's flying escort. There are just thousands and thousands of details, and we work them together as one group, put them together in what we call a common air-tasking order, and it provides a sheet of music that everybody sings the same song off of.

Q: . . . what's happening in Baghdad, but we know very little of what's happening inside Kuwait. Can you give us any picture of what you're attacking and how it's going in Kuwait itself?

SCHWARZKOPF: As I said, I think the best answer to that is it's going just about as we expected. We haven't run into anything we didn't expect. As a matter of fact, the situation is probably a little bit better than what we expected.

Q: With regard to the bombardment yesterday, General, have you information on the type of Iraqi artillery that was used, and roughly the force strength?

SCHWARZKOPF: The estimate was that it was the short-range multiple rocket launcher that we've seen used by many third-country forces. As you know, what it did was just hit one oil storage tank and didn't do any significant damage.

I'd just like to close with one last comment that I think is important to remember. That is that the courage and the professionalism that's been exhibited by all of the people involved in this campaign in the last thirty-six hours is nothing short of inspirational. I think we should all be very very proud, every country should be very proud, of the young men that have been up in these aircraft, of the young women that have been up in the aircraft, and the way they've done their job, and I have every confidence that as they gain more experience they're just going to do better than the great job they've already done. Thank you very much.

★ ★ ★ ★

General H. Norman Schwarzkopf
CENTCOM Briefing
Riyadh, Saudi Arabia
Sunday, January 27, 1991—12:10 P.M. (EST)

GENERAL SCHWARZKOPF: Good evening, ladies and gentlemen. I'd like to start by giving you a brief operational update before I get into the more formal part of the briefing.

Today, as you all know, after nine days, we've flown over 23,000 sorties and air operations. In those air operations we have over 26 air-to-air kills by the coalition air forces. The most recent engagement was 11:20 today, local time. Two U.S. F-15's engaged four Iraqi MIG-23's just southeast of Baghdad. At the conclusion of that engagement, there were four Iraqi MIG-23's destroyed—there were no U.S. losses. The coalition also continues to attack his air force in the air whenever we have an opportunity to do that, and we also attack them in their hardened shelters.

As you probably know, our air campaign has started to force his air force into Iran. Just since yesterday, we have over 39 aircraft that have gone into Iran—to be precise, in the last twenty-four hours, since 1900 hours last night to 1900 hours tonight, we have had 23 aircraft go into Iran. Most of them have been fighter aircraft. We also continue to isolate his forces in the Kuwaiti theater of operation. We're continuing to successfully attack many of the key bridges going into that area. We have had no aircraft losses in the last forty-eight hours.

As far as naval operations are concerned, coalition

forces have been actively attacking enemy patrol and mine-laying craft in the north Persian Gulf and near Bubiyan Island. As of today, 18 enemy vessels have been sunk or badly damaged.

Ground operations continue to be limited to sporadic artillery and rocket-launcher fire by the Iraqis. The U.S. and coalition forces are countering that by employing close air support and artillery counter-battery fire.

As far as air-defense activities are concerned, I'm sure you know that to date the Iraqis have fired 51 Scud missiles—26 at Saudi Arabia and 25 at Israel. The most recent attack was last night at about 10:48 local time. I don't think I need to tell anybody here that we took one Scud missile in Saudi Arabia from southern Iraq, and five Scud missiles were launched against Israel from western Iraq. The Patriot battery at Riyadh, of course, did kill the incoming Scud missile here; and preliminary reports indicate the Patriot missiles also killed all five incoming in Israel yesterday.

I think that concludes just a brief operational update, and I'd now like to talk to you a little bit about the military aspects of this oil spill. The reason why I chose to brief you today is because I heard a lot of questions yesterday from this group here and also the group in the Pentagon briefing, and we had to leave those questions unanswered because we were contemplating some action but didn't want to endanger the air crews that were involved. Those actions have taken place, and so I'd like to now talk to you about it.

(Charts shown)

I'm going to use a technique that General Powell and Secretary Cheney used, and that is to use sketches to illustrate the points I want to make. These sketches all come from hard evidence. They are schematic in nature but pretty accurate.

What you see here is the coastline of Kuwait. This is the Mina al Ahmadi oil fields over here. What you have here is a terminal that goes out on a pier, another terminal goes out on a pier, another terminal. Right down here, these rectangles that you see here are the five ships that were located, and still are located, at those piers. These ships on the 16th of January were low in the water—they were completely full of oil. As of this time, on the 24th of January, these five ships right here were apparently emptied of oil, or almost empty, because they are riding very, very high in the water.

You also have out here a sea island terminal and an oiling buoy. These terminals and buoys are both used to fill the super tankers that can't get into the shallow draft area in this area. As of 1227 local [on 24 January 1991], what you saw here was the sea island terminal intact and a very large oil spill that was coming out of the oiling buoy, and essentially it looked like this, going down the coast.

We have gone back and checked all of our military operations between the time when we last looked at this oil buoy—and nothing was coming out—which was approximately the 16th and the 24th, at the time we found this situation. I can tell you that we see absolutely no indication at all that any U.S. military action caused this to happen. The best estimates we have, based upon the length of the oil spill, is that this probably was opened up about the 19th in order to have what happened between the 19th and the 24th when we got this evidence.

I received this evidence at our headquarters very early in the morning of the 25th of January. We immediately notified the Saudi Arabians of this, and during most of the day of the 25th we consulted with experts from Saudi Arabia, Aramco experts, petroleum engineers, oil field engineers, and also people from the environmental agency of Saudi Arabia. What we were really interested in was number one, how much damage this was going to do to Saudi Arabia and the military operations; we were also interested in anything we could do to assist.

At that time they asked us to try to do two things. They said first of all, about the best thing we could do right away would be to somehow set the source of this oil spill on fire. If we could, it would burn off a great deal of the pollutants that otherwise would go into the Gulf and continue to flow down. The other thing they did is to ask me to somehow cut off the flow of oil to this buoy. That became a major interest of ours because, of course, we are not in the business of destroying Kuwait while we are liberating Kuwait, and we certainly didn't want to go in and completely destroy the oil field or do undue damage. I would tell you that I am no oil expert—I was not then, and I certainly am not now—and therefore we needed the advice of many, many experts as to how to go about doing this. We finally came up with a solution that I'll talk to you about in just a minute.

On the evening of the 25th, after we had gotten the recommendations from these experts, we just happened to have a circumstantial happening out here at the sea island terminal. The United States Navy encountered a small boat. This was a small boat of a type that it suspected of supporting mine-laying craft, also a small boat that has antiaircraft on it, and it's the type of small boat they've been going after out in the area because those boats have been shooting at them. They engaged that boat. That boat happened to be next to the sea island terminal, and as a result of that engagement, the sea island terminal caught fire. So just by circumstance, we did accomplish the first thing we were asked to do, and that is set the source on fire—even though that's not exactly the way we expected to do it. I would tell you that the almost immediate results we saw is we found that the flow of oil out to the oil buoy had been cut off. As a result of this fire, it seemed like the flow of oil from the sea island terminal was considerably less than the flow of oil that was coming out of the oiling buoy.

This is a blow-up of the crude-oil storage terminal

north, and the crude-oil storage terminal south. Basically what we have here is storage tanks, and south of these are two small manifold areas—one here and one here. These two areas, by the way, are about three and a half miles apart, and they're approximately five miles away from the shoreline. The sea island terminal is about eight miles farther out.

What the petroleum engineers and the oil-field experts advised us to do was to take out these manifolds. They said if we could destroy the manifold here, number one, it was the type of damage that could be repaired very quickly once we went back into the area, in approximately two weeks' time was their estimate. But they said if you take out these manifolds, they essentially control the flow of all the oil that comes out of the oil fields into the storage area, and further from the storage area out to the ocean, and the same thing with regard to coming through here. So that's what we decided to do.

Unfortunately, at that time the weather was very bad, and this obviously had to be a very precise military operation, because, as I say, we don't want to liberate Kuwait by destroying Kuwait. So we had to wait until a time when we could go ahead and launch against those two manifolds—at 2230 last night. I'd now like to show you a tape of that operation, and what you're going to see here; I'll be happy to explain.

The type of munition that was used was a GBU-15 precision-guided munition fired from an F-111 aircraft. What you're going to be doing is looking directly through the TV camera in the nose of that aircraft as it goes right into the manifold, and you'll see the manifold area.

Q: General, what is a manifold?
A: A manifold is a system of pipes that controls the out-flow pressure out of the oil fields. That's as far as my expertise goes.

(Tape shown)

What you see here is the manifold area. That's the area that I talked about, and you're looking right through the nose of the guided munition as it's flown straight into the small manifold area to destroy it. This is the manifold area that was destroyed before.

This is the second one.

This next is a tape that was taken late in the afternoon yesterday, prior to the time we destroyed the manifold, and it gives you some idea of what we had. You can see very heavy black smoke: a very large fire out in the area. That is sea island terminal. That is where the fire was occurring and where the leakage was happening yesterday.

This is after the attack—this is early today. You can see that you have an entirely different color of smoke coming out of here, which I am told is because the oil is deeper in the water and it's burning with much less . . . You can see the size of the flame area is much smaller than the one you saw just a few minutes ago.

We have some still shots up here that I'll show you in a minute, that I think are much more dramatic. It will show you the degree of reduction.

(Chart shown)

I know these are hard for you to see—we'll leave them up for you to see afterward. But just as an indication, here is your pier area running out here, and you can see the very large fireball that was out here. This was as of 0913 on January 26th. If you compare that to what you see here, this is a much closer shot of the pier, and I think you'll see by comparison that the fireball is considerably diminished.

The question may come to mind why is it still burning? I've been told that because, number one, as I told you, the manifolds were five miles away from the shore, and then from the shore you have another eight miles of pipeline going out to the sea island terminal, you have thirteen miles of oil in that pipeline that was probably flowing, and the best estimates that we had originally were that it will take more than twenty-four hours before the fire goes out.

I would like to tell you right now that I'm certainly not an expert, and I am not guaranteeing anybody that this fire is going to go out. All I'm showing you is what we have done to date to try to use our military power to solve this very difficult problem. We tried to do it in such a way that we're not out there destroying the entire economy of Kuwait by doing it. I think we've been successful, but only time is going to tell. We'll leave that up for you to see later.

Finally, I would just finish up saying that this is what we think the oil spill currently looks like. I think the estimate you've heard of about thirty-five miles long and about ten miles wide is a correct estimate. It is coming down in this direction. It has gotten almost to Ras al Mishab, and that's what we see at the present time.

I'll be happy to answer your questions now, but before I do, please let me state one more time: I'm prepared to talk about the military aspects of this particular oil spill. I'd be happy to tell you everything I know, but I've got to tell you, from a technical or ecological standpoint I do not know a great deal. So please bear with me if I say I'll have to defer that question to the experts.

Q: General, you've given us a very precise timetable on the war before. You said we're right on schedule, we're this many days into the campaign, and we're right where we want to be. What are the chances that an oil spill like this, that an ecological disaster, could put pressure on the military to try to accelerate the timetable?

A: I don't think there's going to be any acceleration or any pressure at all. Unfortunately, war is not a clean business. Everybody's known that. You all are not old enough to remember World War II—I'm really not either, even though I remember part of it—and I can still remember as a small boy the dirty oil balls rolling up as a result of the type of action that was taking place out in the Atlantic. It's not a desirable thing, but it's certainly not something that's going to impede the progress of the operation, and I don't think it's going to bring pressure to bear to do anything different than what we're doing right now.

Q: We heard from the Saudi Minister of the Environment today that it could be ten to fifteen times the size of the spill of the Exxon Valdez. We've also heard several times from several briefers in the past days that no one expected Saddam would go this far and do something this heinous. Before the war began, there were environmental groups in the United States who were saying let's not go to war because this could be a disaster for the Persian Gulf if he goes ahead with his threats. Did we miscalculate? Did we not expect that he would go this far?

A: I think you've answered your own question. Saddam Hussein did, in fact, say he was going to do this sort of thing before, and we did expect him to do exactly this sort of thing. He has announced all along that he would do things to destroy the Kuwaiti oil fields. He's also announced that he would go ahead and pour oil into the Gulf to try to defeat amphibious operations—which, incidentally, this will not do. As far as the extent of the disaster, I think right now it's far too early to tell what's going to happen.

I've heard as many different opinions on that as there are people who have given me opinions. Some say that the sea states out here are so high that it's going to mix it up a lot. Some say that type of oil is different. There's all sorts of speculation, so I just think it's something that we have to wait and see.

Q: If and when a ground war begins to liberate Kuwait, should we assume that it would be a full-scale operation? Or potentially, is there room for feints and exploratory attacks in your battle plan?

A: I'm sorry, but I don't choose to release any details of the battle plan.

Q: What interpretation do you put on the Iraqi planes going to Iran? Does the Iraqi Air Force still remain a threat, as you interpret it, or has it basically fallen apart?

A: It's tough for me to put any kind of interpretation on what's going on, because there are any number of things that could be. The Iraqi Air Force will always remain a threat if they have one airplane, but as General Powell stated earlier this week, we have gained and maintained air superiority. We have freedom of action to operate anytime we want to up there, and every time they fly, we shoot them down. But the threat is always there, and we're never going to assume away the threat. We're going to be ready for anything that the Iraqi Air Force chooses to throw at us.

Q: Can you talk a little bit about the decision by the Iraqis to fly planes into Iran? Was this a decision made at the high command in an effort to conserve the planes? Do you know anything about it?

A: I have absolutely no idea.

Q: What about the kinds of planes they've taken in?

A: They've taken both. But the interesting part about it is that they're now taking their very best fighters over there. I think that's because they lost an awful lot of their best fighters. And as I say, again, this is speculation, but we have been on a campaign—just as General Powell announced we would be last week—of if they won't fly up to meet us, we will fly down and destroy their hardened shelters one by one. We've been doing that, and we've been doing it very effectively. You'll get more on that this week. It may be they've

decided they can't afford to lose any more aircraft—
but again, that's purely speculation.

Q: About five or six days ago, a refined-products
tanker was sunk, and there were reported to be various
estimates about how big a slick there was from that.
Can you tell us what the status of that refined-tanker
sinking was? Is there any remainder of a spill from that
particular incident?

A: The Navy told me that they monitored that very
closely. Because it was refined product, you have an
entirely different kind of spill, and they said it wasn't
much of a spill. There was a lot of burning, of course,
but not a lot of spilling. As far as I know, there is no
concern with regard to that.

Q: Can you give us a general area where that particular incident took place?

A: That was up in the northern part, up in this area,
I believe—right in here. I'm not absolutely sure on
that. We'll get back to you.

Q: Are you convinced now that this manifolds operation is a success? Is it over? Is more action likely to
be necessary? Also, did you encounter any kind of
opposition from Iraqis while this thing was going on?

A: It's certainly a success because we accomplished
exactly what we wanted when we went in there. No,
we did not encounter any kind of opposition from the
Iraqis, but then again, we seldom do. One of the reasons
why is because we don't let people know what we've
going to do ahead of time.

Q: You said you weren't surprised about the Iraqis
doing what they did with the oil. What, if anything,
about the Iraqis has surprised you, and how concerned
are you about surprises from the other side at this
point?

A: The only thing that's really surprised me, as I've

already stated many times about the Iraqis, is the fact
that their air force, particularly, hasn't chosen to fight,
and also how easy it was to completely take out his
air-defense system in such a way that we have freedom
of action. There are a lot of surprises out there. I, and
my entire staff, spend most of our time trying to think
of what those surprises could be so that we're ready for
them. We're going to continue to do that, and we're
going to try to anticipate every move that he could
possibly make.

Q: We've received calls from people who claim to
have seen Iraqi planes engaged by U.S. fighters inside
Saudi air space, perhaps as far south as Jubail or even
farther south than that. Can you tell us if there's any
truth to that? And also, how far have the Iraqis gotten
inside the coalition air space?

A: There's absolutely no truth to that whatsoever.
I'd also tell you that they'd have to have superb eye-
sight, given the altitude at which these engagements
take place and the overhead clouds that have been out
there for the last . . . It hasn't happened. (Laughter)

Q: Are you assured that the planes going into Iran
will not come back from Iran and be used against the
coalition? And if you're not assured of that, are you
prepared to attack those planes?

A: I think the Iranian government has stated that
they're neutral in this matter, and they have stated
that any planes from either country that come into
Iran will remain until the termination of conflict. As
of this time, we should take Iran at its word. They have
consistently been supportive of the United Nations
resolution, and I see no reason why we should suspect
at this time that they will change. I would also say,
however, that we would be absolutely not worth our
salt as military people if we ignored the fact that those
planes could fly back out of Iran after us. Therefore we

obviously have contingencies that will take care of that situation if it were to occur.

Q: You've referred today and on previous occasions to Saddam in personal terms, and you've talked about his air force and his forces today. Do you think Saddam is listening to your words now, and are you trying to psychologically intimidate him?

A: I've been trying to psychologically intimidate him from long before the beginning of this conflict. I think we have pretty well predicted for Saddam Hussein exactly what would happen if he went to war against us, and he didn't choose to believe it, and I don't know whether he knows what's going on right now. I sincerely hope he knows exactly what's going on. I have no intention of psychologically intimidating him as much as I have of spelling out the simple facts of what's happening and what's going to go on happening.

Q: So you acknowledge that Saddam does what he says he will do. He said he will use chemical weapons, all the weapons at his disposal. Are you therefore expecting him to use chemical weapons?

A: I think that's entirely too hypothetical. Just as we've said all along, he has a vast array of possibilities, and we should watch for those possibilities and be prepared for any of them. I don't exactly agree with you that Saddam has done everything he said he was going to do. Quite frankly, there's an awful lot of things he said very early he was going to do, such as annihilate Tel Aviv. As a matter of fact, he announced himself that Tel Aviv was a crematorium as a result of his own Scud missiles. I think we all know that once again, that's another lie, just like many of the other lies he's told. So I wouldn't necessarily agree with you that Saddam does everything he says he's going to do, but I don't think any of us should discount chemical weapons at all. I think we should be prepared for them.

Q: You said earlier that you're not going to put more resources, I mean, in terms of chasing Scud missiles or launches. Is that still the case? And have you knocked down any launchers in the last five days, for instance?

A: I don't know if we said we weren't going to put any more resources after the Scud missiles. I think I ought to clarify something. I have been quoted as saying he had only 20 missiles and we knocked down 16, and therefore he only have four left. I think that's a slight misquote. I think what I said at the time was we knew that he had more than 20 mobile missiles—we had a wide variety of estimates. I would tell you quite candidly that nobody knows exactly how many mobile missiles he had. I also said at the time we expected that we had damaged 16 of them. We've continued to attack his missiles. We continue to get large secondary explosions. We have counts that go very high in the eyes of some of the pilots that have been attacking those things, and that's normal in the fog of war. We are continuing to attack those missiles, and we will continue to attack those missiles—the launchers, I'm talking about.

Q: Have you knocked down any in the last three or four days?

A: I believe we had a report last night of three that we attacked and successfully destroyed. But again, it's very difficult to confirm that sort of thing because you're talking about a very small target, a very mobile target, and many times you're attacking them at night as well as daytime. So the only time I'm going to be satisfied is when no more are fired, then I can effectively tell you that we've probably taken care of them. We won't be able to tell you that until . . .

Q: In south or west?

A: I believe the ones last night were in eastern Iraq. But we've had the same thing out in the west also.

Q: Do I understand that by your strike of the manifolds today, it reduced the fire and the nature of the oil burning. Do you know for a fact that you've cut the slick, the oil actually getting in the water?

A: The way it was explained to me, once again, is if you want to stop the oil, and the threat was the oil that is in fact inside all of those large storage tanks. In order to stop the oil from flowing out of those large storage tanks, all of that oil must flow through the manifolds. Therefore, if you destroy the manifolds, you interrupt the ability of that oil to flow through those manifolds and out into the sea. That's the way it was explained to me.

Q: The Saudis said earlier, there is at least one other installation in the area, the [inaudible] I think they called it. You said you expected them to do this kind of thing. Can you do anything to prevent them from doing the same thing to the other installation?

A: I don't think there's really much you can do to prevent them from doing that. After all, they're on the ground and we're not. That's one of the reasons why we'd like to get back into Kuwait and put those oil fields back in the hands of the Kuwaitis.

Q: You said the coalition forces are not in the business of destroying Kuwait but in the process of liberating it. In a follow-up to that question, do you feel you will be able to liberate Kuwait before the Iraqis destroy Kuwait completely?

A: I think that's an impossible question to answer. He's already gone after the al Wafra oil fields down in the southern area, tried to destroy them—we passed out pictures of that. And it's entirely likely that he's going to continue to do the same thing, so I don't think there's any way we can ever say that we could liberate Kuwait without any more damage being done to Kuwait.

Q: It's been reported in the Sunday papers today, quoting people in high places in Washington, that a decision has been made that strategic bombing is not going to end this war, and that a ground war is definitely going to be required. Can you give us your own feelings about that?

A: I think the report of the *Washington Post* says that high intelligence officials have come to that conclusion. High intelligence officials are not the people who are going to make that decision. The President of the United States, the Secretary of Defense, General Powell, and I, are going to be the people involved in that decision.

Q: Can you give us an assessment of your air campaign against the Republican Guards? And second, an assessment of how you're doing on the bomb-damage assessment in light of the bad weather we've been having?

A: I think so far I would declare that our campaign against the Republican Guards is highly successful—just based upon the delivery methods and the volume that we've been able to put on them. Being an infantryman, I certainly wouldn't want to be under that type of attack right now. As we said all along, bomb-damage assessment on a tank division or a mechanized division is an extremely difficult thing to come up with, so I don't think we can give it a better assessment at the present time. As far as the rest of the BDA is concerned, I would say that it varies. We have an awful lot of camera shots coming in from the aircraft that show that the ordnance has been placed right on the target. But as you've also seen from the camera shots, what you see is the explosion and then the aircraft pulls off so you don't really see the aftereffect. We're trying to be deliberately conservative. We don't want to mislead anybody. We don't want to tell you we've done something we haven't done. As a result, when we announce something to you that something's happened, you can take it to the bank.

Q: Do you already know, or are quite confident, that you have stopped the oil spill, or will it take the twenty-four hours you mentioned, to know that?

A: I think I said before that we're not going to know anything until at least twenty-four hours. Hopefully the next time we go out there and take a look we'll see a great diminishment. If not, we will go back once again and talk with those engineers and see if there's anything further we can do. I would tell you, when you come up here and look at the picture, this is now the oil slick that's coming out. You can see it absolutely is vastly reduced from the very thick, murky slick that was coming out. You can see blue water in between and what is the oil slick that is coming out. That is much different than what we were seeing before, so that's a very encouraging thing, and I hope that's indicative of the fact that we've been successful.

Q: To clear up another point on the oil slicks, the Saudis say there's a second oil slick that's coming from a tank near Khafji, but the oil from that slick is actually north of the tank at Khafji and there's some confusion about where it's coming from. Is that possibly oil from these tankers that were opened up? Where would that oil be coming from that is creating the slick along the shore that's killing all the cormorants and so forth?

A: I don't know. I do know there was a report of an oil slick a little bit north of al Khafji at one point. We weren't sure where that had come from. We've heard that it might have been, again, an outlet, but I really couldn't give you a good answer on that. I just don't know.

Q: We've heard some reports from some of our colleagues that there's been carpet bombing going on

across the Kuwait border by the B-52's. I know you and
your staff has been deliberately vague about exactly
what the B-52's are doing, but it's a fearsome weapon,
as you well know. Can you give us a little idea—are
you trying to get mainly to the Republican Guards in
southern Iraq, or do you have Kuwaiti targets for
B-52's? Are you carpet bombing, or do you have plans
for carpet bombing?

A: I don't know what the definition of carpet bombing is. Last night I turned to my air-component commander and asked him the same question, and he said
he doesn't know what the definition of carpet bombing
is. I don't think that what we're doing would be described as carpet bombing. Carpet bombing tends to
portray something totally indiscriminate, en masse
without regard to the target. I think we've stated all
along that we're absolutely as careful as we can—not
only in the way we are going about executing our air
campaign, but in the type of armament we're using.
We're using the appropriate weapon against the appropriate targets. We're being very careful in our direction
of attacks to avoid damage of any kind to civilian
installations. It's absolutely going to happen, there's
no question about it, but we're doing everything we
can to prevent it, and that's not carpet bombing by any
definition.

Q: Given the eleven days or so of the air war, could
you give us an assessment of what that air campaign
has done to the Iraqi Army?

A: To the Iraqi armed forces, it's done exactly what
we intended it to do to date, and I wouldn't just limit
it to the army. I'd include the army, the navy, and the
air force. I would tell you that later on I hope to give
you a much more detailed briefing on this than I'm
prepared to give you right now.

Q: Last week you told us that you had neutralized
Iraq's nuclear capability, and that you were going after

the chemical and biological capabilities. How far have you gone?

A: Just to make absolutely sure that we're correct, what we said, I believe, is we have neutralized their manufacturing capability, their nuclear manufacturing capability. I could never say that there is no such thing as a nuclear weapon, although I think that most analysts have said there is not. But what we, in fact, said was that we have eliminated their manufacturing capability, and I would tell you we're continuing to do exactly the same thing to the chemical and biological capability. We're making sure that it will be a very long time before they'll have the capability to build that type of weapon again.

Q: A quick technical question. If you blow the manifold up, does that mean that oil then pumps onto the ground in that part of the country?

A: I already told you, I am definitely not an oil-field technician.

Q: There's been film from Iraqi television of a mass being held in the ruins of a church that I think has been shown on CNN. It seems to have been that the church was bombed. Do you know anything about that?

A: I know absolutely nothing about it, I'll just reiterate what I've said. These things happen. I've been bombed by our own Air Force. I don't think they did it intentionally. (Laughter) I really don't mean to make a joke out of this, but you have to understand that bomb racks get hung up and dropped, and I was bombed by B-52's one time in Vietnam in Manyang Pass. They were coming toward us, they did a marvelous job of dropping all their bombs, and then one rack hung up and it released over my position. I certainly never went back and said why did you do that, I'm angry at you, I know you did it deliberately. I will state once again, we are absolutely doing more than we ever have, and I think any nation has in the history of warfare, to use our technology . . . And everybody should clearly understand this, we are probably endangering our pilots more than they would otherwise be by following this course of action. This is something that hasn't been stated. But by requiring that the pilots fly in a certain direction of flight or use a certain type of munition that requires them to go to altitudes that they normally wouldn't be required to go to, those pilots are at much more risk than they would be otherwise. But we have deliberately decided to do this in order to avoid unnecessary civilian casualties, in order to avoid destroying these religious shrines and that sort of thing, and I think we should be pretty proud of the young men who are out there willing to do that in order to minimize damage of this nature.

Q: When the facility containing biological weapons was hit, the Iraqis made a big point of saying that this was a facility that was manufacturing baby formula. And when General Powell came on, he said that in the back of that was facilities for biological warfare. Do you expect more of that kind of thing to be happening, because the charge has been made that a lot of these kinds of things are happening in civilian facilities? Is Saddam Hussein, in your view, placing these things in civilian facilities, and are you inevitably going to end up bombing civilian facilities going after military targets?

A: I will tell you quite candidly that there are several almost predominantly civilian facilities right now that I would like very much to attack because I know for a fact they're being used by the Iraqis, and we're not doing it for that reason. We knew, in fact, that this particular facility we attacked was in fact what it was. We also used precision munitions on it to make sure that we destroyed that part of it. As General Powell said the other day, it's surrounded by a high military fence, it has guard posts on all four corners, and it was painted with camouflage paint and defended. That's not something you normally do with an infant-formula plant, any more than you put high berms up around an aspirin plant. So I reject the argument that that was only a baby-formula plant, but I would also clearly state that when we went after that facility, we went after it in a precision way, damaged only that part of that facility that we knew or had a very high assurance as given to us by the intelligence community, that it was in fact a research facility for biological warfare.

Q: Doesn't it play somewhere in the decision to go to war that we could be entering a situation in which we, by going to war with Saddam Hussein, would create a situation like this which could have decades-long impact on the environment? Does that not factor in?

A: I can see where some people might want to make that argument. I think that is a ridiculous argument when you think of the cost of human life that the alternative might be also. That's an argument that will probably be argued long after my time and yours, but I certainly don't accept the fact that we should not fight a despot on the basis of the fact that we might for some reason pollute a shore, and I don't take that lightly because, believe me, I'm a lover of the outdoors, I'm a lover of the environment, I'm a conservationist. But I think some great man once said, "There are some things worth fighting for," and I believe that also.

Q: I just wanted to follow up on your precision-munitions answer. We know a lot of these pilots have taken terrible risks in completing difficult missions, and this may be a false assumption, but I've got a mental image of a B-52 at very high altitude dropping gravity bombs. I know they have cruise missiles aboard. I'm just pressing you, once again, to clear up the situation on the use of the B-52's. It's not too surgical at 30,000 feet with gravity bombs, is it?

A: I'm going to give you exactly the same answer I

gave you before, and that's that I'm not going to tell you—

Q: I thought I'd try.

Q: I'd like to know how [inaudible] role of the Royal Saudi Air Force in that—

A: I think the role of the Saudi Air Force speaks for itself. Today we had two pilots that shot down two aircraft. Those pilots are quite proud of themselves tonight, but the first pilot to shoot down two aircraft was a Royal Saudi airman, so I think the role of the Saudi Air Force speaks for itself.

Q: There are reports that between 50 and 60 percent, or some large figure, of Iraqi oil storage and refining capacity have been destroyed. Is this an indication that POL is very high on your list of military priorities?

A: If it's a military target, it's very high on our list of priorities.

Q: You just spoke with some feeling about the care with which you're pursuing this air war. I think I can imagine the answer, but could you say why you're putting your pilots in that risk? And isn't it as much a tribute to the immense political complexity of this region as it is to our humanity, or what is the role of the political complexion of this region in that decision?

A: That's part of it, but that's certainly not the overwhelming part of it. The overwhelming part of it is the fact that we have the capability to do that today. Therefore, since we have the capability, the nations that make up this coalition, have deliberately determined to use that capability to limit the damage against innocent people because we've felt all along our war is not against the people of Iraq. I would contrast that with what the enemy has done and continues to do by indiscriminately using weapons of terror, and indiscriminately doing things like that which make no sense at all when it comes to any sort of reasonable attempt to limit the scope of this conflict and not do damage to innocent people.

Q: Is it not a difficult decision for you personally, if not as a commander, to put your servicemen's lives at risk in return for not hitting . . . You were saying how difficult it is.

A: It's a difficult decision for all of us. But I'll tell you what, that's a tribute to the great young men and women that serve under us, that they understand that it's a difficult decision for us, and they're willing to accept those kinds of decisions, because I think they have a very high confidence that none of us, from the President of the United States all the way down to the lowest platoon leader, is going to do anything to deliberately risk their lives that we don't have to.

Q: There has been a discrepancy between the figures that have been released from Iran and in Washington and here today in the number of planes that have crossed over into Iran. They seem to be consistently lower from Tehran than from Washington or Riyadh. Why do you think that is? Why are the Iranians underestimating the number that have come in?

A: I couldn't answer that question. I have no idea. I would tell you that you're probably going to see different figures from all around because in fact there are many different ways of picking up what airplanes are going out. The weather is bad, and it's not a precise thing. It's not one of these things where you just count everything. So I think those numbers will continue to float on you. I think the important significant thing is the fact that it's going on right now.

PRESS: Thank you, sir.

GENERAL SCHWARZKOPF: Thank you very much.

★ ★ ★ ★

General H. Norman Schwarzkopf
CENTCOM Briefing
Riyadh, Saudi Arabia
Wednesday, January 30, 1991—
1:00 P.M. (EST)

GENERAL SCHWARZKOPF: Good evening, ladies and gentlemen. Thank you for coming.

At three o'clock tomorrow morning, Operation Desert Storm will complete its second week. Last week Secretary Cheney and General Powell gave you their assessment on where we stood at that time. They have asked me to give you a similar assessment at the end of the second week.

Let me start by covering the campaign objectives to date. I realize that some of these may be difficult to read, so I'll go over them quickly.

In our first phase, what we wanted to do was disrupt leadership command and control; destroy centralized air-defense command and control; attack combat aircraft in the air and on the ground to achieve air superiority; damage nuclear, biological, and chemical storage and production capability; and commence attack on the Republican Guards. Once we had that done, we planned to go into a second phase, which was to destroy the air-defense radars and missiles in the Kuwaiti theater of operation to achieve undisputed control of the air; and finally, to sever supply lines in the Kuwaiti theater of operation. Once that phase was completed, we planned then to isolate the Kuwaiti theater of operation, continue our attacks on the Republican Guards, and we had other objectives which I will not discuss further. In order to measure our success to date, I will measure it against the objectives I've just discussed.

Let's first of all start with the leadership objective. You know in the early days of the campaign we did attack many leadership targets. Twenty-six were struck—60 percent of all those were severely damaged or destroyed. We also attacked power plants and telecommunication facilities. One-fourth of Iraq's electrical-generating facilities are completely inoperative, and another 50 percent suffered degraded operations. I think I should point out right here that we never had any intention of destroying all of Iraqi electrical power. Because of our interest in making sure that civilians did not suffer unduly, we felt we had to leave some of the electrical power in effect, and we've done that.

Seventy-five percent of Iraq's command, control, and communication facilities have been struck during our air campaign, and one third of those are completely destroyed or inoperative. As a result, Saddam Hussein and the Iraqis have been forced to switch to backup systems, and those systems are far less effective and more easily targeted.

Let me talk briefly about air defense. First of all, the F-117 remains virtually invisible and is highly effective. But further, we've attacked air-defense nerve systems, striking 29 targets in more than 800 sorties. As a result, the Iraqis have abandoned centralized control of their air defense within Iraq and Kuwait—a very important point. This accounts in part for the very low attrition rate of coalition aircraft. Pilot skill also accounts for that low attrition rate. As you know, we've flown more than 30,000 sorties, and we've lost only 19 aircraft. In the last five days, we've lost only one aircraft to hostile ground fire.

Talking a little bit more about air-to-air combat. As you know, General Powell declared that we had air supremacy last week. We've destroyed 29 Iraqi fighter aircraft, with not one single air-to-air loss on the part of the coalition. Also, I think it's important to remember that not a single Iraqi aircraft to date has penetrated the coalition air space since this war began. In the last three days alone, F-15's have shot down nine MIG-23's and Mirage F-1's. The Iraqi early warning system has completely failed, and their aircraft have been caught totally by surprise when we attacked them.

A subject that's been very much in the news this week is airfields, so I'd like to talk now a little bit about them. We originally targeted 44 airfields—16 primary airfields and another 28 dispersal airfields. We constantly are reevaluating this, based upon where they put their airplanes. To date, based upon where their airplanes have been, we've attacked 38 airfields and we've flown over 1,300 sorties against these airfields. The 38 airfields have all been struck at least once, and many of them have been struck at least four times—at least nine of them are nonoperational. But let me make this very important point. We never had any intention to render all of the airfields inoperable—that was not our intention at all. Our intention is to render the air force ineffective. There have been varying reports about how many of these airfields have been destroyed, and there have been varying reports about how much damage we've done on the ground. I'll tell you we can confirm at least 25 airplanes destroyed on the ground, and I want to give you an example. (Chart)

This is a graphic reproduction of some hard evidence that we have, of the al Taqaddum Airfield on January 23. We went in to al Tagamum and we destroyed three Badger aircraft on the ground. In addition to destroying three Badger aircraft, we did severe damage to an Adnan Candid airplane. This is the equivalent of our U.S. AWACS. When we looked at our results, we found out that there were three more Badgers on the ground, so we flew back the next day and destroyed those three.

As a result of this type of operation, they decided to

put all of their aircraft in hardened structures—they tried to hide their aircraft. Therefore we commenced a systematic destruction of those hardened shelters. At this time, I would like to introduce Brigadier General Glosson. He happens to be the commander of the 14th Air Division. I look upon him as my and General Horner's principal Air Force target planner, and he's going to discuss a little bit of this hardened-shelter attack. Would you start the videotape, please?

GENERAL GLOSSON: What you're about to see are the hardened aircraft shelters at three installations—the first being one of its primary MIG-21 bases of the Iraqi Air Force. That shelter was destroyed by an F-117, as are many of the others in this tape. Again, the F-117.

Every hardened aircraft shelter, obviously, does not have an airplane in it, as you can see by the explosion and the degree of explosion. However, there are a significant number of them that do, and have other things stored in them. That being a case in point. Again, the 117.

Talil Airfield is one of Iraq's major F-1 or Mirage 2000 bases. This hardened aircraft shelter was destroyed by an F-111. (Tape stopped.)

GENERAL SCHWARZKOPF: The result of this type of attack is we have destroyed more than 70 of these hardened shelters, and quite frankly, the Iraqi aircraft are running out of places to hide. We now have reports that many of their smaller aircraft they have moved to roads and hidden them in residential areas that are close to airfields, because they know we're not attacking civilian targets. As you all well know, 89 of their aircraft—and I should say these are their front-line F-1's, Mirages, and their MIG-23 Pencers—89 of them have flown into Iran. The simple fact of the matter is that now every time an Iraqi airplane takes off the ground, it's running away. As a result, Chuck Horner,

my CENTAF Commander, has now claimed air supremacy.

I'd like to talk a little bit about the isolation in the
Kuwaiti theater of operations. One of the ways we do
this is by destroying the bridges that lead into the
operations area. (Chart shown) We've targeted a total of
36 bridges. Of those 36 we have attacked 33 with over
790 sorties. Obviously, by shutting off the bridges, we
shut off the supply lines that supply the forces in
southern Iraq and Kuwait.

I'd like to now show you a little film of the destruction of the bridges numbered one, two, three, and four
in order, and give you an idea of what we're talking
about. Would you show the video please?

The first video is a railroad bridge. Obviously, they
have very limited rail lines, so if we can take a railroad
bridge out, it makes a big difference. We try to hit right
near the shore, I've been told, because that's the most
difficult to repair and does the most damage if you get
in at that point. That's one end of the bridge. You'll
now see the same bridge again. Notice that's where we
hit before—the span's gone. We're now hitting the
other end of that railroad bridge.

Next we're going to show you some versions of
highway bridges. You might ask on this next shot why
it is we're hitting the bridge in the middle. The answer
is, you see how cloudy it is. The pilot just breaks out
of the cloud and doesn't have a lot of time to get a sight
on the bridge, so he just puts the sight where he can on
the bridge and bombs away.

I'd like to point out a couple of things that are
significant about the tape you were just shown. All
those tapes were taken at night. Night is the time
when before he moved the most and resupplied the
most. You'll notice that on all four of those bridges,
you only saw one vehicle. That's another indication of
how we're interdicting his supplies.

Two days ago, we observed a supply convoy backed
up for 15 miles on the road from Baghdad to Basra. It

was backed up on the north side of the road right near the bridge that we had knocked out. Obviously, we attacked that convoy, and we observed countless secondary explosions when we attacked it.

JSTARS and other sophisticated systems give us a measure of just how much damage we're doing to his logistics traffic. This is the main supply route, right here, that comes down into Kuwait City. On any given day in the early part of the campaign, you could look at that supply route, and you'd find about 1,000 trucks on that MSR. Nowadays whenever we look at it with any of our sophisticated systems, the maximum we find is less than 100. That means about a 90 percent degradation in his supply route. If you translate that over to what we know about his supply rate, it takes him about 20,000 tons per day to support the troops in Kuwait. We feel we've reduced them to about 2,000 tons per day.

We've got some anecdotal information that would also demonstrate that we're being very effective. We get many, many reports out of Kuwait that Iraqi soldiers are begging for food from Kuwaiti civilians—in many cases stealing it, also. The enemy prisoners of war that we've taken have told us they're receiving only one meal a day—that meal generally consists of a bowl of rice or a bowl of beans—and they have no water in which to bathe. As a result, many of the enemy prisoners of war that we've taken are infested with body lice, and many of them have open sores on their bodies.

I'd like next to come to nuclear, biological, and chemical. (Chart) We had 31 targeted locations, and we've attacked all 31, with over 535 sorties. We know this is of great interest to the international community. Therefore we are happy to report that we have destroyed all of their nuclear-reactor facilities. Baghdad Nuclear Research Center has been leveled to rubble. Precision guided missiles and TLAM cruise missiles have struck hard at the nuclear, biological, and chemical facilities, as have the many aircraft we've shown.

Over half those facilities have been severely damaged
or totally destroyed. We have absolute confirmation
that we've destroyed over 11 chemical and biological
storage areas. We've also destroyed or heavily damaged
three chemical and biological production facilities, and
we're going to continue a relentless attack on this
heinous weapon system.

Let me turn now to the Republican Guards. We're
targeting them with about 300 sorties a day. We're
using very accurate bombing, and even in bad weather
the many secondary explosions are confirming the fact
that we're inflicting continuous damage on them. Remember, I said 300 sorties a day, but let me give you
some examples. On January 26, 27 B-52's dropped 455
tons of explosives on the Republican Guards. Yesterday,
21 B-52's dropped 315 tons of bombs on them. Today,
28 B-52's dropped 470 tons on them. That's not to
mention the other strikes that we're doing with F-16's,
F-15E's, A-6's, etc.

Just from noon yesterday until 3:00 o'clock this
morning—that's a little bit more than half a day—we
have confirmation of 178 trucks destroyed; 55 artillery
pieces destroyed or damaged; 52 tanks destroyed or
damaged; heavy secondary explosions from revetments; and fires all over the area. We had one spectac-
ular explosion on the 28th of January. Let me give you
a reference. If on a scale of one to ten, the eruption of
a volcano registered ten, and the recent explosion at
the Soviet rocket-propellant plant would register a
nine, the secondary explosion we had the other day
registered a twelve. We now have confirmation that we
destroyed over 125 storage revetments in the largest
ammo storage area in the northern part of the Kuwaiti
theater of operations. Needless to say, we are going to
go back and visit it again to get anything else that
happens to be left there.

We're also attacking very close in to our position,
with over 300 sorties a day. Just to give you some
results this week: on the 28th of January, Marine F/A-

18's and Air Force A-10's engaged three convoys in south Kuwait, with multiple secondaries noted. Frog sites were also struck, with large secondary explosions noted. Convoy of heavy-equipment transports carrying 20 armored personnel carriers and eight tanks was attacked, with 12 of the personnel carriers and all the tanks observed burning. Five to six self-propelled artillery tubes were destroyed in the same area. On January 29th, the Marines sighted 80 to 100 vehicles in revetted positions, and they destroyed at least 34 armored personnel carriers.

I'd be remiss if I didn't mention naval operations. The Navy's done a great job supporting the air campaign, and the Navy has flown over 3,500 sorties from our six carriers. They've also launched more than 260 Tomahawk missiles.

(Chart) We have 170 ships out there that have established sea controls in the waters of the Arabian Gulf and the Red Sea. We have already sunk or disabled 46 Iraqi naval vehicles, and the Navy has captured 74 enemy prisoners of war in two engagements. I also think it's significant to note the very limited area of operations of the Iraqi naval forces. As a result of our naval operations, they really never venture much out beyond the straits here by Bubyan Island up into Um Qasr. Occasionally they get out into Kuwaiti waters, but when they do we certainly go after them. I would tell you even today, British Lynx helicopters, Saudi Dolphins, and U.S. Army helicopters attacked six patrol boats—the result was four sunk. This morning we were also attacking some patrol craft, and at last report we damaged three or four.

I would be remiss if I didn't mention the readiness of our amphibious forces. We have very large amphibious forces over here, and they are continually training and ready to do the job when called upon to do so. Of course, the maritime interception operations are still continuing, with more than 7,000 intercepts to date.

When you talk about Navy, you think about water,

and around here lately when you think about water, you talk about oil, so I'm going to talk a little bit about oil here for a minute.

You remember the pictures I showed you the last time I was here. This was the original oil spill before we took any military action against the manifolds. I told you we weren't sure what we had done, but the next day this was a result where we've already diminished. I am very proud to tell you, yesterday this is the result of that area—blue water, no more oil slick out there, and the United States military is proud of any role we may have played in doing away with this ecological act of terrorism.

Let me now turn to ground operations. U.S. and coalition forces are defending Saudi Arabia, and we're also repositioning. Until last night there were no major ground engagements, although the Marines in their assigned sector were routinely receiving sporadic rocket and artillery fire. In their effort to reduce that, on at least three occasions last week the United States Marine Corps conducted artillery raids on enemy front-line units. The night before last, they were particularly effective and reported severe damage on the enemy, with great loss of life.

I'd like now to sort of report what's been going on last night and today. If you look at this position here, yesterday evening we had an attack in that area by what was estimated to be an Iraqi mechanized battalion. It crossed the border. It was engaged by a Marine light armored infantry battalion and tactical air. Result—ten Iraqi tanks destroyed, four enemy POW's, and the Marines lost two light armored vehicles.

At point number two, right here, later on that same evening another Iraqi battalion came across the border. These were again engaged by AC-130's and Cobras. We destroyed four tanks and 13 vehicles. We have had reports that the Iraqis did go into al Khafji. Of course, as you know, al Khafji has been abandoned and deserted since the very first day of Desert Storm, so there was no one there.

At position number three, in the very early morning Iraqi tanks again crossed the border. This time they were initially engaged by the Saudi Arabian National Guard, and then Marine tac air engaged them and the enemy withdrew.

Early this morning, 40 more Iraqi tanks crossed the border again at the same place they came across before. They were once again engaged by the Marine light armored infantry. This time the results were ten Iraqi tanks destroyed, and they captured nine enemy prisoners of war. At the present time we have reports that the Saudis are moving forces into al Khafji to eject any Iraqis that may be in that area.

This, please, is a very preliminary report because, as you can imagine, fighting all night long and then fighting again today, we don't have final results, but as a preliminary report, the total losses to date—the pilots are reporting rather sensational losses of 41 tanks destroyed; 12 vehicles destroyed; three Frogs destroyed; seven armored personnel carriers destroyed; one 30mm destroyed; four artillery positions destroyed; six bunker positions destroyed. We have confirmed figures of 24 Iraqi tanks destroyed and 13 other vehicles destroyed. The Marines lost two light armored vehicles. Unfortunately, I'm very sad that I have to report to you that they lost 12 KIA in that engagement and 2 WIA. These are the first KIA of any ground conflict.

Now I want to turn, finally, to Scuds, another subject that has been prominent in everyone's mind. As I told you before, I think Scuds are militarily insignificant. After seeing one the other day, I've got to tell you, it's even more militarily insignificant than I thought it was. I went out and inspected one of the Scud bodies. As far as accuracy is concerned, it certainly is militarily insignificant. It's a terror weapon that's been targeted against civilian population centers, and that makes it important, so let's talk about Scuds for a minute.

As you know, the total Scud launches have been 53—27 against Saudi Arabia and 26 against Israel. I think it's significant, however, that in the first week they launched 35 and in the second week they launched 18. I like to feel that we're doing some good.

We've flown almost 1,500 sorties against the Scuds to date, and the Patriot success, of course, is known to everyone. It's 100 percent—so far, of 33 engaged, there have been 33 destroyed.

This chart also shows the sectors from which the Scuds are fired when they go after the major population centers. It's a very large area. Despite this, we have managed to destroy all of their fixed sites—30 sites—and we're quite confident of that. We've destroyed all of their major missile-production facilities. The pilots have reported to us more than 50 kills to date, but again, we won't confirm that until we have hard information.

I told you earlier that we have declared air supremacy. By declaring it that gives us the ability to use some new tactics we were not able to use before. I'm going to have General Glosson come back up here and show you some film that I think will speak for itself.

GENERAL GLOSSON: By way of setting the stage, the first video you'll see is an air-to-air engagement with a F-15C and a MIG-25 Foxbat. What exactly transpires is an attempt to attack a flight of F-16's exiting out of Iraq. The F-15C shoots down the trailer in the Foxbat. When he launched his missile, the Foxbat was doing over 700 knots. The pilot ejected before the missile reached the airplane, but the airplane was destroyed.

When I picked up the tape, you will see the flight lead pulling to shoot down the other lead, or the other MIG-25. Note the radio terminology, if you will, and how he expresses total control of the situation to the extent of telling his wingman, make sure you're not in after burner. Make sure you're only in military [full military power as opposed to after-burner] power, because he's looking at a Foxbat that has a plume of fire coming out the tail, so he wants to make sure that's who it is, because there are friendlies very close by.

The kill box, as we call it, is a rectangular box, and if you'll look in that kill box when it appears in the right-hand corner, you will see the MIG-25 blow up. Roll the tape, please.

I knew this, say January 19th. There's countless footage of these things after that date. Every time I see them I get air sick, I don't know what's going on. But these, I think it's obvious to anybody what's going on.

The bingo fuel call you heard was, obviously, he's getting low on fuel. That's the MIG-25 right there. A heat-seeking missile he launched, and it missed. Now a radar missile. The heat seeker missed, the second one's a radar.

Next, I'll pull you in the cockpit of an F-15E for an air-to-ground sortie. Through the help of a targeting pod and a NAV [navigational] pod on the F-15E, I'll let you look into the night sky of Iraq as we are attacking mobile Scuds and show you how—as General Schwarzkopf said—we have changed our tactics a little bit from the standpoint of being able to do things we could not do earlier because of the SAM threat.

The white indicates hot. You'll see on the FLIR pod that the three erector launchers, or mobile Scuds, are turning into the storage area to join four others. Then, when you notice black, it indicates cold, and you'll see these get darker as this film goes on. Now the pilot is maneuvering to drop laser-guided bombs on this target. There are a total of 11 vehicles in this area. All of these are already loaded with Scud missiles. As you can see, these have already been fired.

Now we'll show you a slow-motion so you can actually see the bomb impacting. Notice the bombs come through, impact, watch this one roll. The next thing you'll see is a secondary explosion in this area, the

AAA firing from that area. The flight lead now clears his number two man in to drop an area-denial munition to take care of the remainder of the four vehicles that were on this side of the road.

GENERAL SCHWARZKOPF: Thanks, Buster.

A little bit of argument going on in the community as to how much damage we did in this film. The minimum damage we did on the 11 vehicles has been confirmed. We have knocked out at least three mobile erector launchers, four Scud missiles on Scud servicing vehicles, and three more Scud servicing vehicles. The other possibility is that we knocked out as many as seven mobile erector launchers in just that one strike.

I would also like to report to you that using similar tactics last night in western Iraq, we also attacked and destroyed three Scud TELs [transporter erector launchers] with F-15's, and I feel we preempted a missile attack on Israel last night.

I certainly can't say there will be no more Scud launches. You can never say that. But I have a high degree of confidence that we're getting better and better at our ability to find them, and I think this tape speaks for itself in our ability to find and destroy them. I assure you that we're going to continue to pursue those launchers.

One last announcement. Today, we went over 500,000 troops in the theater.

Let me just finish up by giving you a brief closing assessment. By every measure our campaign plan is on schedule. There's no way that I'm suggesting the Iraqi Army is close to capitulation and going to give up. I think their actions last night have proven that to all of us, but I'm quite confident that the direction we're heading in is going to lead to exactly the outcome that we all want to see.

That completes the formal briefing. General Glosson and I now would be very happy to answer any questions you might have.

Q: General Schwarzkopf, the Iraqis claimed yesterday that a POW of unknown nationality was killed in one of the bombing raids on a site where he was being used as a human shield. What can you tell us about the human-shield business, and how are you dealing with that when it comes to bombing targets in iraq?

SCHWARZKOPF: I'd really like to tell you how I'd like to deal with it, but I won't get into that. All I can say is that is a gross violation of the Geneva Convention. I think it's very important to state right now that the International Red Cross has inspected all of our POW camps, and I will let their report speak for itself. I would tell you anecdotally that yesterday we transferred quite a large number of Iraqi POW's over to the Saudis, and the Iraqis were being treated so well in our POW camps that many of them said they'd be perfectly delighted to stay right there with the treatment they're getting. It's a funny thing about American troops, but they take pretty good care of their enemy once they're captured. But as I said, the International Red Cross has inspected our POW camps. I challenge the Iraqis right now—challenge them!—to do the same damn thing in their POW camps, and look at how they're treating our people and the other coalition POW's. Thanks for the question.

Q: General, you described heavy B-52 bombardment of troop positions in Kuwait. You described intercepting supply lines, troops that are giving you anecdotal evidence about one meal a day, and body lice. These same troops, it seems, made it 12 miles into Saudi territory last night. Was there any degree to which coalition troops might have been taken by surprise?

SCHWARZKOPF: I don't think we were taken by surprise. As I said, Khafji had been abandoned. We had outposts in this area. The outposts reported exactly what we expected them to report. They made it into Ras al Khafji—12 miles, six miles, it's irrelevant how far it is—because it was considered militarily . . . The reason why it was abandoned by the Saudis very early on is because it's in direct artillery range of the artillery right out here in Kuwait and they didn't want to have bombardments going down on any troops they had in this position. So in essence, the Iraqis went unopposed into this area. The Iraqis that went into the other area were opposed and in fact were turned back. I would tell you, I don't think that battle is over by a long shot. I expect a lot more fighting will probably occur tonight. I would tell you that, obviously, we're ready for whatever comes in there tonight. But I don't think we were surprised.

Q: Could you share with us your views on the threat of Suddam Hussein to use chemical weapons against civilians, to escalate the war? Do you think those threats are credible or not? And what steps, if any, can you tell us that you're taking to meet them?

SCHWARZKOPF: As we've said all along, we don't discount anything on the part of Saddam Hussein. I think some of his other actions he's done to date have demonstrated that he's willing to do anything. So frankly, having seen the accuracy of the Scud missile, I don't think it, from a military standpoint, or even its ability to lay down a dense, wide, long type of gas attack—because it takes many missiles with a certain degree of sophistication to do that—I don't think that's going to happen. On the other hand, there is no telling whatsoever what he might try with a single warhead on top of a single missile, and therefore I would never discount that possibility.

Q: Why do you think the 89 planes have flown into Iran?

SCHWARZKOPF: I come up with three different scenarios. One, they are flying off to husband them for another day. Number two, you have that they are flying in there to launch an attack against us at some future date, although the Iranians claim that is not the case.

To date, I see no reason why we shouldn't believe the
Iranians. Scenario number three, we've had reports that
some of those people were defectors. So it could be any
one of those three things or a combination of all of
them. But I think it's a very good sign that they don't
feel confident where they are—they've got to run
someplace else to hide. I'm delighted with that outcome.

Q: General Glosson, in the film of the attack on the
Scud launchers, you said something about an area-
denial weapon, and we saw quite a large piece of landscape light up there. What kind of weapon is that?
GLOSSON: That was a CBU-87, referred to as a clus-
ter-bomb munition, used for the purpose it was used
for there.

Q: Could you tell us how many Iraqi troops and
tanks have so far come across the border in these
engagements down here?
SCHWARZKOPF: I really can't. I think I told you about
a battalion in each case, and there's about 40 tanks per
battalion. Obviously, we're shooting, not counting,
when they come across.

Q: Given this entire presentation tonight about the
effectiveness of the coalition air forces, is there a
chance that there won't need to be a ground war?
SCHWARZKOPF: There's always a chance of that. But
as a military planner you always plan for the worst case
rather than the best. I'm certainly not going to assume
away the capabilities of the enemy. The mere fact that
they launched this foiling attack, or whatever it might
be, indicates that they certainly have a lot of fight left
in them.

Q: What were the weapons used against the hardened aircraft shelters? And a follow-up question on a
different subject, approximately what was the range of

the MIG interception when the AIM-9 didn't work and he had to go to the radar-guided weapon?

GLOSSON: I'd rather not say the range when the AIM-9 did not fuse, for obvious reasons. The bomb that penetrated the hardened aircraft shelter was an I-2000 weapon that's hardened for that situation.

Q: What about the bridges?

GLOSSON: The same type of weapon that we use with the hardened aircraft shelters.

Q: There's been a late report from Reuters that the Iraqis have opened up another oil spigot in a place called Mina al Bakr. Are you aware of this, and do you have any tentative plans to deal with it?

SCHWARZKOPF: Mina al Bakr has been leaking for several days now. That's an Iraqi oil terminal, in fact, and it's been attacked for several reasons in the past. To date, we've been watching that oil spill very carefully. Frankly, if it gets out of control, I will try to do exactly what we did with the other one. I don't have any other reports other than that.

Q: I think to many civilian minds, the idea of the Iraqi ground forces going over to the offensive as the probing attacks would seem very strange after such an intense aerial campaign. Could you enlighten those civilians?

SCHWARZKOPF: Sure. First of all, we haven't hit this area anywhere near as hard as we've hit the Republican Guards and some of the other areas. We may change our mind now, obviously. Second, there is an old saying that the best defense is a good offense, and sometimes, believe me, when people have been sitting in a hole being hit day after day by air, they decide that rather than sit around and take this any more, why don't we get up and do something about it? It could be that. Third, as I say, the Marines have been conducting very effective artillery raids in this area for about three nights in a row. It's entirely possible that these folks, based upon the severe damage that they had the night before, knew about all the artillery raids have been about the same time. This may have been a preemptive attack to try to get after those forces that had been attacking them three nights beforehand.

Q: I seem to remember a week, or possibly two weeks ago, there being reports saying that these troops down there were virtually left without any soft-skin vehicles to take them back, in fact, had virtually no means of transportation whatsoever.

SCHWARZKOPF: It wasn't these folks right here. It was these folks up here that came down, we think.

Q: Sir, you spoke of the explosion that was a twelve on a scale of one to ten. Can you give us any idea what type of materiel that might have been? To put it in layman's language, what sort of equipment for how many soldiers over what period of time? What sort of ammunition?

SCHWARZKOPF: I wish I could. It's a huge ammunition dump, all of them in revetments. It's a build-up. When they first started building up in the theater, this was an area that they first started their major buildup from, and then they sent equipment down to other units. So all I can say is it was the major ammunition depot that supplied all the forces in Kuwait, and with that level of damage done to it, coupled with the fact that most of the bridges are out now and the fact that we're attacking the convoys that come down, that means that what they've got is what they've got. If they use that up, they're going to be hurting.

Q: If you're unwilling to discuss Iraqi casualties among the Republican Guard, could you perhaps give us an estimate of the degree to which you've reduced the effectiveness of the fighting force?

SCHWARZKOPF: No, because all it would be is a rough

estimate, and I don't like dealing in rough estimates when you start talking about enemy casualties. I told you, I'm anti-body count. Body count means absolutely nothing. All it is is a wild guess that tends to mislead people as to what's going on. That's not the way we do business, so I personally don't like the idea of issuing body counts on a comparative basis. I think it puts undue pressure on commanders to come up with numbers that are unreal.

Q: There are reports in the oil industry that 50 to 90 percent of all of Iraq's refined petroleum adjacent to refineries and to power plants has been destroyed—the storage facilities, basically. Is that the order of magnitude?

SCHWARZKOPF: I told you, we went after militarily significant targets. We didn't want to destroy their oil industry, but we certainly wanted to make sure they didn't have a lot of gasoline for their military vehicles.

Q: There are an awful lot of reporters in Saudi Arabia, particularly in the Dhahran region—

SCHWARZKOPF: You've got about two battalions' worth. I'm going to keep that in mind if we ever need you! (Laughter)

Q: The majority are being barred by the military from access to covering the war. The ostensible reason is mainly a lack of equipment, such as rucksacks and sleeping bags. Even if this is true, there's a large segment of non-pool reporters who are interested in covering things like aviation, supply, logistics, maintenance, things that would not require us to use this equipment and live with the ground troops. My question is, when will the military decide to stop managing the public's impression in league with favored media and allow the American people to get a full—

SCHWARZKOPF: The answer to your question is I will refer you to the Assistant Secretary of Defense for

Public Affairs, who makes those policies. I'm the theater commander. My job is to follow those policies when they're made.

Q: I think the chart showed nearly 1,500 sorties against Scud sites. That's more than a year number of sorties against any other type of target. Do you consider that a proportionate military effort on the allied side to something which you say is militarily insignificant?

SCHWARZKOPF: I'd prefer to think that it's a required military effort, given the circumstances that we're in right now.

Q: Is the central command in Baghdad still giving orders to troops on the ground, or have you destroyed leadership command?

SCHWARZKOPF: No, we haven't totally destroyed it, but they certainly aren't giving the direct orders in the way they have to. There are a lot of circuitous routes they have to go through. I would tell you, even some corps commanders can't communicate directly with their division commanders, and have to go through other division commanders to relay the signals.

Q: Can you tell us what, if anything, you're doing to encourage Iraqi troops to surrender? And following that, can you tell us if you have had any news at all of the missing CBS news crew?

SCHWARZKOPF: First of all, we've got an active psychological-warfare program going. What we're basically telling them is if they stay where they are and fight, they're probably going to be maimed or get killed; and if they come over here, they're going to be treated very well, and they'll live and get to go home. That's basically the message we're sending them. As for the CBS crew, we found their vehicle, and then we got the very best trackers we had. We had those trackers follow their tracks, and their tracks went into Kuwait, and of course that's as far as we could go. We're very concerned about them. I've alerted all my commanders. We're all on the lookout for them, but that's about the best information I can give you at this time.

Q: Three days ago, you gave us a briefing on the military effort to take out those manifolds at the Ahmadi oil fields; you talked about the air strikes that went in. A Washington newspaper ran a story saying that the Navy SEALs were ready and willing to go in and do that job, that that you told them no. Is that true?

SCHWARZKOPF: Normally in response to a question like that I would say that report contains some inaccuracies. However, reverting to my old style, I would describe that report as bovine scathology . . . (Laughter) . . . better referred to by the troops as BS. I don't know who that guy's source is, but he ought to get a new one because his source is a liar.

Q: General, I just wanted to see if I got this right. I get the impression that the Iraqi troops have seized Khafji. It's a little border town there, I know. We've all been up there. And not American troops per se but Saudi National Guard troops, which I don't remember if they have that much armor. Are trying to retake that city, is that accurate?

SCHWARZKOPF: I'd rather leave a question like that to the Saudis because they can give you a lot more details on that. We work very closely together. The Saudis have reported to me that they're mounting an operation to go back into Khafji. I wouldn't really say the Iraqis have seized Khafji. When you walk into an uninhabited place, it's really not much of a seizure.

Q: They're occupying Khafji?

SCHWARZKOPF: The last I heard, there were some there. But again, I have no confirmed evidence that they're still there. Let's wait and see what happens or let the Saudis brief you on that, because they can give you better information.

Q: Without revealing any military secrets, can you tell me what will be the factors or the criteria for you to decide if to begin the ground attack, and when to begin a ground attack?

SCHWARZKOPF: First of all, I do not make that decision. The President of the United States, in consultation with the Secretary of Defense and the Chairman of the Joint Chiefs of Staff will make that decision. The second answer is, no.

Q: What is your reaction to the communiqué out of Washington the other day, with Moscow and Washington talking about a possibility of a cease-fire if Iraq shows any indication whatsoever of pulling out of Kuwait? Do you think it's feasible from your perspective to—

SCHWARZKOPF: I think the correct answer, for my part, would be that we have no intention whatsoever of terminating this military campaign until we've accomplished the objectives that were announced at the outset. I'd refer any other comment to the White House on that.

Q: You talked about the Kuwaiti theater of operations. If you go into Kuwait, expel the Iraqis, are you going to stop at the border, or are you going to pursue them into Iraq?

SCHWARZKOPF: Let's wait and see. This campaign has many different phases to it. There are certain determinations that happen in each one. I'm not going to telegraph any of our punches, but I will repeat once again what the President of the United States has said all along—our argument is not the the Iraqi people. Our intention is not to conquer Iraq in any way, or reduce Iraq to a non-country. It never has been.

Q: The UN resolution says to expel Iraq from Kuwait. You're just leaving the option open that you may pursue them into Iraq, is that correct?

SCHWARZKOPF: I'm not leaving any option open, I'm not leaving any option closed. I'm saying that we have a military campaign that we're going to execute, and I'm not going to go into any of the planning options beyond that.

Q: Sir, you spoke of interdicting the main supply routes. Is it possible that the enemy could shift to secondary supply routes effectively—pickup trucks, jeeps, mule trains, etc.?

SCHWARZKOPF: There's always that possibility, but that's pretty rough to do. They have a very limited road net, and of course, with the Tigris and the Euphrates being where it is, you've got to go across those two rivers. I would expect to see pontoon bridges being put up, but pontoon bridges are pretty easy to find, and they're even easier to take out.

Q: In the Indochiná war the enemy did do exactly that, and their supplies continued to roll south. Granted, there's no triple-canopy forest and we have better night-sighting capability, but do you anticipate the possibility of an extended supply effort down to the more primitive level?

SCHWARZKOPF: I would imagine that they will try, and I can assure you that we will also continue to do what we've been doing. There's a big difference between here and Vietnam as far as air operations and the ability to interdict supply lines.

Q: You mentioned the Marine casualties of 12 dead and two wounded. In your estimation, is that unusually high for an encounter of that size?

SCHWARZKOPF: No, particularly, when you consider the number of tanks that were involved, the number of tanks that were knocked out, and that sort of thing.

Listen, any is intolerably high as far as I'm concerned, but unfortunately, that's going to happen.

Q: Given your destruction of supply routes to Kuwait, and that there are about a hundred thousand Kuwaitis still in Kuwait, what advice would you give to them now?

SCHWARZKOPF: I hope they are continuing to resist in every way they possibly can. I would hope that their spirits are somewhat uplifted by this. I hope they would continue to protect themselves as much as they can. I don't want them to do anything foolish that might get them hurt.

Q: Would you tell them to evacuate?

SCHWARZKOPF: I don't think there's any need for that at the present time. Believe me, if there is a need for that, we'll probably let them know ahead of time.

Q: You have mentioned that you have destroyed all the Iraqi nuclear-reactor facilities. Do you have information about contamination?

SCHWARZKOPF: Every target that we have attacked—be it nuclear, chemical, or biological—we have very carefully selected the destruction means after a lot of advice from a lot of prominent scientists. We've selected the destruction means in such a way that we absolutely, almost to a 99.9 percent assurance, have no contamination. I found one thing—none of the scientists will ever give you a one hundred percent assurance of anything, but they will tell you that there are certain ways that you can limit that contamination, and every one of those targets that we've attacked, we were very careful in the method of attack and the munitions we used to ensure that we didn't have any contamination.

Q: I'm curious about your handling of civilian targets, especially the point you made about power stations and hydro stations. You mentioned you've left them alone because you don't want to reduce Iraq to, I think you described it as a non-country, or to rubble. Can I ask you, the bottom line, if it comes to the big push, is that open? Will those be hit?

SCHWARZKOPF: That's a decision that lies in the hands of the President of the United States.

Q: I wonder if you could generally, from your experience, describe what B-52 strikes of the type you've described can do to troops on the ground, even troops who are well dug in?

SCHWARZKOPF: I don't want to get into too much detail, but I would tell you that the B-52 has a much higher degree of accuracy than it's given credit for. We have different types of munitions that we use also. And the combination of the accuracy and the munitions will have an effect on any kind of target. We vary the munitions based on the type of target—I'd just like to leave it at that.

Q: In 1986 during the Iran–Iraq War, it was generally believed that Saddam Hussein was personally ordering basically every major maneuver against Iran. I wonder if you understand that he is doing the same type of thing today, and given the effect that you've had on his command and control, if that's a factor?

SCHWARZKOPF: I obviously can't tell you whether he's giving every single order, but I would certainly say that his ability to give timely orders has been greatly reduced. In other words, if I'm on the battlefield, the situation changes, and I'm waiting around for an order from high, I'm going to wait a lot longer now than I would have had to wait before.

Q: Besides the fight to retake Khafji, whatever we're calling it—occupation, seizure—is the conflict continuing at the other entry location you pointed out?

SCHWARZKOPF: No. When I came over here, at least, all of those places were quiet. But as I say, I would not be the least bit surprised if we didn't have further action.

Q: Why did Iraqi troops and tanks attack Khafji? Do you have any idea about what they wanted to do?

SCHWARZKOPF: As I mentioned earlier, it may have been to preempt another artillery raid, it may have been for all sorts of reasons. I've already heard it being touted as a major military victory on the battlefield. Moving into an unoccupied village that's six miles inside the friendly lines, I don't consider that a major military victory. If they want to consider it one, that's fine. That's just one battle, that's not the war.

Q: General Glosson, refugees coming into Jordan have been telling tales of convoys of civilian vehicles being strafed, people running in the desert and being strafed, bombs dropping everywhere. Given that frightened people exaggerate, nonetheless, something must be happening. Can you tell us what you're hitting along that road, and what happens if there are a lot of civilian vehicles in among what looks like a military target?

GLOSSON: We're striking only military targets. Having said that, the Iraqi government insists on storing Scuds in culverts and other things along the highway. As you saw on the tape, when we see those type of vehicles go into those facilities, we bomb them. We make every attempt to minimize any possibility of civilian casualties, and that's the best answer I can give you.

Q: General, along those same lines, some of the refugees and Red Cross workers have brought back fragments of bombs identified as cluster bombs, CBU. Are you using cluster bombs along that highway. And if so, how do you reconcile that with your efforts to minimize civilian casualties along, particularly, the refugee route.

GLOSSON: You saw along one of the highways that we just showed you the films, and that was cluster bombs on those four vehicles or Scud missile launchers that were sitting along the highway. Yes, we use the cluster munition to cover a wider area when the military situation dictates that.

SCHWARZKOPF: Let me step in here. We have never said there won't be any civilian casualties. What we have said is the difference between us and the Iraqis is we are not deliberately targeting civilians. There are going to be casualties—unfortunately, that's what happens when you have a war. But we are certainly not deliberately targeting civilians. We never have and we have no intention of doing it in the future. Our enemy certainly is, and I hope that's obvious to everybody in this room since you've been under Scud attack.

Q: If Saddam Hussein were to have a briefing tonight in Baghdad and discuss two weeks of war, he would probably say that we—that is, the coalition forces—have thrown the best at him that they could, and still he is able to launch an offensive. As much of a distortion as that may be, how much, in your own thinking, when you're going into his mental process, is the political dimension of this war a factor—the fact that it is going on, that the Arab people are looking at it, and that you have a political constraint, as well as other constraints, to end the war?

SCHWARZKOPF: This is strictly Norm Schwarzkopf's opinion now, but it's opinion based on discussion with a lot of friends throughout the Gulf area, some of whom tend to be very pro-Saddam Hussein. To date, Hussein has lied to them. He's told them that Tel Aviv was a crematorium—we all know that's not true. To date, he has told them that he has shot down 170 American and coalition aircraft—everybody knows that's not true. He has announced that he is going to do all sorts of wonderful things. The other day he said a prayer for the dead, saying because Riyadh was going to be wiped out that night—that did not happen. He has lied consistently about us damaging religious places—a lot of people know that is not true. So I think that one of the things that's happened out there is a lot of people who were supporters of Saddam Hussein— I'm not talking about the mob in the street, because they're not going to change their opinion—but people who intellectually or at least reasonably thought that he was supporting a cause, have found that he is not delivering on his promises, and that's probably doing him some harm. I think eventually they're going to find the same thing out with this particular attack.

With regard to Saddam Hussein saying he has met the best that the coalition has to offer, I would only say the best is yet to come.

Thank you very much.

★ ★ ★ ★

General H. Norman Schwarzkopf
CENTCOM Briefing
Riyadh, Saudi Arabia
Sunday, February 24, 1991—8:45 A.M. (EST)

GENERAL SCHWARZKOPF: Good afternoon, thank you for coming.

As you know, last night at his briefing, Secretary Cheney mentioned that in the critical early stages of a military operation, it's absolutely imperative to deny the enemy any information on the disposition, actions, or plans of our forces. For that reason he stated that we were going to suspend temporarily the daily scheduled briefings—both in the Pentagon and here in Riyadh. Secretary Cheney also said, however, that he wanted to keep the American public informed whenever possible with periodic updates. The purpose of my comments at this time is to give you a brief assessment of the progress to date of the ground phase of Operation Desert Storm. The contents of my briefing will be limited to release of information which we feel will not jeopardize the progress of our operations. Nor will it in any way endanger the lives of our troops on the battlefield. I know that you will understand our great concern for the operational security, and I also know that the American people would demand nothing less.

Let me first make the point that this is an initial update, and it's based on preliminary reports from commanders in the field. These reports may change or be refined in the hours ahead.

At 0400 hours local this morning, coalition forces

began a major ground, naval, and air offensive to eject Iraqi forces from Kuwait. I want to emphasize, this is a coalition effort. The countries participating so far are the United States, Saudi Arabia, the United Kingdom, France, United Arab Emirates, Bahrain, Qatar, Oman, Syria, and of course, Kuwait.

U.S. forces in this morning's attack were Marines, Army paratroopers, Army air-assault forces, and Army special forces. These forces, along with French and Arab forces, have already reached all of their first-day objectives and are continuing their attack.

Early this afternoon, U.S. Army mechanized and armor forces, along with forces of the United Kingdom, Saudi Arabia, Kuwait, Egypt, and Syria, also launched attacks, and they are moving north with great speed.

With the exception of one early afternoon engagement between a Marine task force and an Iraqi armor unit, contact with the enemy can best be characterized as light. Coalition air forces from the United States, the United Kingdom, Saudi Arabia, Kuwait, Italy, Canada, United Arab Emirates, Bahrain, and Qatar are all conducting surge air operations to support the ground commanders, and they continue to strike key strategic targets.

The United States, the United Kingdom, Saudi and Kuwaiti naval forces are conducting carrier air, minesweeping, naval gunfire support, and of course, amphibious missions along the east coast of Kuwait.

Ten hours into this ground offensive, more than 5,500 prisoners have been captured. We've received reports of many hundreds more north of our positions with white surrender flags.

Friendly casualties have been extremely light. As a matter of fact, remarkably light. So far the offensive is progressing with dramatic success. The troops are doing a great job. But I would not be honest with you if I didn't remind you that this is the very early stages. We are little more than twelve hours into this offensive, and the war is not over yet.

That concludes my prepared comments, and I am now ready to take a very few questions.

Q: General Schwarzkopf, can you give us an idea of how long, based on what you know now and if things go according to plan, how long you anticipate this thing is going to last, and how do you account for the fact that the opposition has been so light so far?

A: I would first of all say that the opposition has probably been so light so far because of the excellent job that all of the forces to date have done in preparing the battlefield. With regard to the second question, it's impossible to say how long it's going to take, but let me put it this way, it's going to take as long as it takes for the Iraqis to get out of Kuwait and the United Nations resolutions to be enforced.

Q: There have been some reports today—and I know this might be an ongoing situation—but can you at least tell us whether we have any forces in Kuwait City? There have been reports of some paratroopers being over Kuwait City—these reports by Kuwaiti residents.

A: I'm not going to discuss in any way the location of any of the forces involved in the battle to date.

Q: Have any U.S. or allied troops encountered chemical or biological weapons?

A: We've had some initial reports of chemical weapons, but those reports to date, as far as we're concerned, have been bogus. There have been no reported chemical weapons used thus far.

Q: Would you say the campaign so far is going better than you expected at this stage, about on par, or slightly worse?

A: I would say that so far we're delighted with the progress of the campaign.

Q: You said with one exception, the contact with the enemy was described, you said, as light. Can you provide any details at all about—

A: This afternoon, about two hours ago, one of the Marine task forces was counterattacked with enemy armor. The Marines immediately brought their own artillery to bear. They also brought their anti-tank weapons to bear. We also brought our air forces to bear. The counterattack was very quickly repulsed, and they retreated. I can't tell you the exact number of loss of tanks, but there were several tanks that were lost in that particular battle.

Q: Has the resistance been light because the Iraqis are retreating, or are they simply not engaging you? Are they surrendering? What exactly are they doing?

A: All of the above.

Q: You say the opposition is light. Is this because you have avoided a frontal confrontation with them? Are you going around or over, and is that why there's little opposition?

A: We're going to go around, over, through, on top, underneath, and any other way.

Q: Are you going to pursue the Iraqi soldiers into Iraq, or are you going to stop at the Kuwait–Iraq border?

A: I'm not going to answer that question. We're going to pursue them in any way it takes to get them out of Kuwait.

Thank you very much.

General H. Norman Schwarzkopf
CENTCOM Briefing
Riyadh, Saudia Arabia
Wednesday, February 27, 1991—1:00 P.M. (EST)

GENERAL SCHWARZKOPF: Good evening, ladies and gentlemen. Thank you for being here.

I promised some of you a few days ago that as soon as the opportunity presented itself, I would give you a complete rundown on what we were doing, and more important, why we were doing it—the strategy behind what we were doing. I've been asked by Secretary Cheney to do that this evening, so if you will bear with me, we're going to go through a briefing. I apologize to the folks who won't be able to see the charts, but we're going to go through a complete briefing of the operation.

(Chart)

This goes back to August 7th through January 17th. As you recall, we started our deployment on August 7th. Basically what we started out against was a couple of hundred thousand Iraqis that were in the Kuwait theater of operations. I don't have to remind you all that we brought over, initially, defensive forces in the form of the 101st, the 82nd, the 24th Mechanized Infantry division, the 3rd Armored Cavalry, and in essence, we had them arrayed to the south, behind the Saudi task force. Also Arab forces were arrayed in defensive positions over here in this area. That, in essence, is the way we started.

(Chart)

In the middle of November, the decision was made to increase the force because by that time, huge numbers of Iraqi forces had flowed into the area, and generally in the disposition as they're shown right here. Therefore we increased the forces and built up more forces.

At this time we made a deliberate decision to align all of those forces within the boundary looking north toward Kuwait—this being King Khalid Military City over here. So we aligned those forces so it very much looked like they were all aligned directly on the Iraqi position.

We also at that time had a very active naval presence out in the Gulf, and we made sure that everybody understood about that naval presence. One of the reasons why we did that is it became apparent to us early on that the Iraqis were quite concerned about an amphibious operation to liberate Kuwait—this being Kuwait City. They put a very heavy barrier of infantry along here, and they proceeded to build an extensive barrier that went all the way across the border, down and around and up the side of Kuwait.

Basically, the problem we faced was this: When you looked at the troop numbers, they really outnumbered us about three-to-two, and when you consider the number of combat service support people we have—that's logisticians and that sort of thing in our armed forces—we were really outnumbered two-to-one. In addition to that, they had 4,700 tanks versus our 3,500 when the build-up was complete, and they had a great deal more artillery than we do.

I think any student of military strategy would tell you that in order to attack a position you should have a ratio of approximately three-to-one in favor of the attacker. In order to attack a position that is heavily dug in and barricaded such as the one we had here, you should have a ratio of five-to-one. So you can see basically what our problem was at that time. We were outnumbered three-to-two, at a minimum as far as troops were concerned, we were outnumbered as far as tanks were concerned, and we had to come up with some way to make up the difference.

(Chart)

I apologize for the busy nature of this chart, but I think it's important for you to understand exactly what our strategy was. What you see here is a color coding where green is a go sign, or a good sign, as far as our forces are concerned; yellow would be a caution sign; and red would be a stop sign. Green represents enemy units that have been attritted below 50 percent strength; the yellow are units that are between 50 and 75 percent strength; and of course the red units that are over 75 percent strength.

What we did, of course, was start an extensive air campaign. One of its purposes, I told you at the time, was to isolate the Kuwaiti theater of operations by taking out all the bridges and supply lines that ran between the north and the southern part of Iraq. That was to prevent reinforcements and supplies reaching the southern part of Iraq and Kuwait. We also conducted a very heavy bombing campaign, and many people questioned why. This reason is that it was necessary to reduce these forces down to strength that made them weaker, particularly along the front-line barrier that we had to go through.

We continued our heavy operations out in the sea because we wanted the Iraqis to continue to believe that we were going to conduct a massive amphibious operation in this area. I think many of you recall the number of amphibious rehearsals we had—including Imminent Thunder, which was written about quite extensively for many reasons. But we continued to have those operations because we wanted him to concentrate his forces—which he did.

I think this is probably one of the most important parts of the entire briefing. As you know, very early on we took out the Iraq Air Force. We knew that he had limited reconnaissance means. Therefore, when we took out his air force, for all intents and purposes we took out his ability to see what we were doing down here in Saudi Arabia. Once we had taken out his eyes, we did what could best be described as the "Hail Mary play" in football. I think you recall when the quarterback is desperate for a touchdown at the very end, what he does is send every receiver way out to one flank, and they all run down the field as fast as they possibly can into the end zone, and he lobs the ball. In essence, that's what we did.

When we knew that he couldn't see us anymore, we did a massive movement of troops to the extreme west, because at that time we knew that the vast majority of his forces were still fixed in this area. Once the air campaign started, they would be incapable of moving out to counter this move even if they knew we made it. There were some additional troops out in this area, but they did not have the capability or the time to put in the barrier that had been described by Saddam Hussein as an absolutely impenetrable tank barrier. I believe those were his words.

So this was an extraordinary move. I must tell you, I can't recall any time in the annals of military history when this number of forces have moved over this distance to put themselves in a position to be able to attack. But what's more important, not only did we move the troops out there, but we literally moved thousands and thousands of tons of fuel, of ammunition, of spare parts, of water, and of food, because we wanted to have enough supplies on hand so if we launched this and got into a slug-fest battle, which we very easily could have, we'd have enough supplies to last for 60 days. It was a gigantic accomplishment, and I can't give credit enough to the logisticians and the transporters who were able to pull this off, for the superb support we had from the Saudi government, the literally thousands and thousands of drivers of every national origin who helped us in this move out here.

And of course, great credit goes to the commanders of these units who were also able to maneuver their forces out here into position.

As a result, by February 23rd, their front lines had been attritted down to a point where all of these units were at 50 percent or below. The second level, basically, that we had to face, and these were the real tough fighters we were worried about right here, were attritted to someplace between 50 and 75 percent. Although we still had the Republican Guard located here and here, and part of the Guard in this area we continued to hit the bridges all across this area to make absolutely sure that no more reinforcements came into the battle. This was the situation on February 23rd.

I shouldn't forget our forces. We put them deep into the enemy territory. They went out on strategic reconnaissance for us, and they let us know what was going on out there. They were our eyes, and it's very important that I not forget those folks.

(Chart)

This was the morning of the 24th. Our plans initially had been to start over here in this area and do exactly what the Iraqis thought we were going to do. That's taken them head-on in their most heavily defended area. Also, at the same time we launched amphibious feints and naval gunfire so that they continued to think we were going to be attacking along the coast, and therefore fixed air forces in this position. Our hope was that by fixing these forces, we would basically keep the forces here, and they wouldn't know what was going on out in this area. I believe we succeeded in that very well.

At four o'clock in the morning, the 1st and 2nd Marine divisions launched attacks through the barrier system. They were accompanied by the U.S. Army Tiger Brigade of the 2nd Armored Division. At the same time, over here, two Saudi task forces also launched a penetration through this barrier. But while they were doing that, the 6th French Armored Division, accompanied by a brigade of the 82nd Airborne, also launched an overland attack to their objective up in this area, al-Faman Airfield. We were held up a little bit by the weather, but by eight o'clock the 101st Airborne air assault launched an air assault deep in enemy territory to establish a forward operating base in this location right here. Let me talk about each one of these moves.

First of all, the Saudis over here on the east coast did a terrific job. They went up against the very tough barrier systems; they breached the barrier very effectively; they moved out aggressively and continued their attacks up the coast.

I can't say enough about the two Marine divisions. They did an absolutely superb job in breaching the so-called impenetrable barrier. It was a classic military breaching of a very tough minefield, barbed wire, fire trenches type barrier. They went through the first barrier like it was water. They went across into the second barrier line, even though they were under artillery fire at the time, and they continued to open up that breach. Then they brought both divisions streaming through that breach. A textbook operation, and I think it will be studied for many years to come as the way to do it.

I would also like to say that the French did a superb job of moving out rapidly to take their objective out here, and they were very successful, as was the 101st. Again, we still had the special forces located in this area.

What we found was that as soon as we breached these obstacles here and started bringing pressure, we started getting a large number of surrenders. I talked to some of you about that when I briefed you on the evening of the 24th. We also found that these forces were meeting with a great deal of success.

We were worried about the weather. It was going to get pretty bad the next day, and we were worried about launching this air assault. We also started to have a huge number of atrocities of the most unspeakable type committed in downtown Kuwait City, including reports that the desalinization plant had been destroyed. When we heard that, we were quite concerned. Based upon that, and the situation as it was developing, we made the decision that rather than wait until the following morning to launch the remainder of these forces that we would go ahead and launch them that afternoon.

(Chart)

This was the situation you saw the afternoon of the 24th. The Marines continued to make great progress through the breach and were moving rapidly north. The Saudi task force on the east coast was also moving rapidly north. We launched another Egyptian–Arab force in this location, and another Saudi force in this location—again, to penetrate the barrier. But as before, these assaults were to make the enemy continue to think that we were doing exactly what he wanted us to do. That meant a very tough mission for these folks.

At the same time, we continued to attack with the French. We launched an attack on the part of the entire 7th Corps where the 1st Infantry Division had gone through, breached an obstacle and mine-field barrier here, established quite a large breach through which we passed the 1st British Armored Division. At the same time we launched the 1st and 3rd Armored divisions. Because of the way our deception plan was working, we didn't even have to worry about a barrier. We just went right around the enemy and were behind him in no time at all. The 2nd Armored Cavalry Division and the 24th Mech Division was also launched out here in the far west. I ought to talk about the 101st, because this an important point.

Once the 101st had their forward-operating base established, they then launched into the Tigris–Euphrates Valley. There are a lot of people who are still saying that the object of the United States of America is to cause the downfall of the entire country of Iraq. Ladies and gentlemen, when we were here, we were 150 miles from Baghdad. What's more, there was nobody between us and Baghdad. If our intention had been to overrun and destroy Iraq, we could have done it unopposed, for all intents and purposes, from this position at that time. That was not our intention; we have never said it was our intention. It was truly to eject the Iraqis out of Kuwait and destroy the military power that had come in.

So this was the situation at the end of the afternoon of February 24th.

(Chart)

The next two days went exactly like we thought they would. The Saudis continued to make great progress on the eastern flank, keeping the pressure off the Marines flank. The special forces started operating small-boat operations in this area to help clear mines, but also to threaten the flanks here and to continue to make them think that we were going to conduct amphibious operations. The Saudi and Arab forces that took these two initial objectives turned to come in on the flank heading toward Kuwait City. The British passed through and continued to attack up this flank. Of course, the VII Corps came in and attacked in this direction shown here. The 24th Infantry Division made an unbelievable move all the way across into the Tigris–Euphrates Valley, and proceeded in blocking this avenue of egress, which was the only one left because we continued to make sure that the bridges stayed down. So there was no way out once the 24th was in this area, and the 101st continued to operate in here. The French, having succeeded in achieving all their objectives, then set up a flank guard position here to make sure no forces could get us from the flank.

By this time we had destroyed, or rendered completely ineffective, over 21 Iraqi divisions.

(Chart)

Of course, that brings us to today. We now have a solid wall across the north of the 18th Airborne Corps consisting of the units shown right here, attacking straight to the east. We have a solid wall here, again of the VII Corps also attacking straight to the east. The forces that they are fighting right now are the forces of the Republican Guard.

Today we had another significant day. The Arab forces coming from both the west and east closed in and moved into Kuwait City, where they are now in the process of securing it. The 1st Marine Division continues to hold Kuwait International Airport. The 2nd Marine Division continues to hold a position that blocks any egress out of the city of Kuwait, so no one can leave. To date we have destroyed or rendered inoperable—I don't like to say destroyed because that gives you visions of absolutely killing everyone, and that's not what we're doing. But we have rendered completely ineffective over 29 Iraqi divisions. The gates are closed.

We continue, of course, high-level air power. The air has done a terrific job from start to finish in supporting the ground forces, and we also have had great support from the Navy—both in the form of naval gunfire and in support of carrier air.

That's the situation at the present time.

(Chart)

Peace is not without a cost. These have been the U.S. casualties to date. I would just like to comment briefly about the casualty chart. The loss of one human life is intolerable to any of us who are in the military. But casualties of that order of magnitude, considering the job that's been done and the number of forces involved, is almost miraculous, even though it will never be miraculous to the families of those people.

This is what's happened to date with the Iraqis. They started with over 4,000 tanks. To date, we have over 3,000 confirmed destroyed—and I do mean destroyed or captured. As a matter of fact, that number is low because you can add 700 to that as a result of the battle that's going on right now with the Republican Guard. That number is very high, and we've almost completely destroyed the offensive capability of the Iraqi forces in the Kuwaiti theater of operations. The armored-vehicle count is also very high, and of course, you can see we're doing great damage to the artillery. The battle is still going on, and I suspect that these numbers will mount considerably.

(Chart)

I wish I could give you a better number than this, to be honest with you. This is just an estimate sent to us by the field today at noon time. The problem is, the prisoners out there are so heavy and obviously we're not going around and counting noses at this time to determine precisely what the number is. But we're confident that we have well over 50,000 prisoners of war at this time, and that number is mounting.

I would remind you that even as we speak, there is fighting going on out there. Even as we speak, there are incredible acts of bravery going on. This afternoon we had an F-16 pilot shot down. We had contact with him, he had a broken leg on the ground. Two helicopters from the 101st, they didn't to do it, but they went in to try to pull that pilot out. One of them was shot down, and we're still in the process of working through that. But that's the kind of thing that's going on out on that battlefield right now. It is not a Nintendo game—it is a tough battlefield where people are risking their lives at all times. There are great heroes out there, and we ought to all be very, very proud of them.

That's the campaign to date. That's the strategy to date. I'd now be happy to take any questions anyone might have.

Q: I want to go back to the air war. The chart you showed with the attrition rates of the various forces was almost the exact reverse of what most of us thought was happening. It showed the front-line troops attritted to 75 percent or more, and the Republican Guard, which gained a lot of public focus when we were covering the air war, attritted less than 75. Why is that?

A: Let me tell you how we did this. We started, of course, against the strategic targets. I briefed you on that before. At the same time we were hitting the Republican Guard. But the Republican Guard, you must remember, is mostly a mechanized armor force that is very well dug in and very spread out. So in the initial stages of the game, we were hitting the Republican Guard heavily, but we were hitting them with strategic-type bombers rather than pinpoint-precision bombers.

For lack of a better word, what happened is the air campaign shifted from the strategic phase into the theater. We knew all along that this was the important area. The nightmare scenario for all of us would have been to go through, get hung up in this breach right here, and then have the enemy artillery rain chemical weapons down. So one of the things that we felt we must have established was as much destruction as we could possibly get of the direct support artillery that would be firing on that breach. That's why in the latter days, we punished this area very heavily, because that was the first challenge. Once we got through this and were moving, then it's a different war. Then we're fighting their kind of war, and that's what we didn't want to have to do.

At the same time, we continued to attrit the Republican Guard, and that's why I would tell you that, again, the figures we're giving you are conservative. They always have been conservative. But we promised you at the outset we weren't going to give you anything inflated, but the best we had.

Q: Hussein seems to have about 500 to 600 tanks left out of more than 4,000. I wonder if an overview, despite these enormously illustrative pictures, you could say how long would it be before the Iraqi army could ever be a threat to the region again?

A: There's not enough left at all for Hussein to be an offensive regional threat. As you know, he has a very large army, but most of what is left north of the Tigris–Euphrates Valley is an infantry army. It's not an armored heavy army, which means it really isn't an offensive army. So it doesn't have enough left, unless someone chooses to rearm them in the future.

Q: You said the Iraqis have got these divisions along the border which were seriously attritted. It figures to be about 200,000 troops that were there. You've got 50,000 prisoners. Where are the rest of them?

A: There were a large number of dead in these units—a very, very large number of dead. When we went into the units ourselves, we even found them in the trench lines. There were very heavy desertions. At one point we had reports of desertion rates of more than 30 percent of the units along the front. As you know, we had quite a large number of POWs that came across, so I think it's a combination of desertions, of people that were killed, of the people that we've captured, and of some other people who are just flat still running.

Q: It seems you've done so much that the job is effectively done. His forces are, if not destroyed, certainly no longer capable of posing a threat to the region. They seem to want to go home. What more has to be done?

A: To accomplish the mission that I was given, I have to make sure that the Republican Guard is rendered incapable of conducting the type of heinous acts that they've conducted so often in the past. What has to be done is for these forces to continue to attack across here and put the Republican Guard out of business. We're not in the business of killing them. We have to psy-ops aircraft up. We're telling them over and over again, all you've got to do is get out of your tanks and you will not be killed. But they're continuing to

fight, and as long as they do, we're going to continue
to fight with them.

Q: That move on the extreme left which got within
150 miles of Baghdad, was it also a part of the plan that
the Iraqis might have thought it was going to Baghdad,
and would that have contributed to the deception?
A: I wouldn't have minded at all if they'd gotten
nervous about it. I mean that very sincerely. I would
have been delighted. Frankly, I don't think they ever
knew it was there until the door had already been
closed on them.

Q: I'm wondering how much resistance there still is
in Kuwait, and I'm wondering what you say to people
who would say the purpose of this war was to get the
Iraqis out of Kuwait, and they're now out. What would
you say to that public that is thinking that right now?
A: I would say there was a lot more purpose to this
war than just get the Iraqis out of Kuwait. The purpose
of this was to enforce the resolutions of the United
Nations. There are some twelve different resolutions of
the United Nations, not all of which have been accepted by Iraq to date, as I understand it. But I've got
to tell you, as a military commander, my job is not to
go ahead and at some point say that's great, they've
just now pulled out of Kuwait—even though they're
still shooting at us, they're moving backward, and
therefore I've accomplished my mission. That's not the
way you fight it, and that's not the way I would ever
fight it.

Q: You talked about heavy press coverage of Imminent Thunder early on, and how it helped fool the
Iraqis into thinking that it was a serious operation. I
wondered if you could talk about other ways in which
the press contributed to the campaign. (Laughter)
A: First of all, I don't want to characterize Imminent
Thunder as being only a deception, because it wasn't.

We had every intention of conducting amphibious operations if they were necessary, and that was a very real rehearsal—as were the other rehearsals.

Q: What kind of fight is going on with the Republican Guard? And is there any more fighting going on in Kuwait, or is it essentially out of the action?
A: No. The fight against the Republican Guard right now is a classic tank battle. You've got fire and maneuver. They are continuing to fight and shoot at us as our forces move forward, and our forces are in the business of outflanking them, taking them to the rear, using our attack helicopters and advanced technology. One of the things that has prevailed, particularly in this battle, is our technology. We had great weather for the air war, but for the last three days, it's been raining, it's been dusty, there's black smoke and haze in the air. It's an infantryman's weather—God loves the infantryman, and that's just the kind of weather the infantryman likes to fight in. But our sights have worked fantastically well in their ability to acquire enemy targets through that kind of dust and haze. The enemy sights have not worked that well. As a matter of fact, we've had several anecdotal reports today of enemy who were saying to us that they couldn't see anything through their sights and all of a sudden their tank exploded when their tank was hit by ours.

Q: Can you tell us why the French, who went very fast in the desert in the first day, stopped [inaudible] and were invited to stop fighting after 36 hours?
A: That's not exactly a correct statement. The French mission on the first day was to protect our left flank. We wanted to make sure we confined this battlefield—both on the right and the left—and we didn't want anyone attacking the main attack on their left flank. So the French mission was not only to seize Al Salman, but to set up a screen across our left flank, which was vital to ensure that we weren't surprised. So

they definitely did not stop fighting. They continued to perform their mission, and they performed it extraordinarily well.

Q: The Iraq Air Force disappeared very early in the air war. There was speculation they might return and provide cover during the ground war. Were you surprised they never showed themselves again?

A: We were not expecting it, but we never discounted it, and we were totally prepared in the event it happened.

Q: Have they been completely destroyed? Where are they?

A: There's not an airplane flown. A lot of them are dispersed throughout civilian communities in Iraq. We have proof of that.

Q: How many divisions of the Republican Guard now are you fighting, and any idea of how long that will take?

A: There were a total of five of them up here. One of them we probably destroyed yesterday. We probably destroyed two more today. I would say that leaves us a couple that we're fighting right now.

Q: I realize a great deal of strategy and planning took place, but did you think this would turn out to be such a cakewalk as it seems? And second, what are your impressions of Saddam Hussein as a military strategist? (Laughter)

A: First of all, if we had thought it would be such an easy fight, we definitely would not have stocked 60 days' worth of supplies on these log bases. As I've told you, it is very important that a military commander never assume away the capabilities of his enemy. When you're facing an enemy that is over 500,000 strong, has the reputation they've had of fighting for eight years, being combat-hardened veterans, has a number of tanks and the type of equipment they had, you don't assume away anything. So we certainly did not expect it to go this way.

As far as Saddam Hussein being a great military strategist, he is neither a strategist, nor is he schooled in the operational arts, nor is he a tactician, nor is he a general, nor is he a soldier. Other than that, he's a great military man. I want you to know that. (Laughter)

Q: I wonder if you could tell us anything more about Iraqi casualties on the battlefield. You said there were large numbers. Are we talking thousands, tens of thousands? Any more scale you can give us?

A: I wish I could answer that question. You can imagine, this has been a very fast-moving battle, as is desert warfare. As a result, even today when I was asking for estimates, every commander out there said we just can't give you an estimate. We've gone by too quickly.

Q: Very quickly, the special-operations folks—could you tell us what their front role was?

A: We don't like to talk a lot about what special operations do, as you're well aware. But in this case, let me just cover some of the things they did. First of all, with every Arab unit that went into battle, we had special-forces troops with them. Their job was to travel right down at the battalion level as the communicators with friendly English-speaking units that were on their flanks. They could also call in air strikes as necessary, could coordinate helicopter strikes, and that sort of thing. That's one of the principal roles they played, and it was a very important role. Second, they did a great job in strategic reconnaissance for us. Third, special forces were 100 percent in charge of the combat search and rescue, and that's a tough mission. When a pilot gets shot down in the middle of nowhere, surrounded by the enemy, and you're the folks required to go in after them, that is a very tough mission. Finally, they also did some direct-action missions, period.

Q: General, there have been reports that when the Iraqis left Kuwait City, they took with them a number of the Kuwaiti people as hostages. What can you tell us about this?

A: We've heard that they took up to 40,000. I think you've probably heard what the Kuwaitis who were left in the city have stated. So I don't think there's any question that a very large number of young Kuwaiti males have been taken out of that city within the last week or two. But that pales to insignificance compared to the absolutely unspeakable atrocities that occurred in Kuwait in the last week. The people that did that are not a part of the same human race that the rest of us are. I've got to pray that that's the case.

Q: Could you give us some indication of what's happening to the forces left in Kuwait? What kind of forces are there, and are they engaged at the moment?

A: I'm not even sure they're here. I think they're probably gone. At most there are pockets of people who are just waiting to surrender as soon as somebody uncovers them. What we're really faced with is fighting the Republican Guard heavy mech and armor units that are there. Basically, what we want to do is capture their equipment.

Q: General, not to take anything away from the Army and the Marines on the breaching maneuvers, but many of the reports from your field commanders and soldiers are indicating that these fortifications were not as intense or as sophisticated as they were led to believe. Is this a result of the pounding that they took, or where they perhaps overrated in the first place?

A: Have you ever been in a mine field?

Q: No.

A: All there has to be is one mine, and that's intense. There were plenty of mines out there, plenty of barbed wire. There were fire trenches, most of which we set off ahead of time. But the Egyptian forces still had to go through some fire trenches. There were a lot of booby traps, a lot of barbed wire—not a fun place to be. I have to tell you, probably one of the toughest things that anyone ever has to do is to walk into something like that and go through it. And while you're going through it and clearing it, at the same time you're probably under fire by enemy artillery. That's all I can say.

Q: Was it less severe than you had expected? You were expecting even worse, in other words.

A: It was less severe than we expected, but one of the things I contribute to that is the fact that we went to extensive measures to make it less severe.

Q: Is the Republican Guard your only remaining military objective in Iraq? I gather there have been some heavy engagements. How would you rate this army you face—from the Republican Guard on down?

A: Rating an army is a tough thing to do. A great deal of the capability of an army is its dedication to its cause and its will to fight. You can have the best equipment in the world, the largest numbers in the world, but if you're not dedicated to your cause, then you're not going to have a very good army.

One of the things we learned immediately prior to the initiation of the campaign—it contributed, as a matter of fact, to the timing of the ground campaign—is that so many people were deserting. What's more, the Iraqis brought down execution squads whose job was to shoot people in the front lines. I have to tell you, a soldier doesn't fight very hard for a leader who is going to shoot him on a whim. That's not what military leadership is all about. So I attribute a great deal of the failure of the Iraqi Army to their own leadership. They committed them to a cause that they did not believe in. They are all saying they didn't want to be there, they didn't want to fight their fellow Arabs, they were lied to when they went into Kuwait, and then after they got there, they had a leadership that was so uncaring that they didn't properly feed them, didn't properly give them water, and in the end, kept them there only at the point of a gun.

The Republican Guard is entirely different. They are the ones that went into Kuwait in the first place. They get paid more, get treated better. Oh, by the way, they also were well to the rear so they could be the first ones to bug out when the battlefield started folding, while these poor fellows up here who didn't want to be here in the first place bore the brunt of the attack. But it didn't happen.

Q: Can you tell us something about the British involvement, and perhaps comment on today's report of ten dead through friendly fire?

A: The British have been superb members of this coalition from the outset. I have a great deal of admiration and respect for all of them and particularly General Sir Peter [Delabiyea], who is not only a great general but has also become a close personal friend of mine.

They played a key role in the main attack. What they had to do was go through this breach in one of the tougher areas. Iraqis had reinforced here, and the Brits had to go through the breach and then fill up the block so that the main attack could continue on without forces over here, the mechanized forces over here, attacking that main attack in the flank. That was a principal role of the British. They did it magnificently, and then they immediately followed up in the main attack, and they're still up there fighting right now. So they did a great job.

Q: The 40,000 Kuwaiti hostages taken by the Iraqis, where are they right now? That's quite a few people. Are they in the line of fire? Do we know where they are?

A: No, no. We were told—and a lot of this is anecdotal—that they were taken back to Basra, and some of them were taken all the way to Baghdad. We were also told a hundred different reasons why they were taken. Number one, to be a bargaining chip if the time came when bargaining chips were needed. Another one was for retribution, because of course, at that time Iraq was saying that these people were not Kuwaitis but citizens of Iraq, and therefore they could do anything they wanted to with them. I just pray that they'll all be returned safely before long.

Q: The other day on television, the Soviet Deputy Foreign Minister said that they were talking already about re-arming the Iraqis. There's some indication that the United States as well needs to have a certain amount of armament to retain a balance of power. Do you feel that your troops are in jeopardy finishing this off when already the politicians are talking about re-arming the Iraqis?

A: I certainly don't want to discuss [inaudible] because that's way out of my field. I would tell you that I'm one of the first people that said it's not in the best interest of peace in this part of the world to destroy Iraq, and I think the President of the United States has made it clear from the outset that our intention is not to destroy Iraq or the Iraqi people. I think everyone has every right to legitimately defend themselves. But the one message came through loud and clear, over and over, to the pilots that have flown in against their military installations: their war machine definitely was not defensive, and they demonstrated that more than adequately when they overran Kuwait and then called it a great military victory.

Q: Before starting the land phase, how much were you concerned by the Iraqi planes coming back from Iran? And do we know what happened to the Iraqi helicopters?

A: As I said before, we were very concerned about the return of the Iraqi planes from Iran, but we were prepared for it. We have been completely prepared for any type of air attack the Iraqis might throw against us, and we're still prepared for it. We're not going to let down our guard for one instant, so long as we know that capability is there, until we're sure this whole thing is over.

The helicopters are another interesting story, and we know where the helicopters were. They traditionally put their helicopters near some of their other outfits, and we tracked them carefully. What happened is despite the fact that the Iraqis claim that we indiscriminately bombed civilian targets, they took their helicopters and dispersed them all over the civilian residential areas just as fast as they possibly could. Quite a few of them were damaged on airfields—those that we could take on airfields—but the rest of them were dispersed.

Q: You mentioned the Saudi armed forces. Could you elaborate about their role on the first day?

A: The Saudi Army, as part of the eastern task force, had to attack up the coast to pin the enemy in this location. We had the Marine attack, and of course we were concerned about those Iraqi forces hitting the flanks. That's one of the things you just don't want to have happen to your advancing forces. The Saudi forces had a tough mission because they were being required to wage the kind of fight that the Iraqis wanted. It was a very, very tough mission. I should point out that the eastern task force wasn't only the Saudis but Kuwaitis, Egyptians, Syrians, the Emiris from United Arab Emirates, Bahrainis, Qataris, and the Omanis, and I apologize if I've left anybody out, but it was a great coalition of people, all of whom did a fine job.

Q: Is there anything left of the Scuds or chemical capability?

A: I don't know, but we're sure going to find out if there's anything left. The Scuds that were being fired against Saudi Arabia came from right here. So obviously we're going to check on it when we finally get to that location.

Q: Could you tell us in terms of the air war, how effective was it in speeding up the ground campaign? Obviously, it's gone much faster than you ever expected. As a second part of that, how effective do you think the air/land battle campaign has been?

A: The air war, obviously, was very effective. You just can't predict about things like that. You can make your best estimates at the outset as to how quickly you will accomplish certain objectives, but a lot depends on how resilient the enemy is, how well dug in they are. In the earlier phases we made great progress in the air war. In the later stages, we didn't make much progress because frankly, the enemy had burrowed down into the ground. That, of course, made the air war tougher, but when you dig your tanks in and bury them, they're no longer tanks. They're now pillboxes. That then makes a difference in the ground campaign. When you don't run tanks for a long time, they have a lot of maintenance problems, seal problems and that type of thing. So the air campaign was very successful and contributed a great deal.

How effective was the air/ground campaign? I think it was pretty effective myself. I don't know what you all think.

Q: As you look down the road, can you tell us what you think would be a reasonable size for the Iraq Army, and can you tell us roughly what the size is now if the war were to stop this evening?

A: With regard to size right now, at one time Saddam Hussein was claiming that he had a 7,000,000-

man army. If he did, they've still got a pretty big army out there. The effectiveness of that army is an entirely different question.

With regard to the size of the army he should have, that's not my job to decide that. An awful lot of people live in this part of the world, and I would hope that is a decision arrived at mutually by all the Arab world to contribute to peace and stability. That's the best answer I can give.

Q: Is there a military or political explanation as to why the Iraqis did not use chemical weapons?
A: We had a lot of questions about that, and I don't know the answer. I just thank God that they didn't.

Q: Is it possible they didn't use them because they didn't have time to react?
A: You want me to speculate, I'd be delighted to. Nobody can ever pin you down when you speculate. Number one, we destroyed their artillery. We went after their artillery big-time and they had major desertions. That's how they would have delivered their chemical weapons. Either that or by air, and we all know what happened to the air.

Other people speculate that their chemical weapons degaded, and because of the damage we did to their chemical-production facilities, they were unable to upgrade the chemicals within their weapons. That was one of the reasons, among others, that we went after their chemical-production facilities early on in the strategic campaign.

I'll never know the answer to that question, but as I say, thank God they didn't.

Q: Are you still bombing in northern Iraq? If you are, what's the purpose of it now?
A: Exactly the same thing we were trying to achieve before. The war is not over, and you have to remember, people are still dying out there. Those people that are

dying are my troops, and I'm going to continue to protect those troops in every way I possibly can until the war is over.

Q: Are you going to try to bring to justice the people responsible for the atrocities in Kuwait City? And also, could you comment on the friendly-fire incident in which nine British were killed?

A: On the first question, we have as much information as possible on those people that were committing the atrocities, and we're using a screening process. Whenever we find those people that committed atrocities, we separate them out. We treat them no diffrently than any other prisoner of war, but the ultimate disposition of those people, of course, may be quite different than the way we treat any other prisoner of war.

With regard to the unfortunate incident yesterday, the only report we have is that two A-10 aircraft came in and attacked two British armored scout cars. That's what caused the casualties. There were nine KIA. We deeply regret that. There's no excuse for it, I'm not going to apologize for it. I will say that because of number of extremely complicated maneuvers being accomplished out here, because of the extreme diversity of our forces, because of the radical differences in language of our forces, and the weather conditions and everything else, I feel that we were lucky that we did not have more of this type of incident. We went to extraordinary lengths to prevent that type of thing from happening. It's a terrible tragedy, and I'm sorry that it happened.

Q: [Inaudible]

A: I don't know, I'm sorry. I don't believe so because the information I have is that a forward air controller was involved in directing that, and that would indicate that it was probably during the afternoon. But it was when there was very close combat going on out there.

Q: The United Nations General Assembly was talking about peace. As a military man, you look at your challenge, and you can get some satisfaction out of having achieved it. Is there some fear on your part that there will be a cease-fire that will keep you from fulfilling the assignment that you have? Do you fear that there will be some political pressure brought on the campaign?

A: I think I've made it very clear to everybody that I'd just as soon the war had never started, and I'd never lost a single life out there. That was not our choice. We've accomplished our mission, and when the decision-makers agree that there should be a cease-fire, nobody will be happier than me.

Q: We were told today that an A-10 returning from a mission discovered and destroyed 16 Scuds. Is that a fact, and where were they located?

A: Most of those Scuds were located in western Iraq. We went into this war with intelligence estimates that I have since come to believe were grossly inaccurate. Either that, or our pilots are lying through their teeth, and I choose to think the former rather than the latter, particularly since many of the pilots have backed up what they've been saying by film and that sort of thing. In any case, last night the pilots had a very successful afternoon and night against the mobile erector launchers. Most of them in western Iraq were reportedly used against Israel.

Q: You've said many times in the past that you do not like body counts. You've also told us tonight that enemy casualties were very large. I'm wondering with the coalition forces already burying the dead on the battlefield, will there ever be any sort of accounting or head counts made?

A: I don't think there's ever been in the history of warfare, a successful count of the dead. That's because it's necessary to lay those people to rest, for a lot of reasons, and that happens. So I would say that no, there will never be an exact count. Probably in the days to come, you're going to hear many, many stories—either overinflated or underinflated, depending upon who you hear them from. The people who will know best, unfortunately, are the families that won't see their loved ones come home.

Q: If the gate is indeed closed, as you said several times, and the theories about where these Kuwaiti hostages are—perhaps Basra, perhaps Baghdad—where could they be? A quick second question: was the timing for the start of the ground campaign a purely military choice, or was it a military choice with political influence on the final choice of dates?

A: When I say the gate is closed, I don't want to give you the impression that absolutely nothing is escaping. Quite the contrary. That doesn't mean that civilian vehicles aren't escaping, that innocent civilians aren't escaping, or unarmed Iraqis—that's not what I'm talking about. I'm talking about the gate that is closed on their war machine.

As for the timing for the beginning of the ground campaign, we made a military analysis of when it should be conducted. I gave my recommendation to the Secretary of Defense and General Colin Powell, they passed that recommendation on to the President, and he acted upon that recommendation. Why, do you think we did it at the wrong time? (Laughter)

Q: I'm wondering if your recommendation and analysis were accepted without change.

A: I'm very thankful for the fact that the President of the United States has allowed the United States military and the coalition military to fight this war exactly as it should have been fought. The President in every case has taken our guidance and our recommendations to heart and has acted superbly as the Commander-in-Chief of the United States.

Thank you very much.

General H. Norman Schwarzkopf Address to Departing Troops at Dhahran

FRIDAY, MARCH 8, 1991

It's a great day to be a soldier! Big Red One, First Team, Old Ironsides, Spear Head, Hell on Wheels platoon, Jay Hawk patrol, today you're going home. You're going home to Fort Riley, Kansas, you're going home to Fort Hood, Texas, you're going home to locations all over Germany. Your country, your countrymen, your wives, your children, and your loved ones are all there waiting for you.

You're all going home as part of the symbolic force of all the soldiers, of all sailors, of all the airmen, all the Marines, all the Coast Guard, all the National Guard, all the Reserves, all who took part in Operation Desert Shield and Desert Storm. And your comrades in arms will be following you.

Hopefully in the weeks to come or the months to come, the last remaining GIs will be returning themselves and all remaining equipment and supplies to the home station. But today you're going home.

I can hear the war stories now. Over Lone Star beer, over Colorado Kool-aid, over some great German beer, a fire water or two and what you drink the most, that

Diet Pepsi and Coca Cola. I know what glorious war stories they are going to be.

Valiant charges by courageous men over 250 kilometers of enemy territory. Along with a force of over 1,500 tanks, almost 250 attack helicopters, over 48,500 pieces of military equipment, moving around, behind, and into the enemy and totally breaking his back and defeating him in 100 hours. It's a war story worth telling, and every one of you deserve to tell it.

I ask all of you when you tell that story, don't forget to tell the whole story. Don't forget to mention the great Air Force that prepared the way for you and was overhead the entire time you fought. Don't forget the great Navy pilots that were there and the great ships that were at sea that embargoed and kept the ammunition out of the hands of the enemy. And don't ever forget to say that the 1st Tank Division of the United Kingdom was protecting your right flank. And don't ever forget to say there was an Egyptian corps protecting their right flank, and there was a task force of Saudi Arabians protecting their right flank. And two divisions of Marines out there making a hard push into Kuwait City with a fine Saudi Arabian force protecting their flank. And don't ever forget to say in your story, there were Kuwaitis, Omrnis, French Foreign Legion involved because you were part of the great coalition determined not to let a petty dictator no matter what size his army, no matter how many tanks he had, no matter how many men he had armed. Despite the fact you were badly outnumbered, you were determined to show a petty dictator that they just can't get away with bullying his neighbors and taking what they want because they think they are so tough.

I think you not only proved that to one petty dictator but to any petty dictator anywhere in the world that should choose to try to pull the same stunt either in the near or far future.

So hopefully you'll tell that war story with a lot of pride in yourselves, but don't forget to make sure that everyone understands that we did it as a part of a joint team, as part of an international team. We all did it together, we all paid the price, we all shared in the victory.

You served in a place I'm sure none of you thought you'd serve. You've been places you never heard of, places you can't even pronounce. But you also better take back with you some free lessons that your family, friends, and the world can hear. You're going to take back the fact that the word *Arab* isn't a bad word. That you do not judge all Arabs by the actions of a few. And I know here that we have a close, wonderful, warm, and thankful people for us being here and have expressed that thanks in many different ways. And you're going to take back the fact there are many soldiers in this world and you worry about them and you greatly respect them. And you are going to take back the fact that Islam is not a religion to be feared, it's a religion to be respected just as we respect all other religions; that's the American way.

It's hard for me to put into words how proud I am of you. How proud I have been to be the commander of this war. I'm proud of you, your countries are proud of you, and the world's proud of you.

God bless you, God's speed for your trip home, and God bless America.

Epilogue

General H. Norman Schwarzkopf's performance as the commander of Operation Desert Storm has made him America's new hero, one that some commentators suggested the country has been looking for since Vietnam. With his impending return to the United States, there has been talk of the traditional welcome for special heroes, a ticker-tape parade up Broadway. In Tampa, Central Command headquarters planned a big reception, as did Valley Forge Military Academy near Philadelphia.

What comes next is unclear.

Schwarzkopf has said many times he planned to retire from the Army in the summer of 1991, ending a career spanning thirty-nine years since he enrolled at West Point.

He has not said whether he would stay on if offered the post of Army Chief of Staff, a possibility raised by some of his admirers within the military. Schwarzkopf has expressed interest in environmental and conservation issues, telling one interviewer, "There's bound to be a great cause out there that could use a tired old retired general to serve it."

There have been suggestions that he be awarded a fifth star. "I can't even begin to visualize myself as a five-star general," he said in one interview. "I think of the people who are five-star generals, and I can't even see myself standing in their shadow. It would be a magnificent honor, one that surpasses anyone's dreams, but I don't see it."

Others see Schwarzkopf as a likely candidate for high office, U.S. senator or perhaps even the presidency. But his political views are not known, as Eisenhower's were not before he decided to run for the White House on the Republican ticket.

Schwarzkopf's father, whom he reveres, was apparently a Democrat, but the general calls himself an independent. When asked about his interest in seeking office, Schwarzkopf said he had "absolutely no political ambition at all," but "I can't say never, okay?"

Whatever the future holds, his act in Operation Desert Storm will likely be a tough one to follow.

There's an epidemic with 27 million victims. And no visible symptoms.

It's an epidemic of people who can't read.

Believe it or not, 27 million Americans are functionally illiterate, about one adult in five.

The solution to this problem is you... when you join the fight against illiteracy. So call the Coalition for Literacy at toll-free **1-800-228-8813** and volunteer.

Volunteer Against Illiteracy. The only degree you need is a degree of caring.